THE COMPANION GUIDES

GENERAL EDITOR: VINCENT CRONIN

*It is the aim of these guides to provide a Companion
in the person of the author, who knows intimately
the places and people of whom he writes, and is able to
communicate this knowledge and affection to his readers.
It is hoped that the text and pictures will aid them
in their preparations and in their travels, and will
help them remember on their return.*

LONDON · THE SHAKESPEARE COUNTRY · OUTER LONDON · EAST ANGLIA
NORTHUMBRIA · THE WEST HIGHLANDS OF SCOTLAND
THE SOUTH OF FRANCE · THE ILE DE FRANCE · NORMANDY · THE LOIRE
SOUTH WEST FRANCE
FLORENCE · VENICE · ROME
MAINLAND GREECE · THE GREEK ISLANDS · YUGOSLAVIA · TURKEY
NEW YORK

In Preparation

OXFORD AND CAMBRIDGE · PARIS

THE COMPA

The Sou

THE COMPANION GUIDE TO

The South of France

Archibald Lyall

revised and expanded by
A. N. Brangham

A SPECTRUM BOOK

PRENTICE-HALL, INC.
Englewood Cliffs, N.J. 07632

COLLINS
St. James's Place, London

Library of Congress Cataloging in Publication Data
Lyall, Archibald, 1904-1964.
  The companion guide to the south of France.

  "A Spectrum Book."
  Bibliography: p.
  Includes index.
  1. France, Southern—Description and travel—Guide-
books.   I. Brangham, A. N. (Arthur Norman)   II. Title.
DC607.3.L9   1983   814.4'804838   82-20479
ISBN 0-13-154641-4
ISBN 0-13-154633-3 (pbk.)

ISBN 0-13-154641-4

ISBN 0-13-154633-3 {PBK.}

First published 1963;
Reprinted 1968;
Second Edition 1972;
Reprinted 1972;
Third Edition 1978
© Archibald Lyall 1963
Limpback ISBN 0 00 216735 2
Hardback ISBN 0 00 211128 4
Maps by Charles Green
Set in Monotype Times
Made and Printed in Great Britain by
William Collins Sons & Co Ltd Glasgow

U.S. Edition © 1983 by Prentice-Hall, Inc.,
Englewood Cliffs, N.J. 07632

A SPECTRUM BOOK

Printed in the United States of America
10 9 8 7 6 5 4 3 2 1

Prentice-Hall, International, Inc., *London*
Prentice-Hall of Australia Pty. Limited, *Sydney*
Prentice-Hall of Canada, Inc., *Toronto*
Prentice-Hall of India Private Limited, *New Delhi*
Prentice-Hall of Japan, Inc., *Tokyo*
Prentice-Hall of Southeast Asia Pte. Ltd., *Singapore*
Whitehall Books Limited, Wellington, *New Zealand*
Editora Prentice-Hall Do Brasil Ltda., *Rio de Janeiro*

Contents

❧

Maps

Illustrations

❧

To S. M. K.,
in whose olive-grove
so much of this book
was written

Introduction

❧

For three hundred and fifty miles the southern coast of France stretches in long, easy, catlike curves, which link Italy with Spain. The plan of this book follows it, in political terms, from the one frontier to the other or, in geographical, from the Alps to the Pyrenees. The five historic regions of the coastland derive a fundamental unity from their position as part of the ancient Graeco-Roman civilization of the Mediterranean shores. Everywhere the peasants speak variants of the same language, the old *langue d'oc* of the South, which is quite distinct from the official French of the North now superseding it. The temperament of the people is vivacious and mercurial, while their physical type, short and dark, contrasts strongly with that of the tall, blond Frenchmen of the North. They are a Ligurian and Iberian mixture as opposed to a Celtic and Teutonic one. Above all, perhaps, they share a civilization of the sunshine, everywhere dedicated to the olive and the vine.

The coast is bisected by the River Rhône, which forms the boundary between Provence on the east and Languedoc on the west. The eastern half comprises also the former Papal territory of the Comtat Venaissin on the Lower Rhône and the County of Nice along the Italian frontier, which belonged to Piedmont for nearly five hundred years. Both these small districts may be included geographically in Provence.

Provence itself is divided into three zones. The historic heartland has always been Lower Provence, which lies to the east of the Rhône delta, mostly in the department of the Bouches-du-Rhône, and contains such ancient cities as Marseilles, Aix and Arles. It is the richest and, from the architectural and archaeological point of view, the most rewarding. With the inland region of Upper Provence, which roughly coincides with the department of the Alpes-de-Haute-Provence (until 1970 the Basses-Alpes), this book is not concerned. It is poor and mountainous, and the population of its little towns and its hill-top villages, unable to live on scenery alone, is steadily dwindling, drained away to the rich and bustling towns of the third

11

zone, the Coast, which is divided between the departments of the Alpes-Maritimes and the Var. In the last century or so this narrow strip between the mountains and the sea has undergone a hardly credible transformation. Previously it consisted of little more than a few scattered fishing villages, living in constant terror of pirate raids. Now it is the most fashionable and at the same time the most popular playground of Europe. It has become, in fact, the Riviera or the Côte d'Azur.

Vast crowds of foreigners, a large proportion of them British, flock to the Coast every year. And that is one of the reasons why nearly half this book is devoted to it. A second reason is that very few good, up-to-date guides to it exist. Yet a third is that it has rapidly become one of the world's principal exhibition grounds of contemporary art, with fine picture-galleries and buildings decorated by Picasso, Matisse, Léger and Cocteau. On the fairly safe assumption that 'modern' art is not a mere passing aberration, the Coast will remain a place of pilgrimage for art-lovers comparable with Tuscany.

Lower Languedoc, beyond the Rhône, bears a close resemblance to Lower Provence. It is a smiling land of endless vineyards, interspersed with famous cities such as Nîmes, Montpellier and Carcassonne. It is divided into the departments of the Gard, the Hérault and the Aude.

Beyond Lower Languedoc lies the Catalan-speaking Roussillon, officially known as the department of the Pyrénées-Orientales, on the Spanish border. It lies under the shadow of the last towering mass of the Pyrenees. We have come to the end of the journey which began where the Alps drop down to the sea at Menton.

Chapter 1

Menton

❧

The Lemon Festival – the Museum – the Mairie – the Old Town – Garavan – the Hills

In **Menton** they will tell you how, when Adam and Eve were expelled from the Garden of Eden, Eve furtively plucked a lemon from a tree as they passed and hid it in her bosom. The Angel of the Flaming Sword was filled with pity for her, pretended not to notice and let her take it with her through the Gates of Paradise. For many years our first fathers wandered over an unfriendly earth, cold, hungry, weary and in want. Adam was bitter and despairing but Eve's heart was still buoyed up by the hope of better things. At last they came to a well-wooded, well-watered place where the high hills came down to a warm blue sea and where it was always spring, and they realized this was the nearest thing to the Earthly Paradise they would ever see. The lemon was yet unwithered, for it was the immortal fruit of Paradise. Eve took it from her bosom, kissed its golden skin and planted it in the earth. Soon all the slopes and valleys were covered with scented lemon trees; and from the lemon brought from Eden stem the myriads of trees which blossom and fruit all the year round in the place which we now call Menton. Such is the ancient legend of the lemon which they will tell you there.

Be that as it may, the oldest known inhabitant of the Riviera lived here some thirty thousand years ago and has left his skull behind for all to see in the Municipal Museum at Menton. He is the famous Grimaldi Man, who was found about a century ago in the caves called Les Rochers Rouges on the shore below the little village of Grimaldi about half a mile beyond the Italian border. So that in time, as well as in space, the French Riviera may truly be said to begin at Menton, the half-way point between Rome and Paris where Gaul and Italy have so long met in peace and in war.

Menton lies on a broad bay which the Romans called the *Pacis Sinus* or Gulf of Peace, but leaving aside the naked troglodytes of the Red Rocks, there is no evidence of any settlement here before the

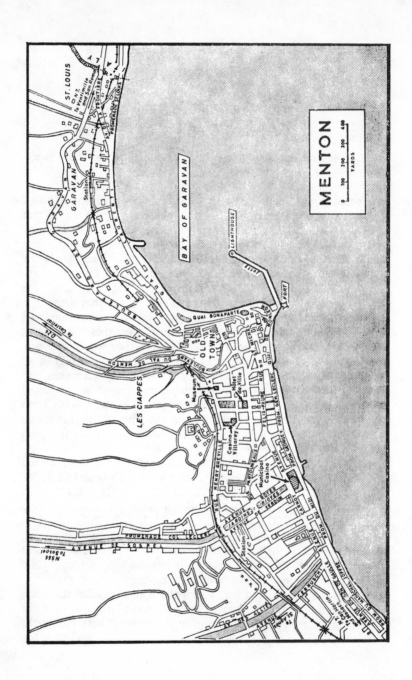

MENTON

middle of the thirteenth century. For the greater part of its history, Mentone, as our grandfathers used to call it, was subject to the Grimaldi, Princes of Monaco. In 1848 it revolted on account of the distress caused by the fiscal reforms of Prince Honoré V and formed a republic called the Free Towns of Monaco and Roquebrune. Prince Honoré, saddened by the disastrous failure of such progressive measures as the state monopoly of flour and corn (advocated many years later in 1893 by Jean Jaurès and the Socialist deputies in the Paris Chamber of Deputies), wrote his own epitaph before he died: 'Here lies one who meant well.' After twelve years of independence the Free Towns voted for union with France by 639 votes to 86.

The Gulf of Peace is divided from the Bay of Garavan by the promontory on which the old town of Menton is built. On the east side is the residential suburb of Garavan, and on the west is the new town, which stretches for a couple of miles along the Gulf coast towards the villas of Cap Martin, now practically a part of Menton. The new town owes its existence largely to the exceptionally mild climate of Menton, which sheltered from the north by a semicircle of mountains, disputes with Beaulieu the claim to the warmest winter climate on the coast. Originally drawn hither by Dr Bennet, a pioneer English physician whose book extolling the climate and virtues of Menton went into five editions in England and was translated into German, Dutch and finally French, and whose monument stands in the Rue Partouneaux, many thousands of English and other Northerners have for a century been coming to winter here in the Balmorals and the Westminsters, the Bristols and the Richmonds, which once lined the Gulf of Peace.

Nearly all the royal and imperial families of Europe, Grand Dukes and Archdukes by the score, have sojourned here at one time or another, and Guy de Maupassant called the Old Cemetery on the Castle Hill 'the aristocratic cemetery of Europe'. To name only two writers, Katherine Mansfield lived in the Villa Isola Bella and the exiled Spanish novelist Vicente Blasco Ibañez made his home in the Villa Fontana Rosa at Garavan. Now the winter season has been surpassed by the summer with its invasion of sun-seeking tourists. Not only are the hotels and pensions of the new town and Garavan full in July and August, when before they all used to be shut, but also thousands bivouac in the camping sites around, such as the Plateau St Michel, La Madone and Cap Martin.

It is the pride of the Mentonnais that semi-tropical fruit will grow here as hardly anywhere else in Europe. In Palermo, for example, the lemon trees produce only one crop a year, whereas in Menton flowers and fruit at all stages of development are on the trees all the year round – some supporting evidence, perhaps, of the Eden legend.

At Carnival time, in February, Menton holds its famous Lemon Festival, when the whole town is decorated and there are processions of floats and carriages festooned with fruit and pretty girls. (Fifteen tons of lemons and oranges are used in the decorations. Afterwards they are either sent to hospitals or made into jam.) In the **Jardins Biovès,** just opposite the Municipal Casino (which take their name from the enterprising mayor who covered over the bed of the Careï torrent to make the gardens) there are great beds of lemons, oranges, tangerines and grapefruit – thousands and thousands of them – arranged in ingenious patterns and mosaics, while others are wired to sticks to form arches and the outlines of urns and vases. Immediately behind, the grey limestone cliffs hang like a backcloth against the vivid blue of the sky.

During the Fête des Citrons there is a show in the gardens of other exotic fruits, such as bananas, avocados, breadfruit and passion fruit, which grow here. I do not think they all ripen, but the bananas in the garden of the now demolished Hôtel des Anglais at Garavan are certainly reputed to do so. There are rarer citrus fruits or *agrumes,* as they are called in French, such as clementines, which resemble tangerines, kumquats (like tiny bitter oranges the size of large olives), and cedrates, which are deformed, misshapen hybrids of grapefruit and lemon. There are 'tree tomatoes'. There are many different varieties of dates and other fruits of the palm.

Menton prides itself almost as much on its enormous, ancient olive trees as upon its ever-blossoming lemons. 'Not this the stunted olive tree met with in western Provence beyond the Var,' boasts a local guide-book scornfully, 'but the royal tree of which the Bible tells us: the trees went forth on a time to anoint a king over them: and they said unto the olive tree, Reign thou over us.' Local shops have fascinating displays of tables, chairs, benches, fruit bowls, bread boards, salad spoons and pepper grinders carved from the local olive wood, which is of a creamy colour, often faintly diffused with pink, and has a grain like marble.

On the east side of the Biovès Gardens, and fronting the Avenue Boyer, is the Palais de l'Europe, behind whose *belle époque* façade of 1909 is the old casino. Its appearance belies the activity inside. Here is a busy conference and exhibition centre connected with the arts; most famous is the Menton Biennale of painting, through which contemporary artists are encouraged. The next Biennale is likely to be held in July 1978. Further east, at the end of an avenue of plane trees is the well modernized **Municipal Museum**.[1] The prehistoric collection on the ground floor stars the Grimaldi Skull. The basement houses local folklore, prints and historical records such as the flags and proclamations of the Free Towns. The picture gallery on the first floor contains a number of copies and school pieces of old masters (some bearing such entirely fanciful and irrelevant labels as Constable and Tintoretto), the collection formed by an Englishman called Mr Wakefield-Mori of modern masters such as Derain, Utrillo, Suzanne Valadon, Dufy, Kisling and Soutine (notice a curious early example of Othon Friesz) and a collection from the Biennale, whose prize-winners are automatically bought by the Municipal Museum. Not all of them deserve it.

In 1965 the **Jean Cocteau Museum**[1] was opened in the bastion of the harbour jetty. It contains drawings from various periods of Cocteau's life, two tapestries and pottery. Graham Sutherland, whose drawings for his Coventry Cathedral tapestry were made in a garage at the port of Menton, was made an honorary citizen of the town in 1968; he spends every winter here.

Not far away is the red and ochre **Mairie**. From the palm-shaded square in front of it the buses leave for Monte Carlo and Nice, while the coaches for Italy go from the arcades of the Rue Honorine just opposite. The Mairie emerged from the habitual obscurity of provincial *mairies* in 1957, when its Salle des Mariages[2] was decorated by Jean Cocteau. On a white background the subjects are painted in what cartographers would probably describe as a series of contour lines. On the ceiling are depicted (suitably enough in the circumstances) Love, Poetry, mounted on Pegasus, and (rather mysteriously) Science juggling with stars which, as he later admitted, would now be sputniks if he had thought of such things in faraway 1957. On the end wall are the grave profiles of two young lovers, she in the wide straw hat, he in the red woollen bonnet, which were the traditional head-dresses of the Menton lemon-girls and fisherlads respectively. Note the curious detail that the man's eye is in the form of a fish, a conceit of Jean Cocteau which may be seen also in his fishermen's chapel at Villefranche. The fresco on the right-hand wall shows a marriage scene in which the figures wear Oriental costume to symbolize the Saracen blood said to run in the veins of the Mentonnais. The young couple are leaving on horseback for their honeymoon while their friends and relations offer them gifts. A blind man proffers a bunch of orchids. Other young people are dancing.

1. Closed on Mondays, Tuesdays and public holidays.
2. Closed on Sundays.

Only the mother-in-law is not content, and at the back a cast-off lover of the bridegroom's is being comforted by her father. On the left wall is the legend of Orpheus and Eurydice. Orpheus having just looked back at Eurydice, she is dying in the arms of her companions. Orpheus drops his lyre and poetry abandons the earth. Men become half-beasts – centaurs – and kill each other. There are even innocent victims such as a bird, pierced by arrows. (Cocteau is clearly against blood sports.) To point the contrast with the austerity of most registry offices Cocteau has furnished this one with an abundance of velvet and gilding, and erected two enormous engraved mirrors in the vestibule.

The main artery of the new town is a long street with many aliases, Rue St Michel, Avenue Félix Faure, Avenue Carnot and eventually, where it runs out towards Cap Martin, the Avenue Général de Gaulle. Parallel to it, along the edge of the sea, runs a long promenade, in no way inferior in the number of its names – the Promenade George V which extends westwards into the Promenade Maréchal Joffre, and eastwards to the Quai Général Leclerc and the Quai de Monléon by the Bastion on the point. From the Rue Clemenceau near the covered market the local buses take off for Gorbio, Ste Agnès, Castellar and the other villages up-country.

The open beach in front of the two Quais, once grandiloquently known as *le port aux grands navires*, was the only harbour which Menton possessed before the present one was begun by Napoleon III in the Bay of Garavan. The lateen-sailed tartanes which exported lemons, oranges and olive oil and traded all over the Mediterranean, had to be laboriously hauled up the pebbly beach. When a tartane arrived safely, bringing merchandise from Marseilles or Genoa, or sometimes even from Syria or Spain, the whole population left their fields and their vineyards and hastened to the shore to man the primitive capstans, haul on the ropes and lug the boat up out of reach of the waves. Once it was in safely the captain would produce some bales of salt cod for a homecoming feast. A fireplace was built between two stones, a great cooking pot was put on the fire and the *stocafi* or stockfish was boiled with tomatoes. Under a sail stretched between two hulls, the fish was eaten with *la crousta*, a local speciality consisting of bread dipped in olive oil and anchovy sauce, and spread with a layer of tomatoes. The food was washed down with large quantities of the heady local wine, and all passers-by were invited to clink a glass. The banquet would go on until far into the night and on the morrow the seamen would disperse with their headaches, each to his own little plot of land (for everyone owned at least a few olive or lemon trees). So the sailor would turn farmer until the next voyage was planned.

Today the harbour on the Bay of Garavan affords a fine safe anchorage for trading vessels, fishing boats and yachts. From the end of the protecting jetty which runs out to the lighthouse there is one of the finest views of the high huddle of the old town. Formerly the houses ran right down to the bay but Napoleon, remembering the difficulties of supplying the Army of Italy, decided to make a by-pass road and for the purpose he built the Quai Bonaparte out into the bay. The extension was not built on solid earth, rock or sand but on the series of sixteen low arches which figure in all the pictures of Menton. Napoleon showed more foresight than he knew, for in the high summer nowadays many thousands of cars a day pass through Menton to and from the Italian frontier.

Some of this traffic is now able to pass by road-tunnel below the old town. Motorists driving to or from Italy and wishing to avoid Menton altogether can take the new Autoroute 8 which curves on a series of viaducts across the Mentonnais valleys to join RN 7 at Roquebrune-Vistaëro.

Much rebuilding has taken place along Quai Laurenti. On the seaward side a new beach and yacht harbour have been created, thus greatly diminishing any aura of old-fashionedness which has been attributed to the resort.

The **Old Town** can be reached by car from the Rue St Michel by way of the Place du Cap and the Rue des Logettes, which leads under a narrow archway into the Rue Longue, or by foot from the Quai Bonaparte. Leaving on the right the little old Palace of the Princes at No. 123 Rue Longue, formerly the main street of Menton, we climb what is locally known as The Ramps, a double staircase paved with black and white pebbles, up to the **Parvis St Michel**, the centre of the old town.

On the left of a large square, paved like the staircase with a pattern of pebbles, is the **Parish Church of St Michel,** an Italianate building of the seventeenth century with a storied campanile of coloured tiles. Ahead a short, wide flight of steps leads up to another mosaic square in front of the Jesuit **Church of the Conception** or the White Penitents. The two figures in the niches of the façade are not the usual Jesuit saints. Indeed, one of them is not a saint at all. On the left is St Isidore the Labourer, the patron of Madrid and a saint so localized that even in Spain I have never encountered him outside the capital. The frock-coated figure on the right is Pope Pius VII, who passed through the city on February 11, 1814, on his way back to Rome from his exile at Fontainebleau. He stayed the night at what is now No. 1 Rue Bréa and gave his pontifical blessing to the people of Menton from the balcony.

This beautiful double square high above the Bay of Garavan is used as the open-air auditorium of the famous Festival of Chamber Music to which *mélomanes* flock from all over Europe in the first half of August. The concerts are given late in the evening, and the ramps leading up to the Parvis are illuminated by thousands of flickering torches, while the belfries and the façades of the two churches are picked out by concealed lighting. It is a very beautiful setting and the acoustics are highly spoken of.

From the Parvis one can wander up to the Old Cemetery at the top of the town through a maze of narrow, twisting alleys, up curving staircases, along dark tunnels and underneath rickety-looking houses built on beams across the mole-runs. The old town of Menton is a Kasbah, one of the few on this side of the Mediterranean. Nobody who has once seen it need spend very much time on the old quarters of Nice or Cannes.

The cemetery occupies the site of the old feudal castle, and just above it begins the **Boulevard de Garavan**, which runs along the high ground towards the Pont St Louis and the Italian border, parallel with the coast road from the Quai Bonaparte. It is bordered by fine villas with exotic gardens and magnificent views. Above rise abruptly the harsh grey cliffs of the Maritime Alps which mark the Italian border, and in particular the massif called Le Berceau, whose highest point, the Roc d'Orméa, is 1129 metres high – between three and four thousand feet.

More than once in living memory the people of Menton have lifted their eyes anxiously to the hills on the border. In 1940, when Mussolini declared war in his attempt to snatch a cheap victory from a France already defeated by the Germans, the Italians broke through the thin screen of Chasseurs Alpins, captured Menton and occupied it until their collapse in 1943, when the Germans took it over. In the summer of 1944, after the Allied landings further along the coast, the Germans had to beat a hasty retreat, blowing up the mole and harbour installations before they went. They stood on the line of the Italian border and right up to the end of the war continued to lob shells into poor, battered Menton, most of whose population had been evacuated for the second time in five years. The reconstruction of the harbour was not finished until 1958.

Perhaps the most beautiful of the villas on the Boulevard de Garavan is **Les Colombières**, built and laid out to the last detail by the writer and painter Ferdinand Bac, who designed many gardens on the coast. It is easy to visit, for it is now run as a restaurant. (I strongly suspect that the Municipality of Menton has covetous eyes on it. If not, they should.) The villa is built in the Hellenic style, sited especially for its views. Immediately in front, framed in cypresses, is the great olive-grove of Le Pian, which the Municipality has bought and turned into a public park to save it from the fate of so many of the fast-vanishing olive-groves of Menton. In the middle distance are the Bay of Garavan and the old town with its *campanili*, silhouetted against the sea with Cap Martin and Cap Ferrat in the distance. The house is entirely classical in style and spirit. One room is the chapel-like Salon des Muses, with Latin inscriptions round the walls. There are the frescoed Venetian Room and the Music Room. Opening out of one arched window is the Garden of Homer, an atrium with a pool and a fountain, surrounded by a frescoed double colonnade.

The fifteen acres of gardens are a perfect haven of peace and quiet. Eschewing the exotic palms and cacti so popular along the coast, M. Bac laid out his gardens in the purest Italian manner. One is reminded of some of the villas round Florence. Tall cypresses rise like pinnacles on every side. Vistas and flights of steps lead down to ornamental pools and balustraded basins such as the Fountain of the Doves, the Fountain of Nausicäa and the Spanish Basin. Statues and urns, busts and benches, break the austerity of the cypress hedges which border the walks. Cleverly designed perspectives and views strike one at every turn. Instead of flowerbeds, borders and flowering shrubs, an occasional urn full of geraniums or nasturtiums breaks the prevailing dark green much as Corot would pick out his tree-scapes with a red petticoat or shawl.

Ferdinand Bac concludes the book which he wrote about Les Colombières: 'And now, farewell! You have contemplated and judged in two hours what took me forty years to dream of and to achieve.'

One of the features which distinguishes Menton from the other Riviera towns is the mountain range which comes down to the edge of the city and affords a variety of walks and drives to the picturesque villages which crown the lower spurs. Most of them were already Saracen strongholds long before the site of Menton, too exposed on its low hill-top by the sea, had been thought of as a place of settlement. Leaving the rich fruit groves (which yield over thirty thousand lemons to the acre) one begins to climb slopes covered with great gnarled olive trees and beyond them through pinewoods and then scrub-oak and *maquis* up to the bare limestone, where nothing grows but a little sparse herbage for sheep and goats.

There are four parallel valleys which run down to the sea at Menton, each separated from its neighbours by a rocky ridge. The Val de Menton itself, carved out by the stream called the Fossan, runs down on the west side of the old town. Violets and anemones carpet the valley in February and March. Seven kilometres up the steep winding road which starts from the Rue de la République near the Mairie is the village of **Castellar** at a height of a thousand feet. You can go up to Castellar by bus, enjoy the view over the sea and the mountains and walk back in an hour down the mule-track which starts from beside the Mairie.

The next valley to the west is the Careï, the torrent which runs under the railway bridge and beneath the Biovès Gardens. About two kilometres along the road, a turning to the left leads up to the Capuchin **Monastery of the Annonciade.** It is on the site of the ancient Podium Pinum or Puipin, from which in the Middle Ages Menton received its first inhabitants. The monastery and the town still preserve their ancient association. Some of the old families yet have their tombs and chapels at l'Annonciade and at the annual pilgrimage on March 25 various confraternities and assorted priests and faithful make the climb from Menton.

The road itself continues to the **Pass of Castillon.** The old Saracen village was ruined by an earthquake in 1887. The new village, built lower down, was destroyed by shellfire in 1944 and has been rebuilt – the third Castillon in less than a century. Thence the road leads through a tunnel to **Sospel,** historically an important road junction on the highway from Nice to Turin, with a fine medieval bridge composed of twin arches with a watch-tower between. The church of St Michel contains a Madonna by François Bréa behind the high altar. Sospel is frequented in summer by the dwellers on the coast – or at least it was in the old days when they used to close their hotels and shutter their shops all through the summer months. North from Sospel, over the Col de Brouis, the Turin road dips into the upper valley of the Roya, where there are some attractive old villages such as Saorge, La Brigue and Tende. La Brigue and Tende only became united with France in 1947, for they were left to Italy when Napoleon III annexed the rest of the County of Nice eighty-seven years before because Victor Emmanuel had a chamois-stalking forest there to which he was greatly attached. Such were international courtesies in the days when crowned heads dealt directly with their 'cousins'.

The next valley to the west, the Borrigo, is reached by way of the Avenue Cernuschi. Seven miles up the bends of a steep and winding road is the village of **Ste Agnès**. Perched on a peak over two thousand feet high and only two or three miles from the sea as the crow flies, Ste Agnès claims to be the highest village of all the Mediterranean coast. Behind it a goat track leads up a three-hundred-foot cliff to the ruins of a Saracen castle. You can go up to Ste Agnès by bus and walk back in half a day by way of Gorbio and Roquebrune.

Gorbio is a hill-top village dominating the valley of that name. The road begins at the western end of the Avenue de la Madone and the Gorbio torrent marks the boundary between Menton and Roquebrune-Cap Martin. The valley, sunnier and less shut in than the other three, is famous for its early vegetables and fruit, as well as for its wine and oil. Over a thousand species of wild flowers have been identified in the valley – more, it is said, than there are in all Ireland.

Chapter 2

Roquebrune

❧

Cap Martin – Roquebrune Castle – the Procession

Beyond the Gorbio torrent lies **Cap Martin**, a promontory whose
rich woods of pine and olive are cut up into a number of magnificent
villas. In the last century Cap Martin was perhaps the most exclusive
place on the whole Riviera. Every winter the Empress Elizabeth of
Austria occupied the ground floor of the right wing of the Hôtel Cap
Martin, and the Empress Eugénie stayed at her Villa Kyrnos. All
round the Cap the roads, where the two empresses went for their
daily constitutionals, were spread with gravel and lit at night with
gas lamps. There are still some very luxurious villas there, although
the Hôtel has long been closed. Cap Martin is never likely to become
a very popular resort, since the jagged rocks which surround it
practically rule out bathing. Roquebrune beach, in contrast, is all
pebbles.

Cap Martin has always been closely associated with the ancient
fortress-village of **Roquebrune**, which towers on a mountain spur
high above it. Once, so the legend goes, there was a nunnery on the
Cap, which the men of Roquebrune had given their word to protect.
It was arranged that if the Saracen raiders appeared, the nuns were
to ring the bells and the Roccabrunasques would come immediately
to the rescue. One night the bells rang out. The men of Roquebrune
hastily armed themselves and ran down the hill to defend the nunnery,
while their terrified wives flocked into the church to pray for their
safety. There were no Saracens. 'We just wanted to see whether you
would really come,' giggled the nuns. A few nights later the nunnery
bells pealed again into the darkness, but the warriors of Roquebrune,
not to be fooled a second time, remained comfortably in bed with
their wives. This time the Saracens had really come. The silly nuns
had cried 'Wolf!' once too often. Next day in the looted convent a
few corpses lay with their throats slit. The more marketable of the
nuns were already on their way to the harems of Algiers.

The *rocca bruna*, the brown rock from which the town takes its

24

name, is a kind of conglomerate or puddingstone thickly embedded with pebbles, and the main square is carved and hollowed out of it. Beyond the square lie the twisted, arched streets of the old town, while a seemingly interminable knee-breaking stairway climbs up to the **Castle.** Conrad, Count of Ventimiglia, built it in the tenth century in case the Saracens should return. (That was for centuries the nightmare of the coast. The Saracens might come back.) Although it is claimed to be the oldest in all France and the sole surviving example of the so-called Carolingian castles, none of the present building can be dated back for a certainty beyond the thirteenth century. All the same Roquebrune demonstrates the evolution of a small fortress-community over a period of a thousand years. It was divided, and the village is still divided, into four wards, that of the peasants, that of the artisans, and that of the men-at-arms, while the fourth was the keep or donjon, where the lord lived. By the fifteenth century the first three wards had become the village and the fourth the castle.

The castle itself, a Grimaldi property from 1350 until the revolution of 1848, was bought in 1911 by Sir William Ingram, an English resident who presented it to the Municipality.[1] It is an interesting example of the residence of a medieval lord. A flight of stairs leads to what appears to be an open courtyard, or first-floor patio, but was in fact the ceremonial hall of the castle, unroofed by a fire during the War of the Austrian Succession. A well in the centre connects with a huge rainwater cistern beneath. Passages lead to the guardroom and to the seigneur's private dungeon. (In the Middle Ages prisoners were kept close at hand, like parrots and canaries today.) On the second floor were the domestic apartments of the lord, a common bedroom for the family, a living-room and a kitchen. One is struck by the extremely small scale of all these rooms. Even the ceremonial reception room downstairs would not be too large for a modern mews-flat. A feudal lord in the Middle Ages lived in a tiny two-room flat with a kitchen – and a prison where we would have a bathroom. The terrace on the third floor affords a vertical view over the red rooftops of Roquebrune below, their planes at all angles to each other like an early Cubist picture.

Second always and only to the Saracens, the plague was the constant terror of this coast, for it was brought in by the ships which traded with the ports of Hither Asia and North Africa. In 1720, for example, it broke out in Marseilles, introduced by the *Saint Antoine* from Syria, and within a year killed a hundred thousand people in

1. Closed on Fridays and in November.

the cities of Provence, forty thousand of them in Marseilles alone. The plague came to little Roquebrune in the summer of 1467 and passed on, in consequence, so the Roccabrunasques devoutly believed, of a vow they made. Every year since, in fulfilment of that vow, a procession takes place through the streets, in which the Passion is re-enacted in a series of tableaux. The 'first Christ' rejects the cup held by an angel and receives the kiss of Judas; the second is insulted and beaten by the soldiers, while Pilate washes his hands; the 'Christ of the Passion' is clothed in red with his hands bound and holding a reed; the 'fourth Christ' falls beneath the weight of the cross; the fifth hangs on the cross, while soldiers pierce his side with a lance and the holy women watch and weep. For five hundred years this procession has taken place every year on the afternoon of August 5, and the roles of the actors have descended in the same families from father to son for many generations.

While Roquebrune's most famous visitor was Sir Winston Churchill, the most remarkable of its modern residents was undoubtedly Hans van Meegeren, the Dutch painter who fooled the whole art world. Tired of painting pictures under his own name which he could not sell, he retired here in 1932, practised hard at the technique and painted a number of pictures such as 'The Disciples at Emmaus', which he sold as a Vermeer to the Boymans Museum in Rotterdam for £52,000. He sold one of his forgeries to Goering, was arrested after the war on a charge of collaboration and saved his neck by pleading, and proving, that he had painted it himself. Although he died in prison, it was not before he had netted himself half a million pounds.

Le Corbusier, perhaps the most widely known architect of modern times, spent many summers at Roquebrune in a small wooden house. Roquebrune has become something of a pilgrimage centre since Le Corbusier's death by drowning at Cap Martin in 1965.

Chapter 3

Monaco

The Town – the Oceanographic Museum – the Casino – the Exotic Gardens

Roquebrune-Cap Martin is one of the largest communes in France. While its eastern boundary severs Menton from its own suburb of Carnolès, its western runs through the town of **Monte Carlo** to form the border between the French Republic and the independent Principality of Monaco. In fact, the coloured parasols and the imported sand of Monte Carlo Beach, the fashionable *plage* of the Principality, are outside its territory in Roquebrune Commune.

The recently constructed Plage de Larvotto and the swimming pools of the Sea Club, almost adjoining Monte Carlo Beach, are within the Principality.

The miniature state is only 375 acres in extent, about half the size of Central Park in New York but its exiguous size is no measure either of its wealth or of its antiquity. Its kernel is the cliff-bound peninsula of Monaco, which juts into the sea like a slightly curved thumb to enclose, between itself and the newer town of Monte Carlo on the opposite shore, a fine natural harbour. (Known to the Romans as Portus Monoeci, the Port of Hercules or Melkarth, it was of little use except as a shelter in a storm, for it lacked any hinterland except steep cliffs and barren mountains.) The Principality consists of three 'towns'; the original settlement of Monaco, with the Palace and the administrative buildings, on the Rock; the cosmopolitan residential and resort town of Monte Carlo; and the commercial centre of La Condamine, which occupies the low isthmus between them.

Monaco became an independent lordship in the year 1308, when the first of the Grimaldi bought it from the Genoese, and it has remained in the family ever since, although passing in the female line, first to the Matignons and then to the Polignacs, who took the name and arms of Grimaldi. As nearly everybody knows, the present ruler is Prince Rainier III, who in 1956 married the American film star, Grace Kelly.

27

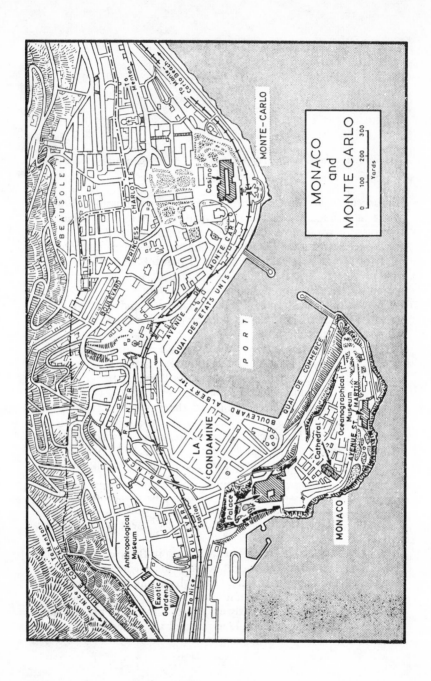

The resident population of the Principality is some 23,000, mostly French and Italian citizens and all of them exempt from direct taxation, which does not exist in this happy land. Some two or three thousand are actual citizens of Monaco, who enjoy the further privilege of freedom from military service. It is hardly necessary to say that there is a long waiting list for citizenship, but by arrangement with the French and Italian Governments this is granted very sparingly – only after long residence and as a reward for signal services to the State. Likewise, of course, all this puts Europe's last absolute ruler in a very strong position, for there is an agreement by which, should his dynasty die out, the Principality would revert to France. That would mean taxes and military service for the Monegasques. So no Republican movement stands much of a chance in Monaco. In a word,

> Prediction's becoming a mania
> But the prophets grow all the time zanier.
> In Monte, they say,
> Where the sun shines all day,
> The political forecast is Rainier.

Most of the actual Monegasque citizens live on the Rock itself. Monaco is almost unique among these little Italianate towns in that its narrow, picturesque streets are all on a level and involve no climbing and no cobblestones. (It was actually at La Garde Freinet in the Maures that, skidding and nearly falling, as I had done in a score of these *villages perchés*, I looked round and found that the name of the precipitous alley was Rue Rompi-Cuou – which is good Provençal for 'Break-your-Bottom'.) In the middle of the last century, after the loss of Menton and Roquebrune, this cliff-top village of two thousand inhabitants was literally all that remained of the Principality. There was one house in La Condamine, while what is now Monte Carlo was nothing but stony fields planted with a few olive trees.

Prince Charles III found himself faced with bankruptcy, for the taxes on the citrus and oil of Menton had been his sole source of revenue. Looking round, he decided to take a leaf out of the book of the Grand Duke of Baden, who made a handsome income out of his Casino. Monaco, whose superb climate was its sole surviving asset, should be for the winter gamblers what Baden-Baden was for the summer. After several false starts and bankruptcies, mainly due to the lack of either decent communications with Nice or of accommodation and amenities in Monaco itself, the concession was taken over in 1860 by François Blanc, the talented ex-Director of the Casino at Bad Homburg. The opening of the railway from Nice in 1868 made the fortune of Monaco, of the Prince and of M. Blanc (who, starting life as a waiter, eventually left over three and a half million pounds).

In the following year the Prince was able to abolish all direct taxation in the Principality. Hotels, villas and furnished houses sprang up almost overnight, and in 1871, 140,000 people visited Monte Carlo, as the rocky shelf of Les Spélugues, on which the new Casino was built, had been renamed in honour of its enterprising Prince. All the English *milords* and other rich people who wintered on the Riviera came over from Nice and even from Cannes. John Addington Symonds denounced the Casino in a fine fruity prose now rare outside Sunday journalism. After referring to the temptresses who lay in wait there, 'splendid women with bold eyes and golden hair and marble columns of imperial throats,' he goes on to sketch the unfortunate croupiers in metaphors more suited to a zoo: 'The croupiers are either fat, sensual cormorants or sallow, lean-cheeked vultures or suspicious foxes. Compare them with Coutts's men. Note the difference.' He had not been lucky at the tables, one feels.

The quality of the visitors soon came to equal the quantity. In the short winter season of 1887 the Hôtel de Paris numbered among its guests the Emperor and Empress of Austria, the Dowager Empress of Russia, the Kings of Sweden and Serbia, and the Queen of Portugal, while Queen Victoria, travelling from Cannes to Menton, drove up to Monaco and ostentatiously refrained from calling on the Prince who, less fortunately situated than herself, was obliged to make his revenue out of one of the more venial, if more foolish, of human weaknesses. It was in that same year of 1887 that an Englishman named Charles Wells became famous as 'The Man who Broke the Bank at Monte Carlo'. He was by profession a confidence trickster, served several stretches in prison and died destitute at the age of eighty-five.

One of the most ancient, and without doubt the most impoverished, ruling families in Europe suddenly found itself fantastically rich. The old sixteenth- and seventeenth-century **Palace** on the summit of the Rock now took on its present look with crenellated fishtail towers and the other trappings of medievalism fashionable in the Ruskin age. Built round a handsome arcaded courtyard and containing some good pictures, it is only open from July to the end of September, when the princely family are not in residence. Otherwise, the public have to console themselves by going up to the great square in front of it at midday to watch the changing of the gaily uniformed guard, which forms no inconsiderable a portion of the two-dozen-strong army of the Principality.

The large pseudo-Romanesque **Cathedral of Monaco** also dates from this period of sudden prosperity. It was built on the site of the thirteenth-century church of St Nicholas, which was demolished to make way for it in 1874 and from which it inherits some good paintings of the School of Nice, including two by Ludovic Bréa, a polyptych of St Nicholas in the right-hand transept and a Pietà over the door of the sacristy.

The profits of the *Société des Bains de Mer*, as M. Blanc's enterprise was euphemistically named, provided Prince Albert I with an income in the neighbourhood of £130,000 a year and enabled him to indulge his favourite hobby of oceanography. On the twenty-four voyages which he made in his yachts, the *Hirondelle* and the *Princesse Alice*, he specialized in the exploration of the extreme depths of the ocean and discovered several hitherto unknown species. In 1899 the first stone was laid and in 1910 the great **Oceanographical Museum**[1] which rises on the seaward cliffs of the peninsula was opened. The most famous collection of its kind in the world, it is now under the direction of Commandant Jacques Cousteau, the pioneer of underwater exploration.

The basement of the Museum is devoted to an aquarium, and as you go down the stone stairs you are greeted by the barking of the seals who dive and swim and swerve in a large basin at the entrance, seemingly untiring in their zest for play. Further on are about sixty glass tanks of brilliant variegated tropical fish, all the colours of the rainbow, as well as such comical local fish as the *mérou*, with the drooping mouth and bulbous eyes of a hanging judge. Turtles flap lazily up and down their tanks. Rays turn up their little white unhappy faces. The long camouflage-dappled bodies of the lampreys sway endlessly like water-plants in a current.

On the ground floor of the Museum are models of luminous fish from the great abysses of the sea, lit up in green, purple, yellow, and red, and many times enlarged and illuminated models of plankton, with colours, shapes and designs which any abstract artist might be jealous of. There are oceanographical instruments and ships' models, and an enormous hall full of all sorts of fish and sea-beasts. The most valuable part of this unique collection consists of the

1. Open daily including the lunch period.

specimens which Prince Albert dredged up from the deep troughs of the sea – at the expense, when all is said and done, of millions of hopeful gamblers who never wished to see a fish in their lives unless it were flanked by a knife and fork. The hall on the left of the first floor is devoted to shells and scientific instruments; that on the right to an ingenious collection of everything connected with the sea and made from its products: a book bound in tanned conger-eel skin; enormous shells a yard across such as are used for holy-water stoups in cathedrals; sponges; mother-of-pearl with the buttons, mirrors, toilet articles, fans, opera glasses and such-like made from it; corals in the branch and coral necklaces, pendants and charms; the skins of sharks and shark-skin shoes and bags.

Prince Albert has perhaps a greater claim to the gratitude of our generation than the discovery of *Grimaldichthys profondissimus* and his scaly cousins on account of his practical support of one of humanity's least known benefactors, a certain Dr Guglielminetti, who, while on a visit to the Principality, invented *goudronnage* or the tarring of roads. The first tarred road in the world was constructed in Monaco in 1902 and with it the death sentence was passed on the dust devil which rendered our macadam roads intolerable to users and neighbours alike in the early days of motoring.

From the height of the Rock you may look across the blue square of the harbour, its edges fringed with the world's largest and most luxurious yachts, and the red roofs of La Condamine to the cliff-top of Monte Carlo. The lower towers of the Casino are dwarfed by the high white apartment blocks clothing the slopes which rise to the limestone cliffs below the Tête de Chien, fifteen hundred feet above. So tiny is the territory of the Principality and so numerous the people who wish to reside there that skyscrapers have been adopted as one solution of the problem; the other is land-reclamation from the sea. This has allowed the creation of the only sizeable bit of flat ground in the Principality – the luxurious Larvotto Beach and Sea Club.

All roads in Monte Carlo seem to lead to the **Casino**, which was built by Charles Garnier, the architect of the Paris Opera House, in the ornate style of 1880, with towers at the corners and great bronze angels sitting on the roof. Inside, it contains a theatre which as an operatic centre soon came to rival the great capitals of Europe. Massenet and Saint-Saëns wrote operas especially for it. Prima donnas were paid several hundred pounds for a single appearance. Many a famous French play had its opening night there, and Diaghilev made it the headquarters of the Ballets Russes de Monte Carlo. There are a restaurant, a night club, bars and, of course, the vast gaming rooms, where almost the only sound is the spinning of the ball in the roulette wheel, the monotonous *'Rien ne va plus'* of the croupiers, and an occasional bark of *'Banco!'* from one of the baccarat tables. The high play is in the inner sanctum, the *Salles Privées*. Even if one does not oneself want to wager, the Casino is well worth a visit, for the student of his fellow-men to watch the gamblers, and for the connoisseur of period decoration to contemplate the frescoes of the eighteen-eighties. Possibly the most remarkable is the ceiling of the bar, on which a number of completely naked ladies puff at cigarettes and cigars but all keep their feet modestly covered. Do not forget to take your passport with you, as admission is granted only to foreign citizens over the age of eighteen.

In front of the Casino are the Boulingrins, formal gardens with tropical trees such as banyans and with cacti the size of oak trees. At the side of the Casino is the famous Hôtel de Paris, built in the same style as the Casino and with another memorable *fin-de-siècle* fresco covering the end wall of the dining-room. A little further up is the cream-coloured Winter Sporting Club in a more severe modern style. (The Summer Sporting Club is out towards Monte Carlo Beach.) Not only the Casino but also both Sporting Clubs, the beaches and most of the big hotels are all owned by the *Société des Bains de Mer*, which even now pays forty per cent of all the salaries earned in the Principality. At the end of the Boulingrins runs the main street of this tiny town. Go a couple of blocks further up the hill and you have already walked out of the Principality into the French suburb of Beausoleil.

Near the point where the Middle Corniche comes in from the west a little museum quarter is growing up round the **Exotic Gardens**.[1] These hang on a cliff-face above the modern industrial suburb of Fontvieille and command a fine bird's-eye view of the Principality. Criss-crossed with paths and bridges, they contain over a thousand different varieties of cacti from Mexico, South America and Africa. There is one particularly wicked-looking plant which seems to be constructed entirely of barbed wire. There is the *echinocactus*, like a giant sea-urchin or a spiny football, which is known to waggish cactus-fanciers as 'mother-in-law's pillow'. *Cereus* winds in evil green serpents across the ground. *Pilocereus polylophus* rises nearly twenty feet high like a green column. Giant euphorbia from Abys-

---

1. Open all day between July and September; closed between 12 and 2 for the rest of the year. The ticket allows entry to the Grotte de l'Observatoire and Musée d'Anthropologie Préhistorique whose times of opening are the same as those for the Jardin Exotique.

sinia reach a height unknown anywhere else in Europe.

After one has wandered among these obscene and unearthly shapes, surely the sets of a mad stage-designer, a visit to the stalactites and stalagmites of the famous **Grotte de l'Observatoire,** which opens at three hundred feet up the cliff, is a slight anticlimax. Neolithic men lived in these caves in the Jardins Exotiques thousands of years before the cacti came, and next door is a **Museum of Prehistoric Anthropology,** with relics from this and other caverns on the Riviera, including the Red Rocks at Menton. Monaco's reputation for frivolity is not neglected. After all, there are fifteen casinos and nightclubs, and clubs for every activity, Scrabble not excluded. Cultural tourism may be an unsavoury phrase, but it is a reality, and Monaco caters for it. There are three theatres and three libraries. Our list of museums is not done with. The National Museum 'De Galea Collection' houses one of the finest collections in the world of doll-automata; the museum is open daily, but the automata are set in action only in the afternoons. In the Palace is a Napoleon Museum. The Sanousrit Collection concentrates on Egyptian archaeology. The Waxwork Museum contains life-size models of all the rulers of Monaco, from François Grimaldi in 1297, to Prince Rainier, Princess Grace and their children. It is closed only between November 26 and December 25.

Chapter 4

The Villages of the Corniche

✿

Eze – La Turbie – Beaulieu – Cap Ferrat – Villefranche

Three roads run at varying levels along the steep coast between Roquebrune and Nice. The Lower Corniche was begun in 1863 after the annexation of Nice, and reached Monte Carlo fifteen years later. It runs for most of the way along the bottom of the cliffs, keeping fairly close to the sea.

The Middle Corniche was begun in 1910 to relieve the congestion on the Lower Corniche and completed in 1928. It has the finest views of the three for one is sufficiently far off to grasp the panorama as a whole and sufficiently near to see the detail. It is the Middle Corniche which serves **Eze**, the most dramatic of all the medieval villages on the coast. Constructed of the local stone, it looks from a short distance like a rugged pinnacle of the mountain top on which it stands. Today only two or three score people live in the old part of Eze, and the houses, the door of one often on a level with the roof of the one below, are given over to a succession of art, souvenir, postcard and antique shops. If one succeeds in dismissing them from one's mind, there is no place which can convey so vivid an impression of a fortified village of the Middle Ages. No wheeled traffic can pass through the narrow gate and one climbs on one's feet up the steep curves of its alleys to the ruins of the castle, set in a cactus garden.[1] From the summit the cars look like beetles crawling along the Lower Corniche thirteen hundred feet below.

The uppermost of the three roads, the Grande Corniche, does not run down into Monte Carlo but joins the lower road at Roquebrune. It was built by Napoleon in 1806 and follows approximately the track of the ancient Via Aurelia, the great highway which ran from Rome to the Rhône Valley and on to such barbarous outposts as Britain. It rises to fifteen hundred feet at La Turbie on the top of the Tête de Chien, the height which overhangs Monte Carlo.

1. Open all day.

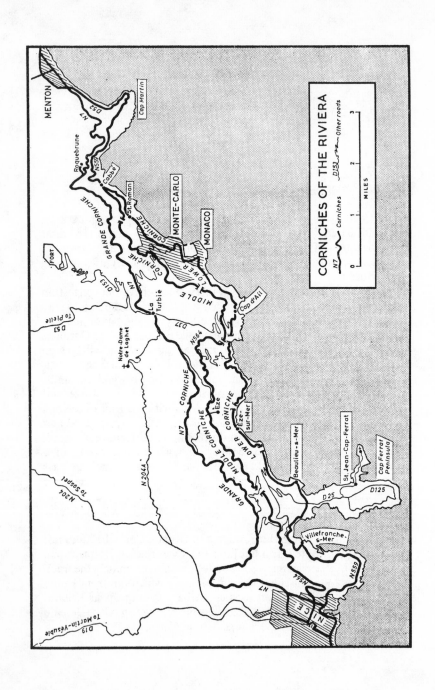

CORNICHES OF THE RIVIERA

N7 Corniches   D153 Other roads

MILES
0   1   2   3

At **La Turbie**,[1] five years before Christ was born, the Emperor Augustus erected a great monument known today as the Trophy of Augustus or the Trophy of the Alps. It commemorated the final subjugation of the Ligurian mountaineers who had for so many years obstructed communications between Rome on the one hand and Gaul on the other. Forty-four conquered tribes were listed in the inscription at the foot of the monument. Originally the Trophy was about 150 feet high on a base 120 feet square and was crowned with a twenty-foot statue of the Emperor himself. It was, however, wrecked by St Honorat, who found the people worshipping it, damaged by the barbarians, used as a quarry for the building of the village, turned into a fort and finally blown up by the French, with other Savoyard castles, in 1705. The heap of ruins remaining by the nineteen-thirties was so far as possible put in order and the monument re-erected to the present height of 100 feet at the expense of a public-spirited American, Mr Edward Tuck. He also built a small but interesting museum containing not only various Roman remains but also models and reconstructions of the monument as it is believed to have originally been. Seaward there is a fine view of the Principality, while landward the ground rises still further to fort-crowned Mont Agel at three thousand feet and the golf course, completed in 1912, which is said to have cost M. Blanc £100,000 to lay out.

Beaulieu, on the Lower Corniche, claims to have had only four days of frost in fifteen years and so prides itself on its sheltered situation that it has christened its eastern section Little Africa. Its other claim to fame is that Gordon Bennett, the eccentric owner of the *New York Herald* who sent Stanley out to Africa, picked on it to found La Réserve, which is still one of the most famous hotels on the Riviera.

Above the delightful Baie des Fourmis is Villa Kerylos, built in the Greek style by the archaeologist Theodore Reinach.[2]

From Beaulieu the road turns off to **Cap Ferrat**, which contains some of the finest gardens and most luxurious villas on the coast. The oldest olive tree in the South of France is said to be in M. Bounin's garden here on Cap Ferrat – and, in case anyone may be interested, the tallest ash in the Place du Frêne at Vence; the biggest mulberry at Roquebrune-sur-Argens in the Pays des Maures; and the largest plane tree the one, over forty feet round at the base, in the main square at Barjols (that strange Mithraic town with the waterfalls

1. Open all day; closed on May 1.
2. Open afternoons; closed on Mondays and in November.

near St Maximin) beneath which, every fourth year at the winter solstice, the citizens play on tambourines and flutes and let off muskets, while forty cooks roast an entire ox, which has been led garlanded and with gilded horns, through the town, blessed in front of the church and sacrificed.

The large Villa des Cèdres in the centre of the peninsula belonged for many years to King Leopold II of the Belgians and is now the home of M. Marnier-Lapostolle, who makes Grand Marnier. His thirty-eight acre garden contains a far finer collection of cacti than the one in the Exotic Garden at Monaco, as well as many other splendid and rare plants. The late Duke of Connaught used to spend every winter at Les Cèdres. Since 1927 Mr Somerset Maugham lived, wrote his books and entertained his friends until his death in 1965 in his villa, La Mauresque, near the end of the Cap. Not far from the attractive little fishing port of **St Jean,** which is the only village on the Cap, is the Villa Ephrussi de Rothschild, which houses the **Musée de l'Ile de France.**[1]

A certain Baroness Ephrussi, born a Rothschild, came to Cap Ferrat, saw and was conquered. She decided to settle there and bought a magnificent site on the high, narrow neck of the peninsula with views over the coast on both sides. Here she levelled off the whole ridge of the isthmus to form a platform and on it built a rather undistinguished Italianate villa and a magnificent garden of some fifteen acres.

The villa she designed both as a residence for herself and as a museum which should be a memorial to her parents. When she died in 1934 she left it with its contents to the Académie des Beaux Arts. It is of particular interest in that it was built especially to house and display the priceless treasures which she brought down from Paris. The painted Directoire panels were not made for the walls; the walls were made as settings for the panelling and the chimneypieces. The ceilings were not made and then painted; they were designed as frames for her Tiepolos. The central hall was expressly constructed as a setting for her Florentine doors and furniture, her *cassoni* and her della Robbias. Around this central hall are Louis Seize *salons* with Bouchers, Lancrets and Fragonards on the walls, contemporary furniture, Aubusson tapestries and Savonnerie carpets. The main theme of the rooms, the Baroness's bedroom and boudoir as well as the more public rooms, is French eighteenth century, but other rooms display the catholic tastes of the Rothschilds. They contain

1. Museum and gardens open in the afternoons; gardens only in the mornings. Closed on Mondays (except at Easter and Whitsun), and in November.

collections of brocaded Louis Seize dresses and costumes; of Sèvres and of Dresden porcelain; of Chinese screens, carpets, hangings, porcelain and pink jade; of cast-iron grilles; of Renoir, Sisley and Monet; of Japanese kakemonos; of Cordova leather . . . Each window has a different view; one over the sea to Eze and Cap d'Ail; another over the cypresses and lily ponds of the lovely gardens to the Temple of Venus on its little hill; yet a third across the Bay of Ville-franche to Mont Boron.

Another attraction on the peninsula is the St Jean-Cap Ferrat zoo (open all day), with its exotic gardens, various animals roaming at liberty, and a butterfly farm.

The deep inlet of the sea which separates Cap Ferrat from Mont Boron has long been a favourite anchorage of the French, as it is now of the American, Navy. What was once the naval harbour of the Dukes of Savoy is on the south-west side of the old fort. It is now reserved for yachts. The Lower Corniche here runs between villas and gardens high above the bay, and beneath it the little town of **Villefranche** clings to the slopes between the highway and the little fishing harbour. (It was so named because it was founded as a free port by Charles II of Anjou, Count of Provence and nephew of St Louis.) Steep alleys and stairways (the Rue Obscure is in fact a dark tunnel) lead down to the broad quays, lined with open-air cafés and restaurants where one may sit in the sun and look at the hanging gardens of Cap Ferrat across the dancing waters of the gulf.

At the entrance to the tiny fishing harbour is the fourteenth-century **Chapel of St Pierre**, where for centuries the local fishermen used to store their nets. In 1957 the Mayor found the fishermen somewhere else for their gear and gave Jean Cocteau, who had coveted it for many years, leave to decorate the building and turn it into a chapel once more. It was an admirable arrangement for everyone. Cocteau had his chapel to paint, the shopkeepers and restaurateurs profit by the trade of the visitors, and the fishermen's charities receive the entrance money.[1]

The little Romanesque chapel is decorated throughout in pale cream, pink, blue and green. The mural on the left of the door shows fishergirls on Villefranche quay in the picturesque old costume of the coast. The panel on the right honours the gipsies of Les Saintes-Maries-de-la-Mer. Against a background of a caravan a fisherman mends his nets and a little girl dances to a guitar. Above is an angel with the Virgin and Child. (In honour of the Bay of Angels, so Cocteau says, angels figure in all the five panels and on the ceilings. It is

1. Open daily.

no fault of his if some of them look rather like the illustrations to *Just So Stories*.)

The remaining three panels represent scenes from the life of the Fisherman himself. On the left is the Denial. St Peter, weeping in bitter humiliation, is being mocked by Pilate's soldiers, the cock is crowing triumphantly and the servant girl covers her face and slips away. The right-hand panel shows the angels delivering the saint from Herod's prison. The apse behind the altar shows him walking on the water, to the immense surprise of the local fishermen, the fishes and, for that matter, of the saint himself, for he cannot see the angel who is supporting him. A faint smile plays over the lips of Christ.

Chapter 5

Nice

۶

*The Old Town – the Modern Town – Carnival – the Battle of Flowers –
the Museums*

In 1887 one Stephen Liégeard wrote a book about the Riviera which, recalling the Côte d'Or of his native Burgundy, he called *La Côte d'Azur*. Doubtless on account of its publicity value, the name caught on in France and it is now much more commonly used than the old word 'Riviera'. By 'the Blue Coast' Liégeard himself meant the whole littoral from Marseilles to Genoa, but the term is now restricted to the section which begins at Menton and ends – well, at Cannes for the straitest of the purists, at St Raphaël for the majority of people, and at Hyères for those who live on the Côte des Maures.

If the limits of the Côte d'Azur are a matter of argument, its capital is not. Nice is the largest, and probably the oldest, town between Marseilles and Genoa. As a tourist resort it has an eighty-year start over Cannes and a century over Menton and Monte Carlo. With more than a third of a million inhabitants it ranks today as the fifth most populous city in France.

It is almost the only town on the Riviera which gives one the feeling that it exists of its own right and not merely by virtue of the visitors. True, Nice has fifteen thousand hotel bedrooms, but, whereas the other places are half-deserted out of the season, life in Nice, with its varied light industries and a high proportion of residents to tourists, goes on much the same all the year round. It no longer draws the aristocratic and fashionable visitors of sixty years ago, but retired people and *rentiers* are attracted to it from all over France, for together with its excellent communications, climate and scenery, it is large enough to provide the cultural, social, commercial, intellectual, gastronomic, sporting and other amenities of a capital. There is an opera house, and the airport is one of the largest and most modern in France. On a spring day it is possible to bathe in the morning, get into a car and a couple of hours later be in the snowfields of Peira Cava or one of the other winter sports

41

resorts in the Alpine foothills at the back of it.

It was doubtless some petty victory over the local Ligurians which led the Greek settlers of Marseilles to bestow the name of Nikêa on the colony which they founded here in the fourth century BC. When the Romans established themselves two hundred years later, they left the little settlement on the seashore to its Greek traders and sailors, and built themselves a new provincial capital on the hill of Cimiez on the other side of the River Paillon. Cemenelum, a city of twenty thousand inhabitants, was destroyed by the barbarians, but at the far end of what is now the Quai des États-Unis the little Greek village somehow struggled on and survived into the Middle Ages. In the eleventh century it became a free town governed by its own consuls.

In 1388, when Provence was ravaged by civil war, Nice and its hinterland became part of Savoy, a hitherto landlocked state whose only coastline was this long-coveted little strip between the mouth of the Var and the border of Monaco. The old town, still very Italian in character, occupies the triangle between the course of the Paillon, the Quai des États-Unis and the Castle Hill. It is a pleasant contrast, when one is weary of the broad straight boulevards, the cars and the buses, of the modern city, to exchange the noise of auto engines for that of shrill disputing voices, the smell of diesel fuel for that of garlic, and to wander round these narrow streets, finishing up with a glass of *vin rouge* at the old dark wineshop opposite the Cathedral of St Réparate or a meal at one of the many excellent, Michelin-rosetted restaurants in its vicinity, some of them specializing in bouillabaisse and other fish dishes. The churches are all seventeenth- and eighteenth-century Italian Baroque in style. Architecturally speaking, the best worth visiting is perhaps the **Chapel of the Black Penitents**, also known as the Miséricorde, especially as it has a good Mirailhet altarpiece.

In the middle of the fifteenth century a remarkable school of religious painting grew up at Nice. It is called the École Niçoise or the École de Bréa after its best-known exponent, Ludovic Bréa, sometimes miscalled by patriots 'the Fra Angelico of Provence'. Other leading members were his brother Antoine, Antoine's son François, Jacques Durandi and Mirailhet. While it does not bear any comparison with the contemporary schools of Florence and Venice, it is marked by a very attractive simplicity and purity of line.

The wholesale **flower market**, just behind the Quai des États-Unis in the Cours Saleya, once the centre of the old town, used to be famous the world over. At the right time of year its two long covered halls held a fabulous combination of colour and fragrance such as no art can produce. From about midday the dealers began to assemble their wares. At two o'clock a signal was given and the trade in beauty was allowed to start.

An afternoon flower market is still held on weekdays, but it is a poor apology now, because the wholesale flower market has been transferred to a modern covered market at Nice-St Augustin near Nice-Côte d'Azur airport.

The Quai des États-Unis, now lined with several of the best restaurants in Nice, such as the Girelle Royale, was formerly the Plage des Ponchettes, where the huts of the ancient Nikêa stood by the shores. The **Galerie des Ponchettes**[1] which still stands along the eastern part, was the old Sardinian naval arsenal, and its name is now better known through the municipally owned picture gallery at No. 77 on the Quai, where exhibitions of modern painters are often held.

At the end of the Quai rises the precipitous hill, the old Greek Acropolis, on which many centuries later the Dukes of Savoy built their castle. In 1706 it was captured and, on the orders of Louis XIV, razed to the ground by an Englishman – the Duke of Berwick, no less, illegitimate son of King James II, kinsman of the Duke of Marlborough, and victorious commander of the French armies during the War of the Spanish Succession (that extraordinary war when the French armies were commanded by an exiled English Catholic, Berwick, and the English armies by an exiled French Protestant, the Count de Ruvigny). Now it is a terraced public garden, planted with umbrella pines, aloes and palm trees, and still referred to as the Château.

Beyond the Castle Hill lies the harbour, **Port Lympia**, which was begun in 1750 and has been several times enlarged. It is from here that the packet-boats sail to Corsica. The red stucco eighteenth-century buildings round it are strongly reminiscent of Italy, and in fact it was in a house on the corner of the Quai Lunel, near the Customs House, that Garibaldi was born in 1807. There are pleasant restaurants round the port, providing good food and views over the harbour. Ane Rouge and l'Esquinade are side by side on Quai Deux-Emmanuel; the more modest La Vedette on Quai Lunel is on the west side of Port Lympia.

The lower course of the Paillon, now covered over, which runs to the sea beneath the Municipal Casino, the Place Masséna and the Jardins Albert Ier, still separates the old town, on the left bank, from the new town which in the middle of the eighteenth century began to arise on the low-lying right bank when wealthy English

1. Open daily except Mondays.

milords realized that there was a place where it did not rain every day and came out to enjoy the delights of the Riviera climate. What had two thousand years before been a Greek colony now found itself faced across the river by a British colony. Politics had something to do with this. The French, like the English, had begun to discover the delights of winter sunshine but, while England was closely allied with the King of Sardinia (as the Duke of Savoy had by now rather mysteriously become), France was on chronically bad terms with him. The English found a warm welcome in Nice, but the French rather naturally preferred their own resort of Hyères.

In 1763 the English novelist Tobias Smollett spent ten months in Nice, occupying a 'ground floor' for which he paid twenty pounds. 'The apartments are large, lofty and commodious enough, with two small gardens,' he wrote. (A furnished house with a large garden then cost £130 a year.) Smollett was indeed the pioneer of the Riviera, if his claim be true that he invented the cult of sea-bathing for health, although women, of course, could not indulge in it 'unless they lay aside all regards to decorum' – as they sometimes do on the beaches round St Tropez today. Smollett was followed by an increasing flow of English noblemen and the Hôtel des Anglais was opened on the site where the Hôtel Ruhl used to stand.

In 1822 a bad frost killed all the orange trees and, to provide employment for those thrown out of work, the English colony financed and organized the construction of a promenade along the shore of the Baie des Anges. The most famous promenade of its kind in the world now runs in a magnificent arc for four miles along the shore of the Bay of the Angels and, commemorating its first creators, retains its original name of the **Promenade des Anglais**. Were Pope Gregory the Great to return from Paradise to visit what King Leopold described as its terrestrial section, his comment might well be: '*Non angeli sed Angli.*'

The tourist boom was not slow to arrive after the union with France and the coming of the railway. An almost unbroken line of smart hotels arose along the Promenade des Anglais from the Hôtel Ruhl et des Anglais on the corner of the Gardens, through the Westminster, Royal, Luxembourg and West End, to the last and most luxurious of all, the Negresco, built on the grounds of a convent next door to the Villa Masséna for six million gold francs in 1912.

Cimiez, once the grand residential quarter of Nice, is still worth a visit. On the right of the Hôtel Excelsior, where Queen Victoria used to stay every winter, is the Parc des Arènes which contains the ruins, partly restored, of one of the smallest amphitheatres of the Roman world, started in the reign of Augustus. There is also a little baptistery, and what may be the best example of Roman baths in Gaul, excavated in 1965. Since then, more of Roman Cimiez has been revealed. All these remains can be visited through the **Archaeological Museum**[1] in the Villa des Arènes, where the ancient history of Cemenelum (Roman Cimiez) and the Nice region is reconstructed.

In the same building is the **Matisse Museum**.[1] The artist had lived, worked and died (in 1954) in Nice and Cimiez since 1917 (with a short stay at Vence between 1943 and 1948). Paintings, drawings, lithographs, pottery, sculpture and personal souvenirs are displayed. If you turn right down the Avenue du Monastère, you come to an ancient **Monastery**, the Couvent de Cimiez, rebuilt in 1860 in a highly decorated Italian Gothic style. (In the cemetery on the left Matisse and Dufy are buried.) Inside there are three Bréa *retables*. On the first altar in the right aisle is Ludovic Bréa's earliest altarpiece, dating from 1475, a *'Pieta'* flanked by St Catherine with her wheel, and St Martin riding a magnificent white horse with red caparisons. Over the third altar on the left is the painter's last known work, a 'Crucifixion' painted in 1512. Opposite, above the third altar on the right, is a 'Descent from the Cross' by his brother Antoine. Both these latter have retained their *predelle*, small scenes below the main picture which should on no account be missed. Often the *predelle* are better than the pictures themselves. (Other Bréas in Nice are in the Masséna Museum, St Augustin, St Barthélemy and the Misericorde Chapel.) On the right of the church is a beautiful Italian garden overlooking the Paillon, from which one can realize the impressive isolation of the rock where the Acropolis and the Castle stood.

As the Boulevard de Cimiez rises towards Cimiez and is joined by Avenue du Docteur-Ménard, there stands the **Chagall Memorial**.[2] This building, opened by Chagall in 1973 when he was aged eighty-six, houses his Biblical Message, seventeen large paintings on the subject of Genesis, Exodus and the Song of Songs. There are also gouaches and etchings on the Scriptural themes that reflect his passionate human and spiritual beliefs.

The old town of Nice meets the new, and the country buses start their runs, in the great palm-shaded **Place Masséna**. Its red-arcaded buildings were erected in 1835 in the handsome Genoese eighteenth-century style to match those of the port. On the east side, on the site

1. Open daily between June 1 and September 30; afternoons only for the rest of the year. Closed on Mondays except between July 1 and September 15, and in November.
2. Closed on Tuesdays; open all day between May 1 and September 30.

of the old municipal casino, is the new Town Hall, and behind it the valley of the Paillon carries the roads into the interior and over the Alps to Turin; on the north the Avenue Jean Médecin (shown on the map by its old name of Avenue de la Victoire), the main shopping street of the town, leads up to the low, villa-covered hills which shield the city from the *tramontana*; southward are the narrow streets of the old town; while on the west the lovely Jardins Albert Ier, with their little open-air theatre, curve down to the waterfront between the Promenade des Anglais and the Quai des États-Unis.

The Place Masséna is the favourite spot from which to watch the Carnival, perhaps the most famous popular festival left in Europe. For a fortnight every February King Carnival holds sway. Stands are erected and thousands of people come into town to watch his procession pass slowly round the square, up to the end of the Avenue Jean Médecin and back again. For all its commercialization, which is undeniable, the Carnival gives a genuine impression of unforced gaiety which somewhere else might require many gallons of liquor to generate. The procession starts at half past two on the two Sunday afternoons and takes an hour to pass. Then it comes round again like the next 'house' in a cinema so that, if you want to, you can sit it out and see it several times. In the evening the procession is repeated and the streets and the floats are brilliantly illuminated by thirty thousand electric bulbs.

The procession consists of the *chars*, or floats, and the *cavalcades*, interspersed with the *groupes à pied*. The *cavalcades* are little processions of gaily dressed eighteenth-century ladies on fine white horses, huntsmen, plumed cavaliers and suchlike. The footmen walk, dance or caper along supporting a papier-mâché framework on their heads and torsos. Many of them are 'big heads', so called because they wear grotesque masks which may weigh anything up to thirty pounds. Some caricature well-known topical figures; some, Janus-like, have faces at the back as well as at the front; others represent vegetables such as artichokes and leeks, birds such as chickens, pelicans or pigeons or figures of pure fantasy. As they caper along the street they look horrifyingly like the creations of Hieronymus Bosch come to life. The floats are often elaborate scenes of fantasy and satire, anything up to thirty feet high. These grotesques and floats are designed by brilliant comic artists, and many sketches and models are sent specially down from the *ateliers* of Paris. The craft of making these extraordinary objects is handed down from father to son. The *carnavaliers*, as they are called, begin work at the beginning of the autumn, for these elaborate confections take several months to produce. An average float uses a ton of waste paper and six hundred pounds of flour and, painted and stretched on its framework of iron and wire, weighs eight tons and may have to take the weight of a number of passengers jigging up and down for hours.

All this takes place in the midst of an indescribable bedlam. Brass bands play in all directions, with *Valencia, Colonel Bogey* and *Le Madelon* competing at short range. The spectators are all buying bags of confetti and throwing the contents at each other, so that soon they are spangled with square and diamond-shaped bits of paper. The great joke is to catch someone of the opposite sex gaping or laughing and stuff a handful into their open mouth, so that it is better to keep your mouth shut – here as indeed so often elsewhere. At the end of the day the Avenue Jean Médecin is ankle-deep in bits of paper. It is like walking through a multicoloured snowdrift. Every year the Municipality sweeps up about a hundred tons of confetti and throws it into the sea.

In the good old days confetti was far from being the only missile used at the carnival. There were bonbons, beans and even eggs – but the gallant threw the flowers which grew so abundantly round Nice and with which rich visitors used to decorate their carriages. In 1876 the flower-throwing became separated from the Corsi Carnavalesques, and the first Battle of Flowers, as we know it, took place on the Promenade des Anglais. Nowadays flower-decked equipages of various sorts parade up and down the Quai des États-Unis on the afternoon of Thursday, the day after Ash Wednesday. The Battle of Flowers is a delightfully pretty spectacle. (I think 'pretty' is the right word to describe it.) The band plays over and over again the gay, jigging Carnival Song (which scans slightly better sung than read):

> If you go to Nice,
> By plane, by train,
> Or by horse,
> If you go to Nice,
> You'll have the sea
> And the carnival lights.

All the *fiacres* of Nice are commandeered for the occasion, and loaded with pretty girls, whose smiling faces contrast with those of the bronzed and misanthropic old cabbies driving them. They throw flowers to the spectators, who try to field them and return them. Flower-sellers on the pavements supply ammunition to throw at the girls, in the shape of bunches of carnations, mimosa and marguerites. Interspersed with the humble horse-cabs are big *chars fleuris* mounted on motor trucks and decorated with banks, canopies, arabesques and arches of flowers, not to mention such conceits as stuffed white doves in cages of blossoms and even little flowering cherry trees. At this season of the year carnations are the predominant flower, but there are many others such as irises, lilies and marguerites. Some present quite a problem in identification, as when, for example, the carnations are dyed blue or green.

The idea of a festival of flowers or fruit has caught on all along the coast. Menton has its Festival of Lemons, Cannes and St Raphaël of Mimosa, Grasse of Jasmine, Cagnes of Carnations, Beaulieu of Tangerines and even Valbonne of Grapes. Villefranche, like Sète far away in Languedoc, has its nautical Battle of Flowers.

The last night of Carnival, Shrove Tuesday, is devoted to a full-dress firework display. They are let off on the quay at the foot of the Castle Hill and the best vantage point is the Quai des États-Unis, where crowds gather on the stands prepared for the Battle of Flowers, and on the beach. In the grand finale flares are set off all the way up the steep ramp leading to the Acropolis and gradually light it as they snake their way up. At the end the pine-tops on the Hill emerge black and ragged from a cloud of illuminated smoke. Then the display finishes, as it began, with the roar of a gun from the castle.

At this point until very recently, when the practice was discontinued for fear of fire, King Carnival was solemnly burned on the beach. Every year a new king succeeded him – like the Priest of Nemi, 'the priest who slew the slayer and shall himself be slain'. The dynasty dates from 1873, when the Comité des Fêtes was formed to take charge of this old medieval custom, but there were two gaps, amounting to ten years, when the Carnival was not held during the German Wars.

Nice is essentially a town for living in and not for sightseeing – unless you include in that term the hundreds of bikini-clad bodies lying on the pebbly beach below the Promenade des Anglais, known to misogynists as 'the meat-slab'. Nevertheless, there are two or three musuems. In the suburb of St Barthélemy is the **Prieuré du Vieux-Logis**[1] where the Dominican Father Lemerre has patiently reconstructed a religious house of the Middle Ages. The thirteen rooms are filled with fifteenth-century furniture, ironwork, household utensils and pictures, each in its appropriate place. The **Musée**

1. Open on Wednesday, Thursday and Saturday afternoons, as well as the afternoon of the first Sunday in the month.

Chéret[1] in the Avenue des Baumettes is called after a local painter, Jules Chéret. Its chief interest is for a student of the Van Loos, the dynasty of Dutch painters who worked in the South of France. (Carle Van Loo was born in Nice.) There is an entire room full of their works on the left as you go in. Sir Thomas Lawrence's portrait of Mrs Anna Brandt and Laszlo's portraits of the Gerliczy-Burian family represent the British School. Upstairs, through the Chéret rooms, is a small collection of modern masters such as Dufy, Braque, Matisse, Bonnard and Marquet. There is a Japanese room, another devoted to the history of the Carnival, another to Carpeaux, and a fourth to nineteenth-century painters. The latter contains a number of Ziems but I found the most interesting the half-dozen works of the diarist Marie Bashkirtseff, who lived at No. 63 Promenade des Anglais. They include a self-portrait, which may be compared with another in the Musée Masséna.

The **Musée Masséna**,[2] next door to the Negresco on the Promenade des Anglais, is an altogether more important museum. Since 1921 it has occupied the palace built in 1900 by the Prince of Essling, grandson of Napoleon's Marshal Masséna, who was himself the son of an innkeeper at nearby Levens. The fine *Empire* rooms on the ground floor, with their *Empire* furniture and carpets, are very rightly used by the Municipality of Nice for important official receptions. Upstairs are a number of primitives, and very notably two fine examples from Lucéram, a polyptych of 'St Margaret' and a 'St John the Baptist' attributed to Durandi, who, slightly older than Bréa, flourished about 1450. A room of Impressionists contains five Renoirs and three Sisleys besides such painters as Boudin and Degas. Two rooms on the same floor are filled with works by Raoul Dufy – twenty-five oils, and many water-colours, drawings, two ceramics and tapestry – left to the town of Nice by his widow in 1962. The rooms devoted to the history of Nice contain a number of interesting prints and water-colours, as well as a curious proclamation by King Victor Emmanuel in 1860, trying to 'throw' the plebiscite and urging his subjects to vote for annexation to France. Other rooms are devoted to relics of Napoleon and to those two martial sons of Nice, Masséna and Garibaldi; others again contain collections of local folklore and customs, armour, Oriental jewellery and ceramics ranging from Moustiers ware to Picasso.

Two other museums catering for more specialist interests are

1. Closed on Mondays and bank holidays.
2. Closed on Mondays and public holidays.

worth mentioning. The **Marine Museum**[1] is at the top of the sixteenth-century Tour Bellanda, on the wooded height of the Château, and contains models of ships. **The Museum of Natural History (Musée Barla)**,[2] 60 Boulevard Risso, displays much local and more general natural history; in 1977 some reorganizing of the museum was started. Barla and Risso were distinguished Niçois naturalists of the last century.

Nice has a more open hinterland than Menton and Monaco, and many of the hill villages are well worth a visit. Beuil, Peille and Peillon are typical 'eagle's nests', perched on their hill-tops. Auron (with four months of good snow a year), Valberg and Beuil are the main winter sports centres. Lucéram, for all its contributions to the Musée Masséna, still has four altarpieces of the Nice School in its church and Lieuche has one. There are some fine fifteenth-century frescoes in the chapel of the Penitents-Blancs at La Tour-sur-Tinée; old Romanesque churches in the high valleys of the Paillon, the Roya and the Vésubie; and fine scenery such as the red rocks of the Daluis Gorges and the Cians Gorges. But all these the reader must explore for himself with the aid of his own legs, of a car or of the admirable local bus services.

1. Closed on Tuesdays.
2. Closed on Tuesdays, public holidays and August.

Chapter 6

Cagnes and St Paul

✋

Renoir's Villa – the Castle of Cagnes – St Paul – Fondation Maeght –
Villeneuve-Loubet

The country immediately to the west of the River Var is even more
thickly peppered with castles and walled fortress-villages than the
rest of this corsair-haunted coast. For many centuries the little river
formed the boundary between Provençal and French territory on the
one side and the dominions of the Dukes of Savoy and the Kings of
Sardinia, who were usually allied with the Spaniards, the English or
the Austrians, on the other.

In 1763 Tobias Smollett wrote that within living memory no fewer
than three bridges over the Var had been destroyed as a result of the
jealousies between the Kings of France and Sardinia so that travellers
to Italy preferred to make the arduous crossing of the Alps or, like
the Président des Brosses, to take ship from Antibes. According to
the Abbé Papon, the historian of Provence, the crossing was ordin-
arily made seated on the shoulders of two stalwart *gaieurs*, but he
adds a warning not to look down into the rapidly-running water for
fear of getting giddy and falling in.

Now there are road and railway bridges and, the Var once safely
crossed, there are several roads westwards. The principal one runs
along the coast; for much of the way it follows the ancient Aurelian
Way, which led from Rome to Fréjus and Aix, and on to Narbonne
and the great cities of Roman Spain, a road where one can almost
hear the tramp-tramp of the legionaries underlying the screech of the
klaxons and the clatter of the lorries and the motor-coaches.

The first place of any importance is **Cagnes-sur-Mer**, the centre of
a countryside rich with fields of carnations and roses. Cagnes-sur-
Mer is really composed of three distinct though continuous villages,
the medieval Haut-de-Cagnes above, the seventeenth- and eighteenth-
century Bas-de-Cagnes, which is really the main village itself, at the
foot of the hill, and the very mid-twentieth-century settlement of Le
Cros-de-Cagnes on the sea.

It was in the middle village that Auguste Renoir, suffering from rheumatoid arthritis and ordered south by his doctors, passed the last sixteen years of his long and fruitful life. His villa, **Les Collettes,**[1] with the ancient olive trees which he loved so much, was bought by the Municipality of Cagnes in 1958 and turned into a museum. There is no signpost to the Musée Renoir from the main road through Le Cros-de-Cagnes. You have to turn off inland at the sign 'Cagnes 2' along the road which leads into the village. From there it is well signposted.

Of the master's original works the museum contains only one oil-painting, three terracottas and half a dozen drawings and bronzes, but there are a number of personal relics – his furniture, his easel, palette and brushes, his coat and cravat, his two invalid sticks and the wheeled chair to which his illness confined him. The last paintings Renoir was able to paint on his feet were the two 'Dancing Girls', commissioned by his friend M. Gaugnat in 1909 when he was sixty-eight and recently acquired by the National Gallery in London. During the last years of his life his brushes had to be tied to his paralysed fingers and he painted with movements of his arm alone. The first two of the bronzes Renoir made here he was able to model with his own fingers but for the later ones he had to use the hands of a clever young amanuensis who worked to his detailed instructions and corrected as he went along every point which the exacting old man found imperfect.

He was looked after by the faithful (and frequently painted) Gabrielle, who came originally as nursemaid to his children and stayed on to tend the old painter, as well as acting as his cook and his favourite model. After his death she married an American connoisseur who had transferred his admiration from the master to the maid.

The great olive trees are still hauntingly beautiful, but the view beyond them to the sea is sadly changed since Renoir's day. A sea of little red-roofed houses, enormous blocks of whitewashed flats and the grey skeletons of other blocks now cover the flat land between Les Collettes and the sea. This is Le Cros-de-Cagnes, which straddles the main road to Antibes, with the Nice racecourse on the left.

The historic Cagnes, **Le Haut-de-Cagnes**, is on the little hill just to the north, which two thousand years ago was a promontory jutting into the sea, like those of Nice and Cannes today. It is typical of these small hill-top villages. Their crenellated walls encase them like the

1. Open every afternoon except Tuesdays, public holidays, and between October 15 and November 15.

armoured hull of a warship, and inside, like its various and complicated inner ducts, is a warren of narrow, twisting alleyways set at so steep an angle that it is a relief when at length they turn into flights of stairs.

Crowning the pyramid-village is a castle built by Raynier Grimaldi, Sovereign of Monaco and Admiral of France, who became Lord of Cagnes in 1309. In 1333 the Grimaldi counted as many as a hundred and ten male descendants and one or other of their branches was, at some time or another, lord of practically every town on the coast except Nice and Cannes. In 1620 Jean-Henri Grimaldi transformed the medieval castle into an elegant Louis Treize château – the equivalent of our English Jacobean style. (It was he who persuaded his cousin Honoré II of Monaco, to transfer his principality from Spanish protection to French.) His descendants remained lords of Cagnes until the last Grimaldi, Marquis of Cagnes, was expelled by the inhabitants at the French Revolution and driven to take refuge in Nice.

The **Castle** was bought by the town of Cagnes for a quarter of a million francs just before the war and turned into a museum[1] – and a model museum at that, with full and interesting explanations of everything displayed on the walls beside the exhibits. The visitor steps into an interior court open to the sky, which was the only source of light and air in the Middle Ages, when there were no windows but only narrow gun embrasures. The Museum of the Olive Tree, which occupies the rooms on the left of the ground floor, is dedicated to that fruit in all its aspects. There are photographs of trees, groves and mills in various countries, old books on olive culture, maps of its geographical distribution, pictures of olive-groves by distinguished painters, old boxes of inlaid 'Nice wood', as it used to be called, olive presses and amphorae, botanical details and everything else anyone could conceivably wish to know about the fruit and its cultivation. The other rooms are historical. The first floor contains the Salle des Fêtes with a *trompe l'œil* ceiling by the Genoese Carlone depicting the Fall of Phaeton; it also houses the so-called Museum of Mediterranean Art. This catholic adjective embraces all the modern painters who have worked on the coast. They range from the Japanese Foujita to the Russian Chagall. The latter has perhaps a better claim than most to be called a Mediterranean artist, since he still lives and works at Vence. Since 1969 an International Festival of Painting is held annually in June at the Castle, under the aegis of UNESCO. Its objectives are to give prominence to contemporary

1. Open daily except Tuesdays and between October 10 and November 15.

development in pictorial art.

Just below the castle on the north-east side, as you turn left by the second car-park, is the old **Chapel of Notre Dame de Protection**,[1] the apse of which is covered by some interesting frescoes. Though the costumes clearly date them from the sixteenth century, they are equally unmistakably 'primitives' and were evidently the work of some local artist or craftsman. These penitentiary chapels were generally built, as this one was, just outside the entrance to a town and dedicated to the Virgin, to St Sebastian or to St Roch, in the hope of warding off the approach of the plague or any other of the many scourges prevalent in the Middle Ages.

From Cagnes three roads turn right-handed up into the hills. Two of them lead to Grasse. The westerly one is the more direct, but we will take the easterly one since it runs by way of the two ancient hill-towns of St Paul and Vence. I use the word 'towns' for want of a better, but it is an all-embracing term in this part of the world, where cities are tiny and villages are large and compact. It must be taken to cover a little episcopal city like Vence, with nearly ten thousand inhabitants, and a big walled village like St Paul with about sixteen hundred. Both alike have the characteristics of small towns.

All the hill-top settlements along the coast – Cagnes, Vence, St Paul, Biot, Mougins – are rapidly spilling into the surrounding valleys. In the old days when perpetual warfare, barbarian invasions, banditry and Saracen raids added up to general anarchy, the farmers tilled their land by day and at night they huddled for safety behind the walls of their fortified villages. Now their houses, rising in tiers above the ramparts and towering magnificently over the sea and the hills, are being bought as summer residences by the bourgeois of Nice and Cannes or by foreign *rentiers* and artists. Many have been turned into antique, handicraft or souvenir shops, or little restaurants and tea-rooms. The owners themselves, only too relieved to be rid of their cramped and insanitary abodes and caring little about the view, have sold out happily and built themselves ugly, roomy, comfortable villas on their properties outside the walls.

St Paul is an old village (there is still a thirteenth-century house standing, just off the main street, and the square watch-tower beside the church is a relic of the twelfth-century donjon) but it owes its present character to Francis I, who in 1537 decided to make it into a fortress countering the Duke of Savoy's stronghold of Nice beyond the Var. His engineer, François de Mandon de Saint-Rémy,

1. Open in the afternoons; closed on Tuesdays, public holidays and between October 15 and November 15.

pulled down six hundred houses to build the great ramparts and bastions which stand intact today, despite many sieges and occupation by Piedmontese, Austrians and even Hungarians.

After the First World War painters flocked to St Paul and many of them presented their pictures as gifts or (for many world-famous masters have in their youth been short of the price of a meal) left them as payment for hospitality to the famous restaurant, **La Colombe d'Or**, which is just ahead of you at the T-fork before you enter the village from the coast road. It bears no sign, but its distinguishing mark is a flock of snow-white doves. In the course of forty years M. Roux, the owner of La Colombe d'Or, accumulated one of the finest private collections of modern paintings in France. They include works by Picasso, Braque, Miró, Rouault, Modigliani, Matisse, Derain, Dufy, Utrillo, Vlaminck, Léger, Bonnard and many others of the École de Paris. When they were stolen in 1960 (and subsequently recovered) they were valued at nearly three million francs.

The price of a luncheon at the Colombe d'Or, which starts with twenty-three different kinds of hors d'oeuvres, all laid out on the table before you, can set you back a hundred francs or more, but one can see these pictures without taking a meal by simply ordering a *pastis* or a vermouth at the bar. Without even going as far as the bar, you can admire the big ceramic of 'The Girl with the Parrot' by Fernand Léger in the front patio.

Wheeled traffic is not possible in the narrow lanes and flights of steps, paved with pink tiles like Siena, of St Paul itself, but there is a car-park at the entrance to the town near the Restaurant of the Golden Dove. The church is nothing much to look at outside but the interior is one of the most attractive in the South of France. The nave, with its three aisles, is so broad as to be almost a perfect square, and in the afternoon it is superbly lit from the light through the west windows.

Near the door is a modern carving of St Antony in olive-wood by Arthur Lutenbacher which must be felt with the palms of the hands for its curves and texture to be appreciated. ('Please do not touch the statues.' What nonsense! All good sculpture should be felt through the fingers as well as through the eyes.) The last altar on the right has an interesting stucco bas-relief of the martyrdom of St Clement and above it a good Italian altarpiece of St Charles Borromeo with the Virgin and St Clement, but the best and most surprising picture is at the end of the left aisle, a St Catherine, which has been attributed both to Lebrun and to Tintoretto. I have not been able to discover how it ever ended up in St Paul but, although the cherubs and flowers at the top betray a later hand, I for one would be prepared to ascribe the central figure to the great Venetian.

The treasury in the sacristy is worth a visit too. Look particularly at a beautiful thirteenth-century Madonna and Child. It is of a harsh power seldom achieved in religious art between the thirteenth and the twentieth centuries.

In 1964 a very remarkable and important museum of modern art was built by the Paris art dealer, Aimé Maeght and his wife Marguerite. The **Fondation Maeght**[1] stands in lovely sloping parkland with glorious views of the coast and hills, just outside St Paul-de-Vence. The little road to it is clearly marked.

Quite apart from the contents, the building itself is fascinating for its whole conception by the architect, J.-L. Sert. The design, the lighting and even the method of humidification to preserve the works of art there are original and stimulating.

There are permanent mosaics by Chagall, Tal Coat and Braque; ceramic sculptures by Miró; bronze figures by Giacometti in the courtyard; in the chapel, windows by Braque and Ubac. Calder's 'stabiles' are placed in the gardens. In addition to its substantial collections of twentieth-century artists, the Fondation presents three major exhibitions a year – either retrospective or contemporary. Each summer a festival, *Nuits de la Fondation Maeght*, is devoted to music, theatre and bailet. The Fondation runs a literary magazine, gives financial aid to artists, has two libraries, a cinema, cafeteria, discotheque and phototheque. Reproductions of the works displayed there can be bought.

The Fondation Maeght, its founders insist, is more than an art gallery, more than a museum; it is an organization aiming to bring about a love and understanding of modern art. It is an audacious and exciting addition to the modern art museums strung along the French Riviera.

Returning to St Paul-de-Vence, in the Place de la Grande Fontaine is the **Musée Provençal de la Grande Fontaine**[2] housed in an attractive sixteenth-century mansion. It contains furniture, costumes and the household utensils once used by Provençal families – a miniature Musée Arlaten which Mistral created in Arles.

If you are making your way back to the coast, you can take the La Colle-sur-Loup road so as to pass by Villeneuve-Loubet. Behind the Place de la Mairie is a place of pilgrimage for gastronomes. It is

1. Open daily throughout the year.
2. Open daily.

the **Escoffier Museum**, the Fondation Auguste Escoffier,[1] the birth-place in 1847 of 'the chef of kings, and king of chefs', who lived until 1935. Photographs, books of recipes, pictures, mementoes and the instruments of the trade all help to retrace the history of the culinary art of which he was an outstanding exponent.

1. Open every afternoon except Mondays, and during October.

Chapter 7

Vence and Gourdon

❧

Vence – the Matisse Chapel – the Gorges de Loup – Gourdon

The full name and style of St Paul is St Paul-de-Vence, and the city
of Vence itself lies some three miles further on. It is a curious drive.
At one point the road skirts a deep gorge, and from the overgrown
depths of it rises to the height of Nelson's Column a single, slender,
stone-built tower, topped (unnecessarily, for it is clearly unclimbable
even by Eiger standards) by a concrete railing. This surprising erection
was the central support of a viaduct, whose two arches were blown
up by the Germans in August, 1944, and which a hundred years ago
carried the old tramway (which in its turn carried Queen Victoria)
from Nice to Grasse. One comes across bits of it shyly emerging
from the scrub and the *maquis* all along this road, but this is by far
the most impressive relic. One feels that a thousand years hence
tourists, if they still exist, will come to gaze at this now neglected
nineteenth-century monument. On the eastern side of the ravine, just
beside the road, may be seen a rusty iron gate and the overgrown
remains of the platform and stairs of a station, carved out of the
cliff, where the line dives into a tunnel.

D. H. Lawrence died of tuberculosis in Vence in 1930 but, apart
from the novelist so suddenly and unexpectedly raised to the ranks
of the world's best-sellers by the British Public Prosecutor, its fame
is bound up almost exclusively with ecclesiastical figures and
religious matters. Historically, it is remembered for a number of
famous bishops astonishing for so obscure a see and, contempor-
arily, it is chiefly known for the Chapel of the Rosary decorated by
Henri Matisse.

The little city is shaped like a pistachio nut and it is wise to leave
your car in the plane-shaded car-park of the Place du Grand Jardin.
From there you enter the old town by the Porte de Peyra and find
yourself in the forum of the Roman city of Vintium, now a delightful
little square with a fountain in the shape of an urn, flanked on one
side by a pottery shop and on the other by a high, square stone
tower.

Ahead is the former cathedral, which is of little interest except for its imaginative and sometimes satirically carved fifteenth-century choir stalls. They are reached by a staircase on the left of the entrance. The door up to them is locked but the key is kept at the presbytery.

The list of the Bishops of Vence, which runs from the fifth century to the end of the eighteenth, includes two saints, St Veran and St Lambert, and a future Pope, the famous Alexander Farnese, who played his part on the world stage under the title of Paul III.

Bishop Godeau, in the seventeenth century, was in his youth known as the wittiest man in France and as a brilliant writer of gallant verses. This ugly brown gnome (whose portrait hangs in the Musée Fragonard at Grasse) was the most popular man who ever frequented the Hôtel Rambouillet, where he was affectionately known as 'Julie's dwarf', Julie being Madame de Scudéry, the daughter of the Marquise de Rambouillet. Cardinal de Richelieu appointed him the first member of the French Academy but at the age of thirty he tired, it would seem, of writing rhymed compliments to pretty ladies, entered the priesthood and was appointed Bishop of Grasse and Vence. Neither diocese displayed so liberal a spirit as Bath and Wells or Sodor and Man. Each refused to share a bishop with the other and both alike repulsed their father in God from their gates at the point of the arquebuse. In the end Godeau opted for Vence, became a model bishop, disciplined his lax clergy, rebuilt his ruinous cathedral and set up tanneries, potteries and scent factories to bring some measure of prosperity to his remote and impoverished diocese. In 1672 he died in an odour of sanctity – and, no doubt, of tanneries and scent factories.

Bishop Surian was called by the Encyclopaedist, d'Alembert, 'the second Massillon of Provence' on account of his silver-tongued eloquence in the pulpit, but he is perhaps better known and esteemed in France for his tart retort to General Brown, who had occupied Cagnes during the War of the Austrian Succession. When the envoy of the enemy commander asked Bishop Surian how long it would take him to get from Vence to Lyons, the Bishop replied: 'I know just how long it would take *me* to get to Lyons, but I have no idea how long it would take an army which had to fight the troops of my master, the King of France.'

Nowadays, the narrow streets and squares of Vence, with the arches and the flying buttresses striding over them, attract fewer visitors than Matisse's **Chapel of the Rosary** on the outskirts of the town. (Follow first the Avenue Henri Isnard, and then swing right into the Route de St Jeannet.) Like so many things in France, a visit to it needs planning ahead, since it is open only on Tuesdays and Thursdays (and not even then if they fall on a holiday of obligation). The chapel is attached to a convent of 'White Sisters', Dominican nuns who nursed the painter during a long and serious illness. Although himself a freethinker, he built a chapel for them and decorated it himself. It was consecrated in 1951, when he was already an octogenarian.

The altar is an oblong block of brownish sandstone from the Gard on a drum of the same rock. With its seven candlesticks and a lean brass crucifix, it faces the nave so that, as is often now the practice in France, the priest celebrates mass facing the congregation. Two walls are devoted almost entirely to window-space, with the glass designed in geometrical patterns of yellow, blue and green. Matisse himself is said to have regarded these windows as his finest work. Whether or not his estimate was correct, there can be no doubt that they excellently perform the primary function of windows by letting an astonishing amount of light into the chapel. It is of a luminosity which one does not expect to find in such a building.

The other two walls are of white faience, decorated with black line-drawings of figures which, faceless though they be, are of a power and beauty which almost make one forget the absence of the colour of which Matisse was so great a master. On the north wall of the chapel is a habited St Dominic, clutching a Bible. On the north wall of the nave the Virgin, surrounded by clouds, holds in her arms a Child with its arms held out to bless. On the rear wall, in three horizontal rows, are the fourteen Stations of the Cross. The Twelfth Station, the Crucifixion itself, is so contrived that it occupies the central position in the top row and therefore dominates the whole composition.

Immediately across the Cagne valley to the east of Vence is the village of La Gaude on the pretty minor road from Cagnes to St Jeannet. La Gaude is interesting because of the architecture of the research centre, built in 1960, for International Business Machines. Shaped like an X with low pillars supporting each arm, the building blends with the rocky landscape which surrounds it and is permitted, as it were, to enter below the building. It is another example of imaginative and fitting architecture on the Riviera coast. Whether the pseudo-Provençal villas round about are as successful is open to question.

From Vence the road runs through **Tourrettes-sur-Loup**, a village of less than a thousand people built round an enormous *place*. It has kept three of the old towers which gave it its name, and at the back of the high altar in the church is a third-century Roman altarstone, such as links so often, in this ancient land, even so tiny and obscure a place with the far past of our continent. Tourrettes has its link also with another and a newer continent, for it was the birthplace of the Admiral de Grasse who forced the British fleet out of Chesapeake Bay and thus enabled Washington to complete the blockade of Yorktown.

Not far beyond Tourrettes the traveller becomes rather suddenly aware of a two-thousand-foot cliff towering in front of him and, on the top of it, some grey houses huddled together like an eagle's nest and hardly to be distinguished from the naked rock of the brink. It is the vertiginous village of Gourdon.

At this point the main road continues through the famous Gorges of the Loup, while the direct road to Grasse forks off to the left through **Le Bar-sur-Loup**. The Gothic church of the village is well worth a visit both for an altarpiece of the School of Nice and for a curious fifteenth-century 'Triumph of Death' painted on wood, popularly referred to as the *Danse macabre*. On the left Death in the form of a skeleton bowman shoots his arrows at the living. In the centre foreground a lady of fashion falls pierced through the heart; on the right a newly-slain man, with an arrow through his chest, has his soul, a tiny, naked, frightened figure – surely the *animula vagula blandula* to which the Emperor Hadrian addressed his poem – drawn from his mouth by a devil, while other demons thrust freshly killed damned into the jaws of Hell. These panels were generally painted in time of plague, as this probably was, but in the background carefree and elegantly dressed lords and ladies dance gaily in a ring, clearly unaware of the figure of Death but all marked on the crowns of their heads with the little dancing black devil which spells their everlasting doom. In the upper right-hand corner an angel with a pair of scales weighs the merits of a soul more fortunate than the others. This *memento mori* is curiously northern in its feeling, one would be tempted to say, did one not recall to mind such paintings as those of Traini in the Campo Santo at Pisa.

The road through the Gorges of the Loup is hacked at many points out of the sheer overhanging cliff, as it runs along the bottom of the canyon. White waterfalls tumble down the precipices and at one point a cascade falls a hundred and fifty feet sheer, without touching the earth, into a basin just beside the road. The gorges are perhaps at their best on a sunny day in early November, for then the river, the waterfalls and the rivulets are lively and full with the autumn rains, while the trees and bushes make up a brilliant, splashing, Gauguin-like palette of russets and browns, bright crimsons and pale yellows, against the monotone of the rockface.

After a few miles the road crosses the Loup to the right bank, turns sharply back on its tracks and rises in steady hairpins to complete the round of the gorges, this time from the western cliff-top. At the end it comes to the little grey village which we saw from so far below, crowning the enormous spur of rock. **Gourdon** has only about three hundred inhabitants and, few though they be, one wonders what indeed they found to live on until the tourists in their motor cars, literally gods from the machine, came to bring some small measure of prosperity, for there is nothing here but bare rock with hardly enough sparse scrub to pasture a few score goats.

Originally a Roman fortress, 'Gourdon la Sarrasine', as its name implies, was long a stronghold of the Moslem marauders who plagued Provence. The thirteenth-century castle,[1] where Raymond Bérenger, Count of Provence, once lived, is built upon a Moorish substructure. The towers and walls of Gourdon, which withstood innumerable sieges, were pulled down in the sixteenth century and in their place the terrace-garden of the castle was designed by the famous Le Nôtre. The half-ruined keep itself was restored by an American lady called Miss Norris. The small museum of medieval objects which it contains is closed for some curious reason on Thursdays (although it is the school half-holiday in France), so that there is only one day in the week when it can be combined with a visit to the Matisse Chapel at Vence. The church is without much interest but the view from the belvedere at the end of the village over the mountains, the Loup valley, and away to the sea, is alone worth the climb to this bleak mountain-top.

1. Open each afternoon except Tuesday.

Chapter 8

Biot, Antibes and Vallauris

❧

*The Léger Museum – Antibes – the Picasso Museum – Cap
d'Antibes – Vallauris – the Temple of Peace*

From Gourdon the road continues straight on to Grasse, but to
follow it would be to enter this ancient scented city by the back door.
One does not go from Gourdon to Grasse. One goes from Grasse
to Gourdon. We will turn back, therefore, to Cagnes so as to explore
the towns of the coast and then return to what the French call the
arrière-pays, the back-country. In any case, this stretch of country
between Cagnes and Cannes is a kind of front garden to Grasse.
Field after coloured field of flowers blossoms in the open, while
others ripen in enormous glasshouses (they cover nine million square
feet in the region of Antibes alone), which look from a distance like
the roofs of underground hangars. Carnations, roses, chrysanthemums, violets, jasmine, tuberoses, anemones, mignonette,
hyacinths, jonquils and mimosa all blossom here in their due and
proper seasons. Unlike flowers elsewhere which, as so many poets
have pointed out, bloom for a week or two and die, the flowers here
attain a measure of immortality.

Some, especially the mimosa and carnations, are shipped to the
markets of Paris and London, but most of them are destined for the
distilleries of Grasse, which is the world centre of the perfume
industry. There they are turned by various processes into the
famous scents which are known and exported all over the world,
the scents which beautiful women use to bewitch their lovers in
boudoirs, bedrooms, drawing-rooms, in restaurants and on dance-
floors all across the globe from Saigon to Saint Louis and from
Stockholm to Santiago. When in due course we reach Grasse we
shall look at the mechanics and the astonishing statistics of the perfume industry. This is neither the time nor the place. Let us just
admire the unplucked flowers as we pass along the twin highway which runs from Nice and Cagnes to Antibes and Cannes.

The Autoroute de l'Estérel by-passes the coastal towns and runs

The harbour at Villefranche

The altar of St Dominic, in Matisse's Chapel of the Rosary at Vence

almost parallel with Route Nationale 7 westwards through central Provence in the direction of Aix-en-Provence.

Two main roads run along the coast almost parallel from the Var to Antibes. The newer and faster of the two keeps close to the sea, but we will take the old road, since we shall be turning inland to **Biot** through the low olive-clad hills where in AD 69 the rival emperors Otho and Vitellius fought out the bloodstained destiny of the Roman Empire. Biot, by the way, happens to rhyme with 'the yacht', although nobody will be able to direct you to Cagnes if you try to rhyme it with 'Skegness'. It is something more like 'Kigh-nyer'.

Close to where you turn off to Biot, at La Brague is a marine zoo, the **Marineland**[1] where dolphins entertain the crowds in a huge pool, while other pools contain other marine mammals, and there is an aquarium in addition.

A short way along the turning to Biot, on a little hill to the right, rises a large white building, half hidden by cypresses. Opened to the public in 1960, this is one of the few picture galleries in France to house the works of a single contemporary artist – Fernand Léger, who with Picasso and Braque was one of the pioneers of Cubism and who lived and worked partly in Paris and partly in Biot. Spacious though the original building was, it has had to be enlarged to accommodate the huge quantity of Léger's work.[2] Most of the pictures were given by his widow, who had been his collaborator for twenty years. In the front garden is a large porcelain abstract called *Le Jardin des Enfants*, while an enormous, coloured mosaic (representing Sport and originally commissioned for the Olympic Stadium in Hanover) extends across the hundred-and-thirty-foot façade of the museum. The painter was, in the words of M. Jean Cassou, 'the great poet of our industrial age' (how Blake and Morris would have snarled at the phrase), but the gallery contains also, especially on the upper floor, a number of the mellower, less severely industrial, works of his old age. The cogwheels, ladders and scaffolding of his earlier periods are replaced by delightful groups of acrobats, musicians, cyclists and picnickers.

The building is a model of what a museum should be – a series of whitewashed rooms lit by wide walls of glass. In fact, M. André Svetchine, the Nice architect who has built many of the best-known villas on the coast, designed the whole museum to serve as a frame for the great mosaic, which was 'blown up' to twelve hundred square feet from a model only sixteen inches by four, and for the enormous

1. Open throughout the day.
2. Open throughout the year.

stained-glass window in the hall.

Biot has several other claims to fame. Up in the hill-top village itself the church contains two altarpieces of the fifteenth-century School of Nice. One is an 'Ecce Homo', and the other, believed to be the work of Ludovic Bréa himself, is a polyptych of 'Our Lady of Pity'. (On her left arm she carries the Child Jesus and in her right hand she holds a rosary. Kneeling at her feet are the Emperor, robed in black, and other lay and ecclesiastical figures. St Bartholomew and St Catherine are on their knees before her, while two angels hold up the folds of her mantle.)

The surroundings of Biot produce, in addition to cut flowers, an average of fifty tons of table grapes a year, which are sent all over France and exported abroad. There are also a number of potteries which, in contrast to the more 'arty' products of its famous neighbour Vallauris, produce mainly household utensils, garden vases and urns. Biot makes the huge Ali Baba pots you see in Riviera gardens. While the local clay soil, which it shares with Vallauris, was originally responsible for the pottery industry, its revival has owed a great deal to the encouragement of Fernand Léger, who here extended his interest from painting to ceramics. It is, on a smaller scale, a success story parallel to that of Vallauris and its good genius, Picasso. A clay soil to start the industry and an artist of talent to revive it just when it needed it most.

Antibes was originally a Greek colony and is said to owe its name of Antipolis – 'The City Opposite' – to its position facing Nice across the Bay of the Angels. It has, in fact, throughout history faced Nice and, when the latter was a fortress of the Dukes of Savoy, Antibes was the corresponding fortress of the Kings of France, backstopping the advanced position of St Paul. Hence the imposing Fort Carré, on the east side of the harbour.

When the young Napoleon Bonaparte was placed in command of the defences of the coast in 1794, he installed his family here in Antibes. Even for a general, pay arrived very irregularly in the revolutionary years, and his mother, the celebrated *Madame Mère*, for all that she was the widow of a nobleman of Ajaccio, had to wash the family linen in the neighbouring stream, while his sisters, princesses-to-be, stocked the larder by raiding the fig trees and artichoke beds of the angry farmers around.

Before the Roman conquest Antibes was what two hundred years ago used to be called a 'factory' – a trading post belonging to the Phoceans of Marseilles. The original Greek town, founded in the fifth century BC, consisted only of the narrow strip along the seafront where today Vauban's ramparts provide a pleasant promenade. Its landward walls ran along what is now the Cours Masséna, where the covered market is, and the treacherous Ligurians were never allowed inside the settlement for fear of a surprise attack. All the chaffering and the trading took place outside the gates.

The medieval Antiboul, as the place was called up to the sixteenth century, spread well beyond this narrow strip and now forms an attractive old town, whose narrow, bustling streets are clearly to be distinguished from the wide, straight boulevards of the recent expansion. Nevertheless, the two chief monuments of the town, whose square Romanesque towers strike the eye of everyone who drives along the highway between Cannes and Nice, are both inside the old Greek periphery. They are the church and, beside it, the Grimaldi Castle, now turned into a museum.[1]

The church faces on to the sea-wall itself. It has a handsome façade flanked by stone flambeaux like frozen torches. At the end of the right aisle is a polyptych of 'Our Lady of the Rosary' by François Bréa of Nice. (To see it you fumble for an electric light switch just to the right.) On the left of the Virgin and Child ecclesiastics, including the Pope, and on the right laymen, including the Emperor in a golden cloak, kneel in prayer, while surrounding the central figures are compartments, each representing one of the fifteen mysteries of the Rosary. The whole altarpiece measures fifteen feet high by twelve feet wide.

The medieval **Castle of the Grimaldi**, for centuries lords of Antibes, rises next door to the church on the foundations of the old Roman *castrum*. Among the more interesting of the Greek and Roman inscriptions are the monument to the shade of 'the boy Septentrion who at the age of twelve danced twice in the Theatre of Antipolis and pleased' (a 'good notice', as they say in the profession) and the votive offering of one Terpon, 'servant of the august goddess Aphrodite', a deity who is still in practice widely venerated all along the coast.

A room on the ground floor contains a very lovely 'Entombment' of the School of Nice, with an elliptical composition which recalls that El Greco's 'Burial of the Conde de Orgaz'. Notice that all the mourning women were apparently painted from the same model, as was so often the case with the Italian masters. Notice, too, the gay domestic scenes in the background, outside the walls of Jerusalem.

But the Museum owes its main fame to Pablo Picasso. In 1945 the exiled Spanish painter left Paris, where he had spent five grey years

1. Closed on Tuesdays in winter.

of wartime, and returned to his beloved Mediterranean. Everything then was crowded and disorganized and he found it hard to work from the hotel bedroom in Golfe Juan where he was living. At this point M. Dor de la Souchère, the Director of the Antibes Museum, came to the rescue, offered Picasso the keys of the Museum and invited him to use it as a studio. Canvas was still unobtainable but Picasso laid in supplies of paints and hardboard and set to work among the dusty Roman inscriptions and the plaster casts.

Inspired by his return to the old Hellenic world of the Mediterranean, he painted innumerable fauns, goats, bulls, owls, centaurs, flautists, dancers and lovers, and notably the famous 'Ulysses and the Sirens'. (To be quite exact, Ulysses' ship is assailed by only one dancing siren and two dancing kids, while her orchestra consists of a centaur and a faun playing pipes.) His parallel inspiration came from his new model, Françoise Gilot, of whom he made no fewer than ten lithographs in a single day. Afterwards, alas, his beloved Françoise left him with the rather unkind remark that she did not want to spend her life tied to a historic monument.

When he migrated to nearby Vallauris, the grateful painter left, on permanent loan, his entire output during the months he had spent in the Château Grimaldi, and later he added a number of his other works, so that now the Museum includes some two hundred of the ceramics which he executed at Vallauris, as well as the paintings, drawings, sculptures and lithographs he actually made in the Château. The first floor is almost entirely devoted to his work and forms one of the most important Picasso collections in the world. Would that every return for hospitality extended in difficult times were so well repaid!

On the stairs up to the second floor hangs a fine black tapestry by Lurçat, and the second floor itself is devoted to paintings by such modern artists as Léger, Atlan and others. In an alcove by itself at the end of the entrance passage, and very easy to miss, is a lovely 'Still Life with a Blue Background' by Nicolas de Staël, the young genius who held a one-man show of his works in this very museum and not long afterwards killed himself. The seven sculptures on the terrace are by Germaine Richier.

The second worth-while museum in Antibes is the **Archaeological Museum**[1] housed in the sixteenth-century Bastion St André on the ramparts. Three thousand years of Antibes' history are displayed, and of especial interest is the Greek and Etruscan material which has been salvaged not far out at sea.

1. Closed on Tuesdays and in November.

To the south of the town of Antibes lies **Cap d'Antibes**, one of those wooded peninsulas, such as Cap Ferrat and Ramatuelle, which lend so much of its beauty to the coast. While most people will probably associate Cap d'Antibes with the photographs in the society weeklies of millionaires, peeresses and film stars sunbathing at Eden Roc or drinking cocktails on the pleasant terraces of the Hôtel du Cap, the Cap is in fact largely residential, divided up into quiet villas with sub-tropical gardens.

On the highest point, in the centre of the peninsula, is the lighthouse and by the side of it is the **Chapel of Notre Dame de la Garoupe**. To reach it, follow the signposts marked 'Le Phare'. This centuries-old sailors' chapel is of particular interest to the student of European primitive and folk art on account of its ex-votos, which are paintings or other objects produced by local amateurs or artisans and offered in fulfilment of a vow or gratitude for deliverance from death.

Curiously enough, the two aisles of the chapel are each dedicated to a different Madonna. The one on the right belongs to Notre Dame de la Garde and contains what one may describe as landsmen's ex-votos. There are pictures of falls from roofs and scaffolding, broken ladders, deliveries from beds of sickness, runaway horses, and gory battles in Tonking. The most vivid of them represents a motor smash. The car is overturned in the ditch, the peccant lorry roars triumphantly off into the middle distance, and the father, mother and two daughters, having learned little road-sense from the accident, kneel in thanksgiving in the middle of the highway. A small boy holds a bicycle with one hand and with the other points heavenwards to Our Lady of La Garde, who has appeared providentially in the sky. (At Valcluse, near Grasse, there is an ex-voto which pillories a black Citroën with a clearly identifiable Geneva number-plate.)

The left-hand aisle is dedicated to Notre Dame de Bon Port, the protectress of the seamen of Antibes, and is covered largely with marine ex-votos. There are model ships, old cutlasses and an eighteenth-century trumpet. Among the pictures are some good marine paintings, such as the victory of the *Intrépide* of Nice, which in 1760 captured in quick succession two well-armed English ships, and the last fight of the *Swiftsure*, which only surrendered to two English ships at the Battle of Trafalgar after losing two-thirds of her crew and shipping five feet of water in her hold. It was painted by a combatant actually present at the fight and probably immediately after the battle. The most exciting, and the oldest of all, commemorates a surprise landing of Saracen pirates at Antibes itself. It is a lively scene, with extremely malignant and turbaned Turks chasing red-bonneted Antibois with scimitars, and shows the town as it was in the sixteenth century. It was offered by the wounded man seen lying at the bottom right-hand corner. Perhaps, however, the most directly human of all the ex-votos is that of the convict Jean Briand who, with his hands locked in a wooden frame like the stocks, gives thanks to Our Lady for helping him to escape from Toulon Gaol and finding him a ship to take him to Martinique. Amateurs of this Grandma Moses style of painting may profitably pursue it to the great pilgrimage church at Laghet, near La Turbie, whose cloister contains no fewer than six hundred of these ex-votos.

Not far from the Sanctuary of La Garoupe, in the centre of the little peninsula, are the gardens of the Villa Thuret,[1] which were laid out in 1866 as one of the earliest acclimatization stations for trees and plants brought to Europe from hot countries. It was there that the first eucalyptus seeds brought from the Royal Botanical Gardens in Sydney were planted. Now these quick-growing trees are to be seen all along the coast roads of the Mediterranean. The mimosa, by now the symbolic flower of the coast, was originally imported from San Domingo no longer ago than 1835. Lord Brougham is credited with the introduction of the palm tree.

It shows how practically and properly the coast, which a hundred years ago consisted of a few poverty-stricken fishing villages, has been able to exploit its great climatic and aesthetic potentialities – or, to put it another way, has put to use its powers for increasing the happiness of such as are able to pay for its amenities. And, after all, these are no longer only the few and the rich and the leisured, for they increase in numbers every year, in proportion as the rich and the leisured grow fewer.

In the seventeenth-century Tour du Grillon is another museum on the Cap. **The Naval and Napoleonic Museum**[2] was opened in 1964, and many of the items relate to Napoleon's return from Elba on March 1, 1815, when he landed at Golfe Juan.

Adjoining Antibes on the west lies **Juan-les-Pins**, which the American millionaire, Frank Jay Gould, created out of a beach of silver sand and a grove of pine trees, to become the most fashionable bathing resort of the twenties and thirties. As an indication of how things have progressed since those days, a work by Joan Miró called *La Déese de la Mer* was anchored to the sea bottom in 1968, and the length of its submarine support is fifty-five feet. Beyond it is the one

1. Closed on Saturdays and Sundays.
2. Closed on Tuesdays and in November.

natural anchorage and beach of **Golfe Juan**, well known to the American Navy. It was here that Napoleon landed with eight hundred men when he came back from exile in Elba in 1815 to reconquer France and rule it for the famous 'Hundred Days'. When the lookout man of the brig *L'Inconstant* shouted 'Land ahoy!' – the longed for, lost land of France – the Emperor called him and emptied into his cap all the money he had in his pockets. General Cambronne, now chiefly remembered for his pungent and monosyllabic vocabulary, was the first to leap to the beach and distribute tricolour cockades for the astonished fishermen to stick in their bonnets. 'The eagle, with the national colours, will fly from steeple to steeple as far as the towers of Notre Dame,' ran the famous proclamation which was nailed up for the first time on the walls of the fishermen's huts of Golfe Juan.

From Golfe Juan a road leads inland to **Vallauris**. Some forty years ago Vallauris meant nothing much to anybody (except the people who lived in it) but a signpost on the road between Cannes and Antibes. Picasso made it a world-famous name. For all its antiquity Vallauris was a very ordinary little Provençal township, where the usual vineyards, the olive-groves and the fields of flowers waiting to be cut for the scent factories nestled among the pinewoods of the low coastal hills. It also had a number of potteries, but these had fallen on evil days when Picasso made his home in the village after the war.

The whole thing was almost as much a matter of chance as his installation in the Castle of Antibes. When he came up on a casual trip from his home at Golfe Juan, three miles away, he found one good potter working among all the mediocre ones. This was a certain Georges Ramié who ran the Madoura Pottery with his wife. In the Ramiés' pottery Picasso, with his ever-active and exploring fingers, twisted some bits of clay into figures and next year, when he returned, was delighted to find that the Ramiés had fired them and kept them. That was the beginning of his interest in ceramics.

Picasso took an ugly little pink villa, with the curious name of La Galloise, The Welshwoman, just outside the village and began to make ceramics with Madoura. Sometimes he would take a newly-thrown pot and twist it into a bird, a woman, a bull, the head of a faun or a bearded man, and sometimes he would just incise it or merely paint on it some pattern or picture such as the now widely famous head of the goat. All these dishes, pots and pitchers, some of them meant for practical use and others as pure ornaments, were copied by the Madoura potters, so that they could be reproduced and sold like prints or etchings, the only difference being that, since every one was made by hand, no two were exactly alike. Picasso thus killed two birds with one stone. He was able at the same time to bring prosperity to the craftsmen of the decaying village and to multiply enormously the circulation of his works among those who could enjoy and appreciate them.

'To see his hands as he moulded the clay, small and feminine yet strong,' writes his friend and biographer Roland Penrose, who used to watch him at work, 'gave a pleasure akin to watching a ballet, so complete was the co-ordination in their unhesitating movements. It seemed impossible for the clay not to obey; in such hands its future form was certain to become impregnated with their life.'

Picasso found himself a disused scent factory, whose enormous workrooms provided even so fecund and fast-working an artist with all the space he needed for painting, sculpture and ceramics, and where he soon established himself as the chieftain of a small tribe of artists and craftsmen. There were the local potters from Madoura and the other establishments, young ceramists who had come to Vallauris to set up their own kilns, painters from Paris who wanted to try their hands at the new game, not to mention the butchers, the bakers, the candlestick-makers of Vallauris, the barbers, the postmen and the fishermen from Golfe Juan. In the ten years he lived here Picasso gave new life to Vallauris and brought prosperity back to the people he loved.

Vallauris is centred on one long street lined on either side with pottery shops. There are said to be a hundred potteries in the little town and most of them have their own shop-windows on the main street. Unlike those of Biot, most of these potteries turn out not household utensils but 'ornaments'. Some of them are good but, to be quite frank, there are many which one would only buy if one were stocking a booth for 'breaking up the happy home' – the Alsatian dogs and such-like which one finds everywhere in country fairs and markets, and the jugs in the form of naked Negresses who pour water out of quite unsuitable places.

There is, however, at least one really fine pottery in Vallauris and that is the original Madoura. In the front display room are a number of pots, vases and dishes most exquisite in colour and shape. Many of them recall the fine ware of China and will almost certainly end up in various museums. These collector's pieces are in the first room. The second is filled with the works which Picasso produced here and which have been copied by the skilful potters of Madoura. The Madoura Pottery is just off the main street and has a sign pointing to it. It is on the right if you drive down the one-way street and on the left if you walk up it.

Apart from Madoura, with its Picasso associations and its room of Picasso reproductions, the Spanish master has left two important original works in the little town of his adoption.

At the top of the main street is the handsome façade of the village church. On the left of the large shady square in front of it is a bronze of a naked, bearded man carrying in his arms a struggling sheep, which he holds by the feet. It was in 1942 that Picasso first conceived this rather curious subject, and over the period of a year he made a number of drawings of the 'Man with the Sheep'. (Christian Zervos has reproduced fifty of them in his *Cahiers d'Art*.) Then very swiftly, in a single day, he made a clay model of it, while Paul Eluard the poet sat beside him writing. It was begun in the morning and finished by nightfall. Then Picasso made a plaster cast of it, which for years dominated his studio and considerably astonished his visitors in Paris. After the war he had it cast in bronze.

Then what to do with it? He offered it first to the Museum of Antibes which had given him its hospitality. After some difficulties and delays the offer was withdrawn. The sculptor then offered it to the town of Vallauris to be set up in the Church Square where, as he said, every day the dogs could water it and the children could clamber over it. The Municipal Council, its gratitude not untinged by alarm, asked cautiously what the 'Man with the Sheep' looked like and accepted it when assured that, as a matter of fact, it looked like nothing so much as a man with a sheep. Only the local blacksmith, rather unexpectedly, remarked: 'What a pity it will be if the statue looks like any other statue!'

On the other side of the square is a small twelfth-century chapel which was 'disaffected', as the French say, at the time of the Revolution and for many years used as a press for olive oil. It consists of a single, windowless, barrel-vault nave leading into a chancel, where the great olive-press is still to be seen. The Municipality of Vallauris offered the building to Picasso to decorate as he liked. He kept putting off the task until one evening when the potters of Vallauris gave a dinner in honour of his seventieth birthday in the old chapel, and he finally gave in and promised to decorate the expanse of stone wall and vaulting above and around him. It is now what he called the **Temple of Peace** (but is variously called by others The Picasso Memorial, or else the Museum of Modern Art, neither title as appropriate as the original),[1] for he had dedicated it to the cause he

1. Open daily.

had nearest at heart, the propagation of peace and the avoidance of war.

The whole interior of the nave, walls and vault, is covered with a single vast painting, **Peace and War**, with Peace occupying one side and War the other. It consists of a number of plywood panels fitted together to form a whole. The local carpenter fixed up a framework on which the completed panels could be fixed when ready, detached from the rough, damp panels of the vault, and in the summer of 1952 Picasso, who had already made a number of drawings of the subject, shut himself up in his scent factory and began work on the panels. For two months he emerged only to eat and to sleep. Nobody was allowed in except his son Paulo, who was placed on guard at the door with strict instructions to keep everyone out even if his father should weaken and invite them in – to act, in a word, as the ropes which bound Ulysses to the mast of his ship. The panels were finished in exactly two months to a day, and the door was at last opened. The painter had made no measurements but when the plywood sheets were put together on the vaulting of the old chapel they fitted to within a fraction of an inch.

The left-hand side, War, shows a black vehicle like a hearse drawn by a team of broken-down black horses. On the vehicle rides a horned and bat-winged demon holding a bloodstained sword in one hand and in the other a bowl of horrid insects or giant bacilli intended to symbolize scientific warfare. In the background other confused and violent warrior-figures advance brandishing weapons. At the far left of the picture the chariot of war is confronted by a serene figure with the dove of peace on his shield. Is he meant to represent Peace? The Kremlin? Who knows? Possibly Justice, for he carries a pair of scales. The colour-scheme, black and red on green, is deliberately intended to clash and to suggest chaos, confusion and unrest.

On the right-hand wall, in contrast, the panels representing Peace are painted in a colour-scheme designed to harmonize and to soothe. They consist of white figures on a blue background (a combination at least as old as the Della Robbia). On the left are a musician playing the pipes, girls dancing and a juggler who balances a bowl of birds and a cage of goldfish to symbolize the precarious nature of peace and of human happiness. In the centre, warmed by a large parti-coloured sun, a boy tills the earth with a plough yoked to Pegasus, and on the right figure the arts of peace such as cooking and writing. A mother suckles her baby in a rather *dégagé* manner while poring over a book.

On the end wall of the Temple of Peace, where the old door on to the square has been blocked up, four figures, a white, a black, a yellow and a red one, representing the races of man, shake hands and hold aloft the dove of peace.

Picasso's original notion was that this windowless cavern should be lit by flickering torches like the caves which primitive man painted in Spain and the Dordogne but, rather fortunately perhaps, the idea fell through and an efficient electric lighting system now shows the panels to good advantage.

Chapter 9

Cannes

✿

St Honorat – Ste Marguerite – Le Suquet – the Harbour – the Croisette

Facing the glittering white *palaces* of Cannes lie two small green islands known to the ancients as Lero and Lerina and to us as **Les Îles de Lerins. Ste Marguerite**, the larger inshore island, and **St Honorat**, the smaller island to the seaward, nowadays mean little more than a bathe or a picnic at the end of a fifteen-minute motor-boat trip from Cannes, but for many centuries Cannes was the property of the ancient Abbey of St Honorat – right up to 1788, in fact, when the tally of monks had shrunk to four and the Pope closed it down, a year or two before the Revolution would have saved him the trouble.

St Honorat founded the island monastery at the end of the fourth century. He ranks with St Cassian as the founder of French monasticism. It is said that St Marguerite was his sister and the Mother Superior of a community of Christian virgins on the neighbouring island. According to the same legend, the austere St Honorat rationed himself strictly to a single annual visit to his sister (for no women were allowed to set foot on his holy island). He promised to come over to see her when the almond tree on the beach came into flower. Missing the pious conversation of her brother, St Marguerite prayed for a miracle, and God caused the almond tree to blossom every month as a summons to him.

St Honorat's popularity as a place of pilgrimage is not hard to account for, since a visit to it carried the same indulgences as a journey to the Holy Land. In the seventh century it numbered nearly four thousand monks and possessed a hundred lordships and priories on the mainland. As well as being rich and powerful, it owned one of the finest libraries in Europe and was among the great centres of pious learning in the Dark Ages. 'In good King Dagobert's palmy days, when saints were many and sins were few,' St Honorat produced over twenty saints and six hundred bishops. Among its *alumni* was St Patrick, the Apostle of Ireland, who spent nine years on the island and there received his religious training. Today the monastery, bought by the Cistercians in 1869, may be visited on weekdays by men only (you turn to the left at the landing stage and then to the right through the arch inscribed 'L'Abbaye') but with the exception of the cloister it has been completely rebuilt in the last century and contains little of interest. The monks manufacture, to their own recipe, a sweet liqueur called Lerina, which comes in both green and yellow. It is not at all bad but I have noticed that few of the bottles on the local bistro shelves seem to have had their corks drawn. Adjoining the *abbaye* is the eleventh-century donjon of the old fortified monastery, where the monks, after lighting a beacon to be taken up by the watch-tower on Mont Chevalier, used to run for safety when a Saracen sail appeared. Now there is a flight of steps up to the door, some twelve feet above the ground, but formerly it could be entered only by a ladder which the monks could draw up after them. The keep is still in excellent preservation. Standing honey-coloured against the blue sky, with the Mediterranean lapping against the rocks at its base, it could easily be one of the smaller Crusader castles of Syria or Cyprus. To the left of the entrance there is an attractive little two-storied cloister with arcaded galleries and a Roman cistern in the middle. The chapel on the first floor served for a time as the drawing-room of the Comédie Française actress who bought the place at the time of the Revolution. A formidable spiral staircase leads up to the battlements and a good view over the sea and the coast. The entire island belongs to the monastery, and visitors are confronted with notices reminding them that they are on holy ground and ought to dress and conduct themselves with modesty.

Apart from the cultivated fields and vineyards surrounding the monastery, both islands are covered with thick woods of Aleppo pine intersected by forest paths. They afford a favourite Sunday excursion for the Cannois. From the landing stage on Ste Marguerite it is a short walk up to the fort, which has housed a number of distinguished prisoners from the Man in the Iron Mask to the pusillanimous Marshal Bazaine, who surrendered Metz to the Prussians in 1870. One can visit the cell of Bazaine, who escaped in 1874 by the simple process of bribing his guards to open the gate, although the authorities put out a face-saving story to the effect that he had climbed through his window and slid down a rope (which everyone knew he was too corpulent to do). In another cell is a statue by the Danish sculptor Viggo Jarl in memory of six Huguenot pastors who returned clandestinely to France after the Revocation of the Edict of

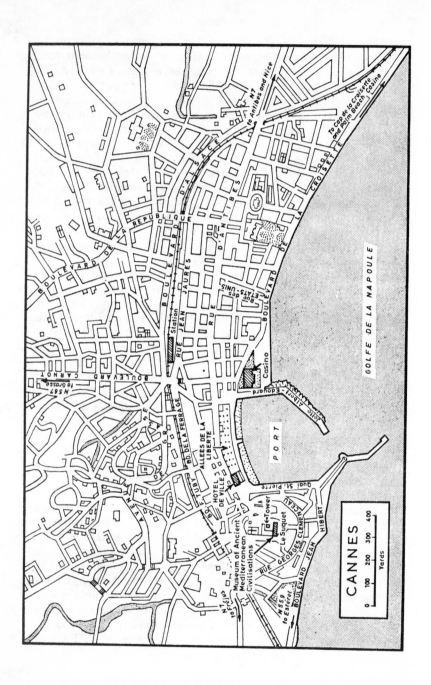

CANNES

0 100 200 300 400
Yards

PORT

GOLFE DE LA NAPOULE

BOULEVARD

RUE DE LA CROISETTE

To Cap de la Croisette
and Palm Beach Casino

N7
To Antibes and Nice

BOULEVARD D'ALSACE

BOULEVARD DE LA REPUBLIQUE

RUE JEAN JAURES

Station

RUE D'ANTIBES

Rue des ETATS-UNIS

Casino

Jetée Albert Edouard

BOULEVARD CARNOT

N567
To Grasse

AVENUE

Bd. DE LA FERRAGE

G. R. I.

Bd. D'UBY

ALLEES DE LA LIBERTE

HOTEL DE VILLE

Quai St. Pierre

Tower

Le Suquet

Museum of Ancient Mediterranean Civilisations

N7
To Fréjus

RUE GEORGES CLEMENCEAU

BOULEVARD JEAN HIBERT

N59
To Estérel

Nantes and were sentenced to solitary confinement in this fort. They lasted, the shortest five and the longest thirty years thus. There are letters from Louis XIV directing the Governor, M. de St Mars, that the only one who had preserved his sanity was, if possible, to be converted to Rome, while the five who had gone mad were to be as well treated as was consistent with their isolation from the outside world – although naturally these *opiniâtres* could not be allowed to indulge their habit of singing psalms at the top of their voices unless they were first removed to cells out of hearing of their fellow-prisoners.

Among these fellow-prisoners was the famous Man in the Iron Mask (actually a velvet one), who was immured there from 1687 until 1698, when M. de St Mars, bored to death on the Île Ste Marguerite, procured himself the governorship of the Bastille and took his mysterious captive with him. The identity of Louis XIV's state prisoner has never been established. He has been thought to be Louis's twin brother, born several hours after him; Count Mattioli, a minister of the Duke of Mantua, who had double-crossed him in some negotiations over Casale in Piedmont; a priest who had interfered between the King and Mme de Montespan; a court page who had been an accomplice of the poisoner Mme de Brinvilliers; and, according to the latest theory, the indiscreet son of Anne of Austria's doctor who, when he held a post-mortem on Louis XIII, had found him incapable of producing children.

The monks of St Honorat did their rather inadequate best to protect their humble subjects at Portus Canis, on the mainland opposite, from pirate raids, by erecting walls and building a watch-tower and refuge on the little hill variously known as La Castre (the *Castrum*), Mont Chevalier and Le Suquet. Besides the eleventh-century tower and some walls, the summit of Le Suquet, rising on the western side of Cannes harbour, contains a seventeenth-century church, which, possibly on account of a miraculous Madonna, attracts large congregations for Sunday mass. There is also a **Museum of Ancient Mediterranean Civilizations**, otherwise known as the Musée de la Castre.[1] This consists for the most part of the collections presented by the Dutch Baron Lycklama in 1873 and was completely modernized, rearranged and re-illuminated in 1961. The first of the Baron's two gifts consists of antiquities from the Eastern Mediterranean, mainly Roman, Etruscan, Greek, Egyptian and Phoenician, and the second of an ethnographic collection from all over the world, from Polynesia to pre-Columbian South America.

1. Closed on Mondays, public holidays and in November.

There is a remarkable picture of the Baron himself in Oriental costume. (There is no municipal picture gallery in Cannes, but there are good commercial galleries at 65 Boulevard de la Croisette and in the Rue des États-Unis, while the Madoura Pottery of Vallauris has a showroom at 81 Rue d'Antibes.)

Cannes had a population of three or four thousand fishermen and farmers on that fateful day in 1834 when Lord Brougham and Vaux, on his way to the Italian Riviera with his ailing daughter, was turned back at the Var. There was an outbreak of cholera in France at the time and the Sardinian authorities had closed the frontier. The ex-Chancellor settled down to wait for the lifting of the quarantine in the solitary hostelry at Cannes, M. Pinchinat's Hôtel de la Poste-aux-Chevaux, on the point where the recently-built Sofitel Méditer-ranée stands at 1 Boulevard J. Hibert. (Now there are eight thousand hotel rooms in Cannes.) Delighted with the climate and the scenery, he decided to settle there and built himself the Villa Eléonore Louise on the Fréjus Road, to the west of Le Suquet. The villa was so named in memory of his daughter who died before it was finished. A recent writer, Mr Roderick Cameron, says that the villa still stands, 'and on its walls can be found the poems inscribed to the young girl for whom it was built; one by her father, and the others by Lord Wellesley and the Earl of Carlisle respectively'. Lord Brougham spent thirty-four winters there, and before he died at the age of ninety had seen Cannes develop from a fishing village into a fashionable winter resort, for other English noblemen followed him and built villas where the Croix des Gardes runs down to the sea. To their fury the railway was extended to Cannes in 1863 and ran across the bottom of their gardens, cutting off their villas from the sea. With the coming of the railway, hotels began to spring up on the other side of the town, where the earth from the railway cuttings had been used to construct the Boulevard de l'Impératrice, now the Boulevard de la Croisette. Cannes swiftly became 'the rage' in Europe's highest circles and in 1890 a local citizen was able to count no fewer than sixty foreign royalties living there.

When Lord Brougham discovered it, Cannes had only an open anchorage, and the perfumes of Grasse, instead of being shipped from the obvious port, were sent by road all the way to Marseilles. Having adopted Cannes for his own, Lord Brougham, with all the magnificent assurance of a nineteenth-century English grandee, wrote and asked King Louis-Philippe to supply funds for the construction of a harbour. Sure enough, the King produced two million francs and in 1840 the present jetty was built out from the point

Above, Alphonse Daudet's mill at Fontvielle.
Below, the castle at La Napoule, west of Cannes

The Pavillon de Vendôme at Aix-en-Provence

where Pinchinat's hotel then stood. Thereby Lord Brougham gave a twist to the development of Cannes second in importance only to the one he had given it when he first settled there for, more than any town on the coast (unless one is to include St Tropez), Cannes now centres round its harbour, which is the first port of the Mediterranean so far as pleasure yachts are concerned. The creation of a second yacht harbour at the eastern end of the Boulevard de la Croisette has made Cannes still more important as a sailing resort. The year 1860 saw the first of the regattas which made the Prince of Wales call Cannes rather patronizingly 'the Mediterranean Cowes', and shortly afterwards the Yacht Club was founded.

As late as 1887, however, Guy de Maupassant wrote of Cannes as 'a dangerous port, unsheltered . . . where all vessels are in peril', and it was not until 1904 that the protection of the harbour was finally assured by the construction of the Jetée Albert-Edouard. The name was bestowed in honour of the Prince of Wales, who first came out in 1872 to stay at Mr Gray's new Hôtel Gray d'Albion and used to play baccarat at the fashionable Cercle Nautique on the Croisette, where the Festival Hall now stands. All along the Jetée Albert-Edouard and the Quai St Pierre opposite, yachts are moored side by side as though in a car-park. It is here, even more than in Monte Carlo, that one can see some of the world's most luxurious yachts at close quarters. Many are laid up here all through the winter.

At the base of the Jetée Albert-Edouard the large pink **Winter Casino**, with its gaming rooms, its theatre and its fashionable Ambassadeurs' restaurant, divides Cannes neatly into two halves. To the west is the Cannes of the Cannois and to the east is the Cannes of the foreigners. Beside it, at the corner of the harbour, is the Gare Maritime where the *vedettes* take off for the islands, and beyond that is the Pantiero, the beach where the fishing boats are pulled up, the nets are spread to dry and the local men play *boules* ever since their old pitches (or *boulodrome*) under the plane trees of Les Allées de la Liberté have been asphalted and turned into a car-park. Behind and beyond the Allées is the crowded quarter round the market (which, it is very well worth knowing on a summer afternoon when the other car-parks are full, has a car-park on its roof). From the Place de l'Hôtel de Ville, where the coastal buses start from, the Rue St Antoine winds through the old town up to the hill of Le Suquet.

It is no longer true to say that Cannes west of the harbour is the preserve of the Cannois, for it is also the Cannes of the yachtsmen. The Quai St Pierre is lined by ships' chandlers, small restaurants and sailors' bars, where bronzed yacht-owners meet prospective clients to fix up a charter to St Tropez or Porquerolles or to call on the hospitable nudists at the Île du Levant. Beyond the Quai St Pierre, the Boulevard Jean Hibert, once a jumble of little old buildings and unexpectedly cheap restaurants, now caters for international tourism. There is the four-star Sofitel-Méditerranée, for instance, and comfortable restaurants like the Mariner and Eugène. On the east side of the Casino, between the Rue d'Antibes, the main shopping street of Cannes, and the Croisette, are all the smartest hotels of Cannes. Some, like the Suisse and the Gray d'Albion, date from the last century. In 1912 the great M. Ruhl of Nice built the Carlton with its four hundred rooms, still after sixty-five years one of the crack hotels of Cannes. The foundation stone was laid by the Grand Duke Michael, who had performed the same godfatherly office for the Casino in 1906. At the end of the twenties, just as the Wall Street crash broke in America, the Majestic, the Miramar and the Martinez were added to the long line of hotels on the Croisette. Architecturally, these *palaces*, as the French call them, are pretty deplorable but they undoubtedly make an impressive background to one of the most elegant promenades in the world. There was a time when the Niçois used to sneer at the Croisette as '*la promenade des puces*', but for several decades at least Cannes has easily surpassed Nice as far as fashion and chic are concerned.

When I used to visit Cannes as a young man I was taught a rhyme which arrogantly summed up the four main resort towns of the Riviera:

> Menton's dowdy.
> Monte's brass.
> Nice is rowdy.
> Cannes is class!

It is only fair to add that Menton, Monte and Nice had their own versions of this jingle less complimentary to Cannes.

The life and economy of Cannes, like those of everywhere else on the coast, have been transformed by the advent of the summer season, which came into existence about the end of the nineteen-twenties. A nineteenth-century French writer said that one should always try to see a country at its most characteristic and therefore visit it at its climatic extreme; thus one should go to Sicily in high summer and Sweden in mid-winter. Until some thirty years ago his advice was ignored by transhumant pleasure-seekers, who pursued an equable climate round the seasons, wanting logically enough to be warm in winter and cool in summer. Now, on the contrary, they flock to broil themselves on the Mediterranean beaches in the summer, and in the winter churn up the virgin snow of the Alps, those *horridos montes* of which Julius Caesar himself could write only with a shudder.

In the nineteen-twenties the season lasted from November to April, and the resort towns lived on the winter visitors, whereas in summer the hotels shut their doors and the coast was deserted except by such unfortunate natives as were compelled to live and work there. None of the 'villa people' would be seen there after the beginning of May on account of the heat, which was known to be unbearable by any northerner, although none had dared to put it to the test. Now the seasons are reversed. All through July and August the beaches are crammed with bathers in the sea and in the sunshine, so that the hotels are crowded, while in the winter many of them do not find it worth-while to stay open. Nevertheless, the expensive jewellers and *couturiers* on the Croisette will tell you they sell very little during the summer season and rely on the February custom to make their money, for Cannes, with its reputation for elegance and its many rich villa-owners, has been very successful in preserving a winter clientele. Cannes, like Monaco, Nice and Menton, arranges a year-round season. Its festivities and sporting events are legion, as are its business and professional congresses at the major hotels, and its artistic and literary manifestations. The International Film Festival in May, for which the Festival Palace was specially built, is world famous, or, as some might think, notorious.

It is equally well situated to take advantage of the summer season for, unlike Nice, it has two long beaches of fine silver sand, off the Boulevard du Midi on the west of the harbour and the Croisette on the east. The mile-and-a-half long **Boulevard de la Croisette** takes its name from the Cap de la Croisette at the eastern end, which separates the Bays of La Napoule and Golfe Juan and which formerly had a cross upon it. On the point is the very symbol of the summer season, the **Palm Beach Casino**, a low white building which looks rather as though a Foreign Legion fort had had a flirtation with the Doge's Palace. The Winter Casino closes from April to October and is replaced by the Palm Beach. Gamblers may care to know that the Palm Beach is the tenth biggest casino in France for turnover, the Palais de la Méditerranée at Nice being the second, the Casino d'Hiver at Cannes the fourth and the Municipal Casino at Nice the eighth.

Beyond the Rue d'Antibes and the railway line rises the hill known as the **Californie**, where some of the finest villas are embowered in the exotic vegetation which has been introduced to replace the original *maquis*, broom and scrub-oak. Now many of the estates have been broken up and blocks of luxury flats built in their place. A number of the middle-rank hotels all along the coast have also been converted into flats, much to the annoyance of the local people, for they are sold or let at figures which they cannot themselves afford to pay, while the Parisians and others who own them come only for a month or two in the year and so create little employment and bring little benefit to the tradespeople. On the thousand-foot summit of the Californie are a modern observatory and a hotel. Every half-hour a bus leaves from the Place Général de Gaulle opposite the Casino for the starting point of the funicular which takes visitors up to Super-Cannes, as the hill-top has been not very happily christened, to enjoy the magnificent view over the coast and the mountains. For the round trip you should allow at least an hour and a half.

Behind Cannes are the two old hill-top villages of Le Cannet, now a part of the town, and Mougins, where Picasso lived and died. Beyond Mougins is the Cannes Country Club, with one of the four local golf courses. Mougins is reckoned the smartest and you are liable to find people like the King of the Belgians playing there, but experts consider Mandelieu, at the mouth of the Siagne near the airport, to be the most interesting course. Mougins closes down in the summer when golfers can choose between Mandelieu, Valbonne and Biot, which has the advantage of a clay soil. All have eighteen holes.

Between Mougins and Valbonne is Castellaras. It is worth looking at the outside of the carefully reconstructed Provençal-style village which is used as a holiday village. Below it the architect, Jacques Couelle, has designed highly original individual houses which harmonize excellently with the surroundings. These houses are sculpted rather than just built.

Chapter 10

Grasse

✤

*The Scent Factories – the Fragonard Museum – the City – the
Gorges du Verdon – Moustiers-Ste-Marie – the Fountain of
Vaucluse*

The sandy slopes behind Cannes and Mandelieu, such as La Croix
des Gardes, La Roquette and the Tanneron, are a blaze of gold in
January and February, for then the mimosa forests which cover them
are blooming in all their glory. Interspersed among the wild mimosa
are orchards of cultivated or 'grafted' mimosa. The grafted mimosa,
which lasts better than the wild, is cut, packed in waterproof con-
tainers and sent to England, its principal market, and the other
northern countries. Some even goes to America and Canada. Out of
an average crop of three thousand tons seventy per cent is exported,
but production fell when the mimosa, a very delicate plant, was so
badly damaged by the great frost of 1956 that a number of *mimosistes*,
rather than wait several years for their stricken trees to revive, preferred to grub them up and sell the land for building lots. Since then,
the mimosa industry revived, only to be hit again by a devastating
forest fire in the Tanneron hills some years ago. While the florists
prefer the grafted, the scent factories of Grasse use only the wild
mimosa on account of its stronger scent. The yellow blossom is
stripped from the branches in February and sent for the extraction
process in the *parfumeries*.

The perfume industry was introduced into Grasse from Italy by
Catherine de Medici, and the city is now the world's scent capital.
In all, the coast produces some twenty thousand tons of mimosa,
carnations, roses, jasmine, mignonette, narcissi, jonquils, tuberoses
and violets a year. While the cash value of the cut-flower industry in
the Alpes-Maritimes is rated far above that of the perfume flowers,
the latter are at the base of the great scent industry which is worth
vastly more than both industries together. More than half of its
value is in dollars and sterling, and provides France with its most
valuable single item of export.

Scent is not made from flowers alone. Grasse uses ambergris from whales, musk from Tibetan deer, civet from Ethiopian cats, patchouli oil from Java, ginger from India, vanilla from Réunion, aniseed from Spain and sandalwood from the Solomon Islands. The art of scent-making was well known to the Egyptians, Phoenicians, Greeks and Romans, but the invention of Grasse was to mix alcohol with the antique oils. There are some twenty factories in the town where the flowers are reduced to the concentrated 'essence' or 'absolute', and sent to Paris for the making of the final perfume. Several of these, such as Molinard, Fragonard and Galimard, are open to visitors and it is interesting to go round and watch the different processes at work. They fall into three main categories; distillation by steam, which is used for the orange blossom: *enfleurage* by steeping in animal fats, which is used mainly for jasmine and tuberose: and extraction by means of hydrocarbons such as ether and acetone, which is the method used for mimosa. You give a franc or two to the girl who shows you round. You are encouraged to buy something but are not obliged to.

Mimosa is far from being the only flower crop which feeds the voracious scent factories. The country round Grasse produces several hundred tons of jasmine, four hundred tons of roses, and a thousand tons of orange blossom a year. This orange is not the sweet, eating orange but the bitter Seville orange or *bigarade*. The flowers are plucked in May and hurried to the factories, where they are distilled as soon as possible (for all these flowers lose their scent very quickly) in enormous copper alembics, each of which contains a ton of flowers and a hundred and seventy gallons of water. The 'essence' or neroli is then separated from the orange blossom water. The high price of scents will be understood when it is realized that it takes a thousand kilos, that is to say, about a ton, of blossom to produce one kilo of the neroli, which enters into the composition of eau-de-Cologne and the majority of fine perfumes. (Similarly, twelve hundred rosebuds weigh a kilo and it takes seven hundred and fifty kilos to make one kilo of the pure essence, which in turn suffices for four or five hundred bottles of scent. It costs twice as much as gold.) Some of the orange blossom is left on the trees and allowed to become fruit, which is picked in the autumn and made into marmalade and the preserved fruit which is now the second largest industry of Grasse.

If Grasse is no longer the fashionable resort it was in Queen Victoria's time, it has gained in quantity what it has lost in quality; for example, the famous Rothschild villa and gardens above the town are now a camping ground where hundreds of visitors live in tents and caravans in the summer. A thousand feet above the sea and sheltered by the Préalpes from the north winds, it has a high reputation as a health resort. In the winter invalids and convalescents go there to regain their health, and in the summer the dwellers on the coast go up at weekends to enjoy the mountain air, while many visitors like to base themselves there and go down daily to the sea for their swim.

The most prominent feature of Grasse is the Cours Cresp, the enormous terrace with magnificent views rolling right down to the sea. At one end of it the Hôtel de Cabris, built in 1773 by Mirabeau's sister, the Marquise de Cabris, houses the **Museum of Provençal Art and History**[1] which used to be more familiarly known as the Fragonard Museum. When it was turned into a scent factory, the lovely old panelling was taken out and sold, but in 1921 it was restored and made into a museum. In the first two rooms on the ground floor are three Fragonards, Madame du Barry's 'Three Graces' and two interesting self-portraits with a fifty-year gap between them, one of 1750 and the other of 1800. There are also a number of his original drawings and prints, pictures of the period by other artists and original furniture from the Hôtel de Cabris. The other artists whose works are on view here include his sister-in-law and pupil Marguerite Gérard, and his son Evariste. There are thirty paintings and drawings by the Aixois painter Granet, and water-colours by Prosper Mérimée. Original furniture from the Hôtel de Cabris is also housed in the Fragonard Museum. The Marquise's bathroom still contains two baths and two bidets of the period. In the basement is a regional museum devoted to local costumes, pottery, furniture and household utensils. There is a very complete historical collection of old Grasse scent bottles and labels. The first floor contains collections of faience and glassware and relics of Admiral de Grasse, of Mirabeau and of the Revolution.

From the end of the Cours the Rue Jean Ossola leads into the narrow lively streets of the old town, which can hardly have changed in two or three hundred years. One may either turn left up the hill to the lovely, arcaded Place des Aires or right to the **Cathedral**, which dates from the end of the twelfth century. Grasse at this time was an independent republic closely allied with Pisa, and the façade shows clear Lombardo-Pisan influence. (The double stairs up to the door are an eighteenth-century addition.) The interior is very impressive,

1. Open daily in July, August and September; at other times afternoons only. Closed on Mondays, the third Sunday in each month, and in November.

with enormously thick round columns, heavily scarred where the Baroque altars have been removed. The building is Romanesque with *berceau brisé* arches which already foreshadow ogives. In a chapel off the right aisle is a 'St Honorat with Six Saints' attributed to Ludovic Bréa. At the end of the aisle is the skull of St Honorat himself, who is the patron of Grasse. Over the sacristy door is a large 'Washing of the Feet' by Fragonard. One of the very few religious paintings by this frivolous, not to say licentious, artist, it has hardly more religious feeling than Goya's San Antonio frescoes in Madrid. It was commissioned for seven hundred *livres* by a confraternity of penitents during the lean years after the Revolution, when the old painter had lost his fashionable clientele in Paris and returned to live in poverty in his native town.

If the Côte d'Azur is the front garden of Grasse, Grasse is one of the main doors to the Côte d'Azur, for the famous Route Napoléon connects it directly with Lyons and Paris. Route Nationale 85, as it is officially called, follows more or less the route which the Emperor took when he marched on Paris after his landing at Golfe Juan in 1815. When the Mayor of Cannes refused him entry into that town he spent his first night bivouacked on the sand dunes where the church of Notre Dame de Bon Voyage now stands, not far from the Casino. At the news of his approach Grasse sounded the tocsin to call the citizens to resistance, and Napoleon by-passed the city to spend the night at a spot on the hills above which is still called the Plateau Napoléon.

The westward road out of Grasse runs past the handsome irrigation reservoir of St Cassien, created in 1964 by damming the Biançon stream. For those with long memories it is strange to see a sheet of water on the Riviera coast which was once so barren and parched, but the lake, when viewed from on high, as from Cabris, lends both charm and diversity to the scene. The road past St Cassien connects Grasse with Draguignan and the heartland of central Provence.

Another, lesser known, road connects Grasse directly with Avignon and is especially to be recommended in July, for then the fields and hill-sides are a mass of purple lavender and the air is pervaded with its scent. The flower is cultivated for the factories, but it also grows wild and gives its peculiar flavour to the local lamb. (For this is all sheep country and is famous also for almonds, truffles and, needless to say, honey.) A man I met in a bistro in Valensole, the other side of Moustiers, assured me his village was the world's lavender capital – '*le capital mondial de la lavande*,' he repeated proudly.

Though narrow and winding, the road has the advantage of passing along the famous **Gorges du Verdon**. The Grand Canyon of the Verdon is said to be the finest in Europe, thirteen miles long and over two thousand feet deep. The Corniche Sublime, built in 1947 and designed specifically to serve the viewpoints which meet one at every turn, follows the southern edge but there is an older road on the northern side which is less vertiginous and whence footpaths wind down into the gorge itself. My advice to travellers who, like myself, prefer to drive on the inner rather than the outer side of precipice roads, is to leave the Route Napoléon at Castellane and follow the northern road, if they are coming from Grasse, and to take the southern road through Aiguines and Comps, joining the Route Napoléon at Le Logis du Pin, if they are coming from Moustiers-Ste-Marie at the western end of the gorge. In recent years, the Aiguines end of the Gorges du Verdon has been transformed through the creation of an enormous artificial lake, the Barrage de Ste Croix, which involved drowning a Roman bridge and some hamlets. A new village, Les Salles-sur-Verdon, is beginning to look established.

Moustiers is a little town with a twelfth-century church, and famous since the seventeenth century for its faience, generally characterized by grotesques in the manner of Callot. The secret of its fine white glaze is said to have been brought by an Italian monk from the eponymous town of Faenza itself. In the eighteenth century a dozen potteries flourished here and every year four hundred mules and asses carried their products down to Beaucaire to be sold at the annual fair. One by one the potteries closed down, the last in 1873, but in 1925 the writer Marcel Provence set up a kiln and restarted the industry. The ceramics of Moustiers may be seen in the museums at Nice, Grasse and Aix and in a little museum, formerly the mansion of the Lords of Moustiers, in the town itself.[1] The other feature of Moustiers is its remarkable situation at the foot of a great cliff wall, like the background of a Mantegna, cleft by a gorge four or five hundred feet deep. Almost at the top, where the eagles soar, an iron chain, seven hundred feet long and with a gilded star swaying in the middle, spans the chasm from one side to the other. According to legend, the 'Chain of the Star' was put up (Heaven knows how) by a local nobleman called the Chevalier de Blacas, who was captured at Damietta in the Seventh Crusade, in fulfilment of a vow and in gratitude for release from his long captivity among the paynim.

The road to Avignon winds on through the lavender fields to **Riez,**

1. Open daily in summer; closed between November 1 and April 1.

a Roman town with a Merovingian baptistery (one of the half-dozen buildings of the period surviving in France) and a striking row of four antique columns from a temple, still standing erect and isolated in a nearby meadow (sign-posted Les Colonnes). Crossing the Durance, the road runs through Manosque and Apt. Some five miles off the Avignon road is a turning to the **Fontaine de Vaucluse**, the classic example of a phenomenon not uncommon in limestone country where an underground river, in this case the Sorgue, gushes full-grown out of a cave at the foot of a rockface. Two other well-known examples of these *sources vauclusiennes*, as geologists call them, are the Timavo near Trieste and the Ombla near Dubrovnik. Except for devoted Petrarchophiles the Fontaine de Vaucluse is nothing to turn off the road for; the approach to it is first ruined by a series of stalls of the most meretricious Vallauris pottery and then blocked by a paper-factory, which works on the water-power. A better idea of the fountain as it must have been in Petrarch's time can be had from the two views of it in the Musée Calvet at Avignon.

But the diversion is worth-while if you happen to be passing along the road at lunchtime, for there are one or two pleasant restaurants where you can eat fresh-water crayfish and trout and watch the great blue dragonflies wheeling over the swiftly flowing water, clear as crystal and a vivid green from the water plants beneath it.

Chapter 11

St Raphaël and Fréjus

୬

*The Estérel – St Raphaël – Fréjus – the Cathedral – Thoronet –
St Maximin*

On the west, Cannes is sheltered from the worst of the mistral, and
the view across the bay is embellished and dramatized by the jagged
mountains of the Estérel, a very ancient formation of eruptive rocks,
a single great block of porphyry, in fact. It is said to be not only the
most ancient piece of Europe, but one of the oldest land masses on
the earth. It has, however, been so worn down by millions of years
of erosion that it nowhere rises much higher than a couple of
thousand feet.

Until the beginning of the century there was only one road con-
necting Cannes and Italy on the one hand with St Raphaël and the
Rhône valley on the other – the present Route Nationale 7. In the
eighteenth century these wooded ravine-riven hills had a sinister
reputation for brigandage, and lonely travellers breathed a sigh of
relief when they were safely past the inn of Les Adrets, for it was a
favourite haunt of the bandit Gaspard de Besse, who was broken on
the wheel at Toulon in 1781. In the nineteenth century the Estérel
was a haven for convicts escaped from the hulks at Toulon, and in
the twentieth a base for the fighters of the French Resistance. Nineteen sixty-one saw the opening of the new double-track motorway,
the *Autoroute de l'Estérel* (A8) which now carries the fast through-
traffic from Paris to the Italian frontier at Menton where it links
with the great Italian *autostrada*.

Along the rocky and deeply indented coast many enticing little
bays and beaches nestle at the foot of the red porphyry cliffs. It was
practically unknown and uninhabited until 1903 when, on the
initiative of the Touring Club de France, a new road along the
cliffs was built to connect Boulouris at the St Raphaël end with La
Napoule on the Bay of Cannes, where the Corniche d'Or, as the
tourist brochures like to call it, begins to climb out of the alluvial
plain at the mouth of the Siagne.

At **La Napoule** a large reddish-purple château confronts the shallow waters of the bay. Two towers and a gateway alone survive of the medieval castle of the Villeneuves. The rest has been rebuilt by the remarkable American sculptor who bought it during the First War. He died in 1937 and is buried in the château. The **Henry Clews Foundation**, as it now is, is open each afternoon though not on Sundays, and it is also closed between December 1 and 21. The gardens are alone worth the trouble of a visit, and the castle is filled with Henry Clews's own sculptures and paintings. While the latter are fairly typical of the middle-brow taste of the early twentieth century, the former consist mainly of grotesques inspired, one would judge, by medieval sculpture and Negro carving. They combine a vivid, not to say a tortured, imagination with a mastery of rare and intractable materials, for Henry Clews, being a rich man, was able to command the most exotic marbles from all over the world. It is worth pausing on the main road, even if you cannot go over the château, to look at some of the gnomes, owls, monkeys, pelicans and scorpions with which Clews has adorned the main gateway of his dream-child. I have seen this New York banker's son described as the greatest sculptor America has produced. Even if he is not that (for Epstein was also an American) he is almost certainly the most original. Cultural exchanges between France and the United States are arranged by the Foundation, and on summer evenings concerts are given in the château.

A long string of little bathing resorts, practically all creations of the last thirty years or so, extends along the Estérel coast, through Théoule, Le Trayas and Anthéor to where the perpendicular red peaks of Le Rastel d'Agay overhang the wide, majestic bay of Agay and to Le Dramont with its high semaphore-rock, its castle-crowned island and the stele which records the landing of the twenty thousand men of the 36th American Division on August 15, 1944. Last of all, and quite different in character, is the older resort of Boulouris, whose luxurious villas and lush gardens almost merge with those of St Raphaël. Between Théoule and Miramar is a striking example of a modern architectural style that is being employed along this coast. In this case it is discreet. Port-la-Galère looks like a cluster of pink and white cave dwellings, sculpted out of the rocks rising steeply out of the sea. They are summer residences, and one of them is Hôtel Guergy with a reputation for good sea food.

St Raphaël became known to the world about a century ago when the pamphleteer Alphonse Karr, one-time editor of *Le Figaro*, made his home there and wrote enthusiastic descriptions of it to all his friends in Paris. (Gounod was among the first to respond, built a villa at Boulouris and composed *Roméo et Juliet* there.) A long series of villas and hotels confronts the sea until the road turns abruptly right by the Hôtel Excelsior (a good halt for luncheon or a night, with a bar where they understand gin-and-tonic) and runs into the centre of the town itself. On the right of the main road, past the railway bridge, the narrow streets of the old fishing hamlet which Karr discovered are grouped round the little twelfth-century **Templar church.** The single-arched Romanesque interior is of an extreme simplicity, for the church was designed not only for worship but for defence and as a refuge for the villagers in time of danger. Its belfry served as a watch-tower against pirates, for the Templars were charged with the defence of the coast until the dissolution of their Order in 1308. By the side of the church is a Roman milestone from the Aurelian Way – *lou camin aurélian*, as the peasants still call the N.7.

Further on, the road runs through the pinewoods, villas and hotels of **Valescure.** What a happy name, one cannot help thinking, the old Vallis Obscura or Dark Valley has chanced on for a health resort where valetudinarians seek a cure! It has long had a reputation as a winter station for invalids, and its golf course, founded in 1891 by the Grand Duke Michael, provides an attraction for the healthy and athletic also.

The Casino on the point of St Raphaël is built upon the site of a luxurious Roman villa, doubtless the summer house of some rich citizen of nearby Fréjus, and just beyond it is the harbour. There are no 'picturesque bits' here, for it was blown up in the war and all the buildings round it are new. Napoleon disembarked here in 1799 after leaving his plague-stricken army in Egypt, and in 1814 he returned, this time a prisoner escorted by Austrian dragoons, on his way to exile in Elba. There were no such things as war crimes trials and 'Hang the Kaiser' campaigns in those days and the English frigate on which he sailed received him with a salute of twenty-one guns.

Beyond the harbour stretches a long sandy beach known as Fréjus Plage, immensely popular in summer, and all much built up now. At the end of it, just before you come to the naval air station, the road turns sharp right to **Fréjus** itself, for this ancient port, where Octavius once moored a hundred galleys, is now nearly a mile from the sea.

There are two well-known Roman towns called Forum Iulii or Julius's Forum. The one in Italy has given its name to Friuli, while the one in France has come down to us as Fréjus. The oldest Roman city in Gaul, it was founded by Julius Caesar in 49 BC, some six years after his first invasion of Britain. (Agricola, who conquered Britain over a century later, was born here in Fréjus.) Augustus erected this little town on the Aurelian Way into a naval base and built here many of the swift ten-banked galleys which defeated Antony and Cleopatra at Actium. He planted a colony of discharged soldiers from the Eighth Legion, and before long the population numbered twenty-five thousand people, which is roughly its present figure. The ancient harbour lay to the south of the present Avenue Aristide Briand. Of its great basin, its two kilometres of quays, its lighthouse, towers, baths, warehouses and shipyards, hardly anything is left. The port, long silted up, was filled in by the farmer who bought it at the time of the Revolution. The so-called Lantern of Augustus, where the ship canal to the sea issued from the basin, is a medieval construction erected on the base of a Roman tower.

The best preserved of the Roman ruins of Fréjus is the **Arena**,[1] which lies on the right where the road to Brignoles leaves the town. Although only a few tiers of seats are left, the ellipse is still complete. Bullfights take place here in the summer when the Arena is not flooded, as it used to be, by the waters of the Reyran. This unruly river killed several hundred people in the lower part of the town in December, 1959, when the Malpasset Dam broke a few miles upstream. An entirely new reservoir system has been created by damming a tributary of the Siagne, called the Lac de St Cassien. The Arena is built of a curious, rather sickly, greenish stone rare in the South of France, although the city of Berne is largely constructed of it. Just outside the town, the road to Cannes passes among the ruins of the aqueduct which brought water to the town from fifty kilometres away in the mountains. The arches may be seen striding purposefully away in single file towards the Estérel until eventually they vanish among the umbrella pines.

Destroyed by the Saracens in the tenth century, the city was rebuilt by Bishop Riculph, and his cathedral, with its cloister, crenellated tower and chapterhouse, form a square block like a fortress in the centre of the town. From the Place de Formigé one enters it through a pair of fine Renaissance doors, carved with sixteen panels, sacred and profane, representing the heads of knights and ladies, and scenes of the Annunciation, the Nativity, the Last Judgement and the Marriage and the Coronation of the Virgin. To have the shutters which cover them opened and to get into the baptistery and the

1. Closed on Tuesdays.

cloister you ring a bell on the left of the narthex, at the foot of the stairs, but there will be no response in the lunch period, nor on a Tuesday.

From this point the Cathedral is on the right, the cloister straight ahead, and the octagonal **baptistery** on the left. The last is an early Christian building believed to date from the beginning of the fifth century, when converts to the state religion were enrolling *en masse*, the Roman Empire was rapidly breaking apart, and the hard pressed Emperor Honorius was withdrawing his last troops from Britain. There are two doors to the baptistery, a large one (the iron grille was the gift of Louis XV's minister, Cardinal Fleury, who was Bishop of Fréjus) and a narrow one through which catechumens had to enter for baptism. After the bishop had washed their feet in the terracotta basin fixed into the floor near the door, they were immersed and baptized in the octagonal font in the centre. Then, white-robed and regenerate, they passed through the large, or triumphal, door to their first communion in the cathedral just across the narthex.

The **Cathedral** is a contemporary of the one at Grasse and in the same style. On the first pillar to the left is a fine painted wooden crucifix of the sixteenth century and at the entrance to the choir a mid-fifteenth-century polyptych on wood representing St Margaret surrounded by saints, the work of Jacques Durandi, one of the masters of the Nice School, who flourished about 1450. The curious picture on the right of the nave with the view of Fréjus in the background represents St Francis de Paul, who afterwards became its patron saint, being welcomed to the city.

The little twelfth-century **cloister** was beautifully restored in 1925, and has a garden of oleanders and a well in the middle. It is surrounded by an arcade of slender marble columns. Grotesque fourteenth-century paintings adorn the wooden ceiling. The staircase on the far side leads to an upper storey and a small but good **museum of local archaeology**. On the floor of the first room is a perfectly preserved Roman mosaic with a leopard in the centre. There are fragments of sculpture and Greek and Gallo-Roman pottery and glassware. In the next room are autograph letters of Napoleon and of the Abbé Sieyès, who was a native son of Fréjus and who, when asked what he had done in the Revolution, answered laconically: 'I survived.' For a member of the Directoire, it was an achievement.

The Christianity of the cathedral does not represent the only religion here, nor are the Roman ruins the sole reminders of a vanished and far-flung empire. Fréjus has long been a garrison town and was the focal point of enormous camps of colonial troops. A kilometre and a half along the Brignoles road, a road turns right to Fayence and on the left of it, where it runs through the former Senegalese camp of Caïs, rises a reproduction of the famous Missiri mosque at Djenné. It is made of concrete, even to the imitation logs which project like scaffolding from the walls, and is coloured to imitate the red mud of the Sudan. Today it is rotting, empty and deserted, for the many thousands of Moslems in the South of France do not seem to consider it worth keeping up. But there is an even more exotic excrescence on this quiet Provençal landscape three and a half kilometres along the road to Cannes where an Indo-Chinese temple rises at the crossroad to Valescure. The slope leading up to it is a stucco menagerie, populated with dragons, fish, lions, cows, deer and tortoises. The pagoda itself is newly painted, with dragons on the outside wall, and, unlike the Sudanese mosque, shows signs of being still in use. It stands in the Galliéni Military Cemetery, surrounded by the graves of five thousand Annamese soldiers killed in the First War, and it was evident when I visited it on a grey afternoon in November that there had been some sort of a service there on All Souls' Day. There were still fresh chrysanthemums in the vases and half-consumed joss sticks in the bowls before the altar, where a bronze Buddha sits flanked by images of birds with flowers in their beaks riding on the backs of tortoises. On either side, the tall statue of a warrior stands on guard.

Further inland beyond the Galliéni Cemetery is a new residential suburb, Domaine de la Tour de Mare. The chapel of St Sépulcre was designed in every detail by Jean Cocteau and executed after his death in 1963.

From Fréjus the N.7 runs direct to Aix-en-Provence and thence on to Lyons and Paris. From Vidauban a comparatively short detour rejoins the main road at Brignoles to take in the **Abbey of Thoronet.**[1] It is one of the famous 'three sisters' of Provence, the others being Sénanque and Silvacane. All three are Cistercian houses of the twelfth century. It was well built in a wooded, well-watered but solitary spot, according to the Cistercian practice, in the purest style of Provençal Romanesque. The church, the cloisters and the monastery buildings, all of a reddish local stone, are now the property of the State. They fell into a state of dilapidation when the monks were driven out at the Revolution, but the novelist Prosper Mérimée, who visited Thoronet in 1834 in his capacity of Inspector-General of Historic Monuments, set to work to restore them to their

1. Closed on Tuesdays.

original condition. The eighteenth-century accretions have been cleared away and the interior of the great church now displays all its pristine majesty and purity of line. On the left of the church are the impressive double-arched cloisters. The chapter-house is a little later, early Gothic with palm-tree vaulting; the floral designs on the capitals of the columns are the only decorative sculptures in this austere abbey. The dormitory and the cellar are also of interest.

Between Brignoles and Aix the road passes the great **Abbey of St Maximin**, the most important Gothic monument in Provence. Although its façade and towers were never completed, the high interior is very impressive and reminds one of an English Gothic cathedral. Long a place of pilgrimage, its full name is St Maximin-la Sainte Baume. This has nothing to do with Holy Balm, but is derived from the Provençal word *baoumo*, a grotto or cave, and is closely bound up with the legend of Les Saintes-Maries-de-la-Mer. St Maximin was believed to have landed there with the three Maries and been martyred at Aix, while St Mary Magdalene settled in La Sainte Baume, a cave in the wooded heights to the south, and there spent her latter years and died. The two saints were buried side by side and round their tomb the settlement of St Maximin grew up. The crypt where the tombs lay was covered in for safety, lost at the time of the Saracen invasion and 'rediscovered' in 1279. The present church was built a few years later and from then on St Maximin entered into keen competition with Vézelay in Burgundy, which possessed a rival set of the bones of the Magdalene. Ruined at the Revolution, the abbey was only saved from demolition by the resource of Lucien Bonaparte, who happened to be stationed in the town and hastily commandeered the abbey as a military warehouse. When Barras wanted at least to melt down the pipes of the organ, Lucien saved them by inviting the *conventionnel* for an inspection and greeting him with the strains of the Marseillaise, hurriedly learnt by the organist. The abbey was bought back by the Dominicans in 1859 and it was there that the famous preacher Lacordaire wrote his *Life of St Mary Magdalene*.

The polygonal apse with its many high windows is strikingly beautiful, and the Gothic vaulting of the nave, which rises to a height of sixty feet, is of a singular purity of line. Do not on any account miss the picture by the Venetian Ronzen in the fourth chapel on the right, for into the twenty-two panels of the Passion at Jerusalem the painter has incorporated the earliest known view of the Papal Palace at Avignon, not to mention the Piazzetta at Venice. The gadget below marked *minuterie* will turn on the electric light for sixty seconds, and the same with the next chapel, which contains a lovely thirteenth-century cope.

The pilgrimage point is the crypt, which was actually the burial vault of an early fifth-century Roman villa. Even if the tombs to be seen there do not actually contain the remains of SS Mary Magdalene, Maximin, Sidonius and Marcella, at least they are among the oldest Christian relics in France, being Gallo-Roman sarcophagi of the fifth century. A gilt-bronze reliquary contains a skull venerated as that of St Mary Magdalene.

Chapter 12

St Tropez

❧

The Maures – St Tropez – the Bravade – the Annonciade – the Harbour – the Old Town

The Massif des Maures, separated from the Estérel by the Fréjus Gap, forms another 'island' of very ancient rock, quite unrelated to the limestone formations of Provence. Although it was for over two centuries the main Saracen stronghold in Provence, it derives its name not from the Moors but from the late Greek ηαῦρος, through the Provençal word *maouro*, 'black', an epithet applied to it on account of its thick forests of Aleppo pine, ilex, Spanish chestnut and cork-oak. The double link might not seem immediately apparent between a smart West End wedding and a village in the Maures, but the principal manufactures and exports of Collobrières, the largest centre, are corks and *marrons glacés*. They grow up side by side in their forests and, in a far country, they attain fulfilment and perish together. But perhaps this is carrying the pathetic fallacy rather too far.

Between Fréjus and Hyères, the two extreme limits of the Côte des Maures, the only place of any consequence is St Tropez. For hundreds of years the coast was rendered uninhabitable by the corsair raids which continued up to Charles X's capture of Algiers in 1830. (In the eighteenth century ransom prices for prisoners ran as high as 10,000 *livres* a head.) The scattered natives huddled in walled villages such as Ramatuelle, Grimaud, Gassin and Bormes. They were built on hill-tops at a safe distance from the sea, where the watch-towers on the coast could give them long enough warning to bring their families and their cattle in to safety, and prepare their defence.

Now the movement is seaward. The whole shore south of Fréjus is cut up into *parcs*, *domaines* and *lotissements* for sale as building lots, and a number of little villa-settlements such as St Aygulf (named after the seventh-century abbot who introduced the Benedictine rule into St Honorat and whose skull may be seen in the

Cathedral at Grasse), Les Issambres and La Nartelle already dot the coast as far as **Ste Maxime** on the Gulf of St Tropez. Here a small fishing village sprang up as soon as the coast was fairly safe, at the end of the eighteenth century, and its sheltered position, its fine sandy beach and the golf course at nearby Beauvallon, where the poet Paul Géraldy lives, have earned Ste Maxime a faithful clientele, especially of British visitors with families in tow.

Facing it on the opposite side of the gulf is a very different place, the ancient port of **St Tropez**. It owes its curious name to one Torpes, a Christian officer of Nero, who was martyred at Pisa in AD 68. (A large picture of his decapitation still hangs in the cathedral of that city.) The headless body of the martyr was put in a boat with a dog and a cock and set adrift. After a voyage of nineteen days it landed safely here in the Sambracitan Gulf, where a pious lady named Celerina, to whom all this had been revealed in a dream, gave it decent burial. The head of the saint is still venerated in Pisa, but the body was taken from the church at St Tropez to save it from the Saracens and hidden so securely that, less fortunate than that of St Maximin, it was never found again.

Two other versions of the St Tropez legend exist. One maintains that on a stormy night the figurehead of a ship in perdition was washed up on the shore. Local fishermen built a chapel and venerated the figurehead, calling it *san trovato*, 'the found saint'. This became *San Tropato*, hence St Tropez.

The other – it runs a poor third for credibility – says the saint was in fact a statue of Hermes whose most striking feature was his massive sexual organs. These were removed by the blow of an axe so that the pagan god could become acceptable as a Christian one and the patron saint of the town.

St Tropez was destroyed by the Moors in 739, rebuilt, again destroyed and lay abandoned and a temptation to any invader, when in 1470 the Seneschal of Provence, who happened to be the neighbouring Count of Grimaud, invited a gentleman of Genoa, one Raffaelle Garezzio, to rebuild, fortify and repopulate it. This he did by importing twenty-one Genoese families, and in return King René of Provence exempted the inhabitants from all taxes and feudal dues except responsibility for the defence of the coast. The French monarchs recognized these privileges and the little town enjoyed a kind of autonomy under its Capitaines de Ville for nearly two centuries. Its fleet was strong enough to go to the help of Fréjus, Antibes and the Lérins when they were hard pressed and in 1637 it put to flight an attacking force of twenty-one Spanish ships, a victory still celebrated every year on June 15.

The custom of the *bravade* is peculiar, as far as I know, to this part of France. In addition to the Fête des Espagnols in June, there is a more important *bravade* in honour of St Torpes, which has taken place every May for four hundred years. On the afternoon of May 16 about a hundred men in eighteenth-century uniform form up in the beflagged and decorated Town Hall Square to the sound of drums, bugles and fifes. The bust of the saint, helmeted, garlanded and beribboned, is brought from the church. Escorted by a guard armed with blunderbusses, and by the clergy, mayor, town captains and other civic officials, the saint heads a procession round the town. The banners wave overhead, the drummers and the buglers play their loudest and the musketeers discharge volleys into the ground until the streets are thick with acrid smoke.

The commanders of the *bravade* are the two Capitaines de Ville. They wear full naval uniform with swords and are attended by two small boys similarly attired, who weave graceful salutes with the standard of St Torpes. (On one side it bears the likeness of the saint himself and on the other of his boat with its three strange passengers.) These four are very grave and dignified figures, but the same cannot always be said of their troops. The *bravadeurs* are dressed in the French colours – white trousers, blue tunics and red facings. On their heads they wear shakos, tricornes and a kind of fore-and-aft affair, half-way between an Iraqi cap and a fisherman's bonnet. Some of them wear horn spectacles, some smoke cigarettes and some chew gum. They laugh and chat with their friends in the crowd and I was glad to see that thirsty warriors were free to break parade for a quick drink when they felt like it. Nothing would be easier than to make cheap jokes about the Awkward Squad or to describe the *bravade* as *War and Peace* played as a Laurel and Hardy farce. It would be a mistake, however, to laugh, for its strength lies precisely in its casual character. That is the guarantee of its spontaneity, one thinks to oneself as one watches the parade in the Place de l'Hôtel de Ville. The very fact that there is no drill is the proof of its genuineness, that it is a tradition kept up by the Tropéziens for themselves, their own pride and tradition and not to attract tourists – which, anyhow, they do not need to do. There are no tickets, no admission fees, no *tribunes d'honneur*, no official guests, no stands and, perhaps most important of all, no drill or discipline. Any visitor is welcome to watch but it is not laid on for him. If the world were to sink into the sea and only St Tropez survive, there would be a *bravade* the following year. When the *bravade* was over, I trotted out a tactless quotation to a Tropézien friend: '*É finita la commedia.*' '*Non è una commedia,*' he replied rather coldly.

The theme-song is *La Marseillaise des Bravadeurs* with its chorus:

> Aux armes, bravadeurs,
> Formez vos bataillons.
> Marchons, marchons,
> Et sans repos
> Déchargeons nos tromblons!

And discharge their blunderbusses without repose they do indeed. Deafening volleys succeed each other. The air is thick with smoke and the falling paper wadding of the muzzle-loaders. The stones of the Place de la Mairie, where the main parades take place, are soon blackened with the powder from the point-blank volleys. The dogs all get hysterics and have to be taken away, and if you place yourself strategically you may be in time to catch a pretty girl swooning in your arms. Apart from the deafening volleys, the *bravadeur* has the habit of firing off isolated shots – perhaps from just behind your ear when he is going back on parade after a well-earned beer – just to keep the public on its toes. Until late at night stray shots ring out all over the town. You imagine desperate gunners on the rooftops and find yourself forming phrases like 'isolated pockets of resistance'.

The *bravade* originated soon after Garezzio's resettlement of the town. On account of the perpetual danger from pirate raids (for St Tropez was the arsenal and warehouse of the whole Côte des Maures) the early settlers always kept their weapons at hand. They even carried them in the annual procession of their patron saint – which would otherwise have afforded an ideal opportunity for a surprise attack, the more so since it involved a procession to his chapel outside the town. Now, when young men in festive mood carry loaded firearms their fingers itch on the trigger. A salute of gunfire has been regarded as a mark of honour ever since gunpowder was invented. What more natural, then, than that the Tropéziens should fire off volleys in honour of their saint? Such at least is the explanation put forward by the Abbé Espitalier, the learned biographer of St Torpes, and it seems a likely one enough.

In 1677, the lordship of St Tropez passed by marriage to the Suffren family, whose most famous scion, the Bailli de Suffren, became the greatest admiral in French history. For two years, during the American War of Independence, he harried the Atlantic and the Indian Oceans, where he made himself (according to a patriotic French guide-book) 'the terror of the English'. The other martial son of St Tropez, after whom the main street is named, was General Allard, who organized and commanded the armies of Ranjit Singh, King of Lahore, and died in India in 1839.

St Tropez lies at the dead end of the road, leading on to nowhere. Nobody passes through St Tropez on the way to somewhere else; they only go *to* St Tropez and then return the way they came. One can imagine the isolation of the peninsula before the coast road was built, let alone motor cars to run on it. When Guy de Maupassant came here in his yacht, St Tropez was connected with the outside world only by an old sailing boat from St Raphaël, the *Lion de Mer*, and a dilapidated *diligence* which brought the mail over the ridges of the Maures.

Apart from Maupassant, the first person to discover the little town was the Neo-Impressionist painter Signac, who settled down here in 1892. He started a fashion which many were to follow. Bonnard, Matisse, Marquet and Dunoyer de Segonzac came to live here, and many others of the École de Paris arrived in the summer with their easels, their palettes and their canvases. Dunoyer de Segonzac was the last of this illustrious band.

Some of the most representative work of these talented visitors has been harvested, garnered and preserved in the town, thanks to the taste and generosity of a local connoisseur. M. Georges Grammont, by origin a Lyonnais, was a wealthy manufacturer of submarine cables who lived and died at St Tropez. He proved himself a discriminating patron of the local artists' colony Eventually he purchased the de-consecrated chapel of **L'Annonciade**,[1] which lay at the western end of the port near the shipyards, and his architect, Louis Sue, converted it into a magnificent home for his collection. On his death in 1955 he left it all to the town, which is now challenged only by Grenoble among provincial towns for one of the best collections of early twentieth-century painters in France.

Well lit and well arranged, the museum contains, in addition to half a dozen bronzes by Maillol and Despiau, ninety-seven pictures, all well-chosen examples of the generation which immediately followed Cézanne and Van Gogh. Signac, with his nine pictures, is the chief ornament of the gallery. (Notice that he departs entirely from his mosaic technique in his water-colours.) Of special interest to Londoners will be the two Derains, both painted in his wildest *fauve* period, of Westminster Palace and Waterloo Bridge. There is an exquisite little Seurat, 'The Port of Gravelines', on the staircase landing. Of the three Matisses, look at No. 46, 'Interior at Nice' and

1. Open daily except Tuesdays, and closed in November.

No. 71, 'Corsican Landscape', an interesting example of his early work before he developed his characteristic style. Of the six Bonnards my favourite is the 'Nude by the Fireplace' on the upper floor. Marquet and Vuillard are here at their best. Notice the latter's 'Two Women by Lamplight' (No. 70) and 'Interior with Two Chairs' (No. 63). Among the other painters here are Cross, Friesz, Vlaminck, Braque, Dufy, Lhote, Van Dongen, Suzanne Valadon, Camoin, Roussel, Utrillo and Dunoyer de Segonzac. The mere list of names will give an idea of the quality of the gallery – as it was when I saw it and as it has become again, for in July 1961, burglars came with a *camionnette* in the middle of the night and stole fifty-six out of its ninety-seven pictures, all of them uninsured and valued by the Curator, M. Dunoyer de Segonzac, at five million francs on the market in Paris or eight million in London. The solitary painting left on the walls of the first ground-floor room was No. 17, 'The Country House at St Tropez', a delightful little tree-piece in the manner of Cézanne which, being by the little-known Urbain, the robbers left behind. They overlooked also the most valuable picture in the collection, the small Seurat on the landing. Happily, everything was recovered.

The second period in the development of St Tropez began after the First War, when it was discovered by the Bohemians and cosmopolitans and became a sort of Montparnasse-on-Sea, full of artists, writers, hangers-on and what a tactful English writer on the Riviera has described as 'the morally and politically unconventional of France, Britain and the USA'. (It is no good trying to think up puns about Tropeze Artists or Daring Young Men, for the z is silent. St Tropez rhymes with *trompez*.) Something of the old tradition of the thirties survives today; painters have returned and hold open-air exhibitions round the harbour. The existentialists have faded out; Colette was replaced by Brigitte Bardot. In the summer endless carloads of visitors pack the little town, the women dressed in boleros and bare almost everything, or whatever uniform is decreed for the season, and all apparently, having come to look at the celebrities (who seldom stir from the gardens and swimming pools of their villas, anyhow), reduced to looking at each other. Most of them presumably live in the enormous tented fields along the bay, some of which house thousands of campers each. St Tropez has six thousand inhabitants, two hundred hotel rooms, and on a fine Sunday in August may, it has been estimated, have a luncheon population of anything up to fifty thousand.

The shortage of hotel accommodation in St Tropez is probably due to the fact that it is wellnigh the only place on the coast with a single season. In the summer it is crowded out, gay and glamorous and sophisticated; in the winter even the residents go away. I once spent November and December there and was literally the only outsider in the deserted town. All the hotels, nearly all the eating places and many of the shops were closed. After nightfall the town, which in summer goes to bed at dawn, was given over to a few stray cats. The fact is that St Tropez has the sad distinction of being the solitary place on the coast which faces due north. Everywhere one must be prepared for the winter rains when the wind blows from the east – *le vent d'Italie*, as it is called – but St Tropez is exposed also to the force of the north-westerly wind, the *mistral*. Even the enormous Hôtel Latitude 43 has been forced to give up and turn itself into a block of flats, for which it can at least get a rent all the year round.

For the Tropéziens the centre of town life is the Place des Lices at the end of the Rue Gambetta, where the market is and where the men, of all ages and seemingly inexhaustible leisure, play *boules* all day in the shade of enormous plane trees. (Camoin has a pleasing picture of the Place des Lices, No. 85 in the Annonciade.) For the visitors, naturally enough, life centres round the harbour, which is perhaps the most attractive on the coast. Yachts and fishing boats fill the little square of water, which is surrounded on two sides by quays, on the third by a small ship-repairing yard and on the fourth by the mole where the fishing boats moor and the nets are spread out to dry. From the Annonciade the broad Quai de Suffren, with the bronze statue of the admiral in front of the Café de Paris runs to meet the Quai Jean Jaurès, which is lined by cafés and restaurants and backed by a row of high, narrow houses, colourwashed in cream, pink and yellow ochre. With its unmistakable Genoese influence, it recalls Portofino and Camogli. The quay is wider, however, and on close inspection the houses reveal themselves as clever reproductions of the old ones. When the Allies landed on August 15, 1944, the Germans blew up the port before retiring into the citadel, where they surrendered in the afternoon. The houses on the quays lay in ruins except for the Quai Mistral near the round Daumas Tower and a few houses at the far end of the Quai Jean Jaurès. They are recognizable by their lower storeys, which project slightly outwards, whereas the new houses are perpendicular. A row of little restaurants line the quay and look rather like a line of wildbeast cages in a zoo, separated from each other by wire trelliswork, their front parts open to the sunshine and disappearing into dark cavernous interiors.

When all is said and done, life has few more agreeable experiences to offer than to dawdle over a meal in the sunshine outside the Rascasse or sit over an apéritif on the terrace of the Café Sénéquier and watch the masts of the yachts swaying lazily from side to side, with the mountains in the background and a gay cosmopolitan crowd on the quay in front. Once on this same Quai Jean Jaurès I saw cars from Iceland and Andorra parked side by side. Behind them was moored a yacht registered in far Penang and another little boat rumoured to have sailed round the world before coming to anchor in St Tropez.

Behind the Quai Jean Jaurès is the old part of the town. At the end of the quay, by the remains of the former mansion of the Suffrens, a street leads into the Place de l'Hôtel de Ville. (The elaborately-carved door on the right-hand side, by the way, is not Provençal but was brought by a sailor from Zanzibar.) If you continue through the narrow streets beyond the square you come to the old fishing harbour called La Ponche. If you want to have a leisurely tasting of the wines of Provence and a bite to go with them, make for La Vinothèque at 7 Place de la Mairie.

Built out into the waters of the Gulf of St Tropez is Port Grimaud, a *cité lacustre* of recent construction. Each house has been individually designed to create a harmonious and colourful total effect; each has its own jetty on the 'canals'; and so Port Grimaud is a highly fashionable place for the yachting community. The whole village is wonderfully quiet, as the only way of getting about in it is by boat. Its hotel, the Giraglia, is in the same style as the rest.

To the right, on a hill, is the seventeenth-century citadel, a double line of walls enclosing a moat and a hexagonal donjon with a courtyard in the middle. The first floor is now a maritime museum.[1] There are model ships, engravings and some interesting seventeenth-century maps of the Mediterranean. In summer the citadel is the setting for the Festival of St Tropez when both classical and jazz music is performed. On a clear winter's day (a day of mistral, for choice) there is a magnificent view over the whole Peninsula of Ramatuelle, the Gulf and the Estérel, while the snowy peaks of the Alps stand like a white wall on the far horizon.

While St Tropez itself has no *plage*, a number of roads radiate out to the many sandy beaches which girdle the peninsula – La Bouillabaisse, La Baie des Graniers, Les Salins, Tahiti and the three-mile-long strand of La Pampelonne near Cap Camarat. The Baie des Canoubiers, a mile or two out of town, has the reputation of being

1. Open throughout the day; closed between November 15 and December 15.

one of the safest as well as the most beautiful anchorages for yachts on this part of the coast. Colette lived there from 1923 to 1936. Her famous house, *La Treille Muscate*, on the Route de Salins, is now forlorn and dilapidated, and her much-loved garden neglected.

In the centre of the pleasant wooded peninsula to which it has given its name rises the enchanting hill-top village of **Ramatuelle**. It is a tangle of narrow alleys and stairways like its neighbour, **Gassin**, which looks from below like some scaly grey-brown monster rising on a ridge out of the thick foliage of the oak woods. There is a magnificent view from the terrace in front of the church, where once the beacon gave warning of the corsairs to Grimaud, to be relayed thence further inland.

Both Gassin and Ramatuelle were old strongholds of the Moors who swept up through Spain to conquer Southern France some twenty-five years after Tarik crossed from Africa. It was not until 973 that Duke William the Good of Provence, ably seconded by Gibelin de Grimaldi, finally drove them from their almost impregnable fastness of Le Frassinet on the main crest of the Chaîne des Maures. Today what is now called **La Garde Freinet**, a prosperous village which lives largely on its surrounding forests of cork, chestnut and mulberry, shows no trace of the Arabs unless it be that the people will greet a stranger with a polite '*Bonjour, monsieur*', a courtesy now becoming rare in Europe.

For his services Gibelin de Grimaldi was given a fief near the head of the Gulf of St Tropez, on which he in turn bestowed his name. **Grimaud**, as it is now called, is a village of marked character, with an eleventh-century Templar church and a long, arcaded Gothic House of the Templars in the Rue des Templiers. The alleys wind up the hill and under the houses, and at the top come to the wide enceinte of the castle walls. The ruined keep is a landmark far around, for two or three high towers still stand and lift gaunt fingers to the sky.

Three kilometres south of Grimaud lies the village of **Cogolin** on N. 98, of unusual interest because briar pipes, carpets, and silk yarn from silkworm cocoons (in the nineteenth century silkworm rearing was a cottage industry throughout Provence) are manufactured there, and the factories can be visited.

A guide at *Les Tapis et Tissus de Cogolin* in Boulevard Louis Blanc accompanies visitors round the carpet and linen workshops, mornings or afternoons, but not on Saturday afternoons or Sundays.

Chapter 13

Hyères

❧

The Coast – the Îles d'Or – Hyères

From Cap Camarat to Hyères stretches a string of euphonious little summer resorts, with names as silver as their sands; Cavalaire with its woods of oak, pine and mimosa and one of the finest beaches on the Mediterranean, Le Rayol perched on its terraces, Le Canadel, Pramousquier, Cavalière, Aiguebelle and St Clair nestle among the woods between the coast road and the shore. Umbrella pines and mimosas, oleanders, myrtle, thyme and cistus, still form a background to miles of golden beaches. But nature is having to give some ground, of course, to the encroachments of houses, restaurants and shops. Even yet, these little places delight the sun- and sea-worshippers, where other attractions are minimal. The seclusion they enjoyed for the first few postwar years after the little local railway line had been abandoned, is gone. The sad fact is that Mediterranean-faring is growing at such an enormous rate that very soon there will not be enough coast to go round.

The road dips to sea-level again at **Le Lavandou,** which twenty or thirty years ago was a prosperous fishing village and has now become a flourishing seaside resort, surrounded by summer villas. With its long sandy beach, its sheltering woods behind, its jetty with the long quay where the fishermen spread their nets to dry, and its broad tree-shaded promenade, it bears a strong family resemblance to Ste Maxime. Just above it perches the picturesque old village of Bormes (or Bormes-les-Mimosa, as it likes to call itself on the analogy of Juan-les-Pins, Hyères-les-Palmiers and St Pons-les-Mûres). It is pushing southwards to link with La Favière and the hillside developments of the village-groups of Village des Fourches on Cap Bénat. At La Favière, the new yacht marina of Bormes-Favière has been completed, and a small section of sandy beach has been preserved.

Apart from the fishing and the tourist trade, Le Lavandou is the port for the islands of Port Cros and the Île du Levant, the eastern group of the Îles d'Hyères – or the Îles d'Or, as they are also called, probably on account of a yellowish rock common there, which takes on a peculiar metallic sheen and was at one time mistaken for gold. To the east the long, almost cliff-bound, Île **du Levant** is divided between the Navy and the nudists. The eastern half (closed to the public) is an experimental rocket station belonging to the French marine, and the western half (open) is the setting for one of the most famous *naturiste* colonies in Europe. From the little landing stage a red Land-Rover *camionnette* takes passengers and their belongings up to the village of **Héliopolis,** which has its own post office, hotels, shops and even estate agents, on the top of the cliff. The morning boat from Le Lavandou touches there and passengers who are not going to stay can either disembark for a few hours to visit the nudists (they do not like cameras, by the way) and take the boat back to the mainland in the afternoon or continue to **Port Cros,** the wildest and in some ways the most beautiful of the group. It is hilly and densely wooded, with numerous walks under the over-arching pines and cistus shrubs. It is private property and there are 'No Smoking' notices everywhere, although this does not prevent matches and cigarettes being on sale in the *bar-tabacs* in the little port. In 1963 Port Cros was declared a National Park, which means that all animal and plant life is protected, as well as marine life immediately surrounding the island. On arriving at Port Cros, visitors can buy a well-illustrated and instructive guide-book in French to the island's natural history.

The western island, **Porquerolles,** is the largest of the Îles d'Or. It boasts several good hotels, is covered with pine-woods and, though the south coast is cliff-bound, the sandy beaches on the north are much frequented in the summer. To foster the lush, sub-tropical vegetation has for sixty years been the especial care of its proprietrix, for Porquerolles, like Port Cros, is private property.

The fourth island is no longer an island at all, though geologically a part of the group. The boat runs several times a day between Porquerolles and La Tour Fondue on the southernmost tip of **Giens,** a hilly, wooded, little peninsula, where in 1961 a local resident, the poet St John Perse, received the news that he had won the Nobel Prize. The former island (which became an island again for a short time after a great storm in 1811) is now attached to the mainland by two narrow strips of sand, enclosing a lagoon and saltpans where high white hillocks of salt glitter in the sunshine. A road runs along the eastern neck of land to the modern little harbour and bathing beach of Hyères-Plage and inland to the diadem of medieval walls and towers where Hyères itself rises on a little hill.

Hyères. the oldest resort in the South of France, was already frequented in the eighteenth century when the English were beginning to discover Nice but, like Grasse, it has fallen out of fashion since the days when Queen Victoria stayed there. (Robert Louis Stevenson, who had been banished by his doctors to the South of France and detested it, wrote: 'I was only happy once; that was at Hyères.') Surrounded by numerous villas, it is celebrated for its mild winter climate and its avenues of tall date palms. The **Olbius Riquier Gardens**, to the left at the bottom of the Avenue Gambetta, are particularly agreeable, with their many different varieties of palms and other exotic plants. The only museum is the **Municipal Museum**[1] in the Cité Administrative, Place Lefèvre. It is small and of interest to archaeologists, for it contains remains of the Greek colony of Olbia, an offshoot of Greek Marseilles, excavated at nearby L'Almanarre (and that name is one of the few Moorish relics hereabouts, from Al Manar, or lighthouse).

The old town is now some three miles from the sea but in the Middle Ages it was a favourite port for pilgrims sailing to the Holy Land, and it was here that St Louis landed in 1254 on his return from the Seventh Crusade. His first act was to pray in the church which now bears his name. In the Place de la République at the entrance to the upper town, St Louis has a handsome Romanesque particoloured façade, with a rose-window, in the Italian style. The interior with its *berceau brisé* vaulting resembles the Cathedrals of Grasse and Fréjus. The centre of the old town is the Place Massillon, where the covered market is and where a twelfth-century Templar church is now used as a law court. Thence the precipitous Rue Ste Catherine leads up to St Paul's church with a magnificent view over the town, the Salins and Porquerolles. Beside it a turreted house bestrides one of the city gates, for in the eleventh and twelfth centuries, when Hyères was a tiny independent state, the city walls ran along the brow of the hill and what is now the Rue Barbacane.

Modern Hyères has spread eastwards across the alluvial plain created by the Gapeau river, towards the Hyères saltpans. New yachting and water-sports centres have sprung up – Ayguade-Ceinturon, Berriau-Plage, Port Pothuau and Port-de-Miramar.

1. Open afternoons only; closed on Tuesdays.

Chapter 14

Toulon

❧

The City – the Museum – the Coast – Cassis

It was Louis XIV who created the great arsenal and made Toulon into the principal French naval base, a position it has retained ever since. Its naval eminence brought Toulon a sinister fame as the Devil's Island of its day, for criminals and vagabonds, Turkish prisoners and Negro slaves (and after the Revocation of the Edict of Nantes large numbers of recalcitrant Protestants) were assembled in their thousands to row the galleys of the King's navy, which had twenty-five oars to a side and four slaves to each oar. Each *galérien* lived, ate and slept at his bench, chained by one wrist to his oar and one leg to the gangway. It is surprising to learn from a Parisian traveller, writing in 1630, that 'the principal amusement of strangers in Provence is to gaze at the galley slaves and visit them in their galleys. There one sees all the misery, filth, dirt, stench and diseases of humanity.' It is an even more remarkable commentary on the conditions of the time than this macabre taste in sightseeing that these wretches should actually have included a number of volunteers, who were distinguished from the others only by the right to wear moustaches. In truth the symbol of Toulon might well be Puget's two muscular 'Caryatids' (or, more correctly, Atlantes) who almost audibly groan beneath the weight of the town hall balcony on the Darse Vieille.

It was in Toulon that the modern world's most famous military reputation was born in 1793 – that of Napoleon Bonaparte. The inhabitants had declared for the Royalists against the Republic and handed the city over to the English, who entrenched themselves in a commanding position on the peninsula between La Seyne and Tamaris. The youthful Captain Bonaparte captured their stronghold and the city and was straight away promoted to brigadier-general. His sergeant at the attack on 'Little Gibraltar' was a certain Junot, who now set his foot also on the ladder which led him to within grasp of a marshal's baton.

111

As a great naval fortress, it was inevitable that Toulon should suffer severely during the last war. In 1942 the Vichyist Admiral Laborde blocked the harbour by scuttling sixty ships of the French fleet. Later on, the Allied bombers flattened the Old Port. In August 1944, when General de Lattre de Tassigny's forces were attacking the town from the heights above, the Germans blew up the citadel, the dockyards and the harbour installations before surrendering.

The main axis of the town is the Boulevard de Strasbourg, which connects the two main centres of life, the station quarter on the north-west, whence the road runs up to the heights of the Faron and where many of the hotels and restaurants are, and, to the south-east (turn right at the theatre), the old town stretching down to the waterfront and the Vieux Port. The picturesque Quai Cronstadt, named in honour of the visit of the Imperial Russian Navy in 1893, was destroyed, together with the red-light quarter behind, in 1944, rebuilt in a rectangular contemporary style and rechristened, more topically, Quai Stalingrad. (It was sitting in a café on the Quai that Bernanos wrote several of his novels.) The narrow streets of the old town are grouped round the cathedral, which is almost pitch-dark and has nothing in it anyway. Especially delightful and *méridional* are the Place Puget, with its dolphin fountain, and the flower, fruit and vegetable markets in the Rue Lendrin and the Cours Lafayette. The Rue d'Alger and the Quai Stalingrad are the gay evening promenades of the town.

I whiled away a wet afternoon very pleasantly in the **Museum of Art and Archaeology**[1] but there is nothing in it worth breaking a journey for, except perhaps for amateurs of model ships, of which there is an elaborate collection on the ground floor. A Pieter Breughel version of the 'Flemish Proverbs' holds the place of honour in the picture gallery on the first floor. I admired also two very pleasant Solimenas and two Annibale Carracis of Ariadne displaying her ample charms on Naxos, as others do nowadays on the Île du Levant. On the second floor are paintings by moderns, including Vlaminck, Othon Friesz and Ziem.

For inveterate sightseers, mention may be made of the Old Toulon Museum[2] at 69 Cours Lafayette, and the Maritime Arsenal[3] for a conducted tour of the harbour installations (hardly anything ancient here); for the latter it is as well to be in possession of your passport as a means of identification.

1. Closed on Mondays and Wednesdays.
2. Closed on Mondays and Wednesdays.
3. Open daily except during military holidays.

On the north, Toulon is sheltered by the precipitous ridge of Le Faron, served by a scenic road, La Corniche du Faron, and by a funicular to the summit which starts from the Hôtel La Tour Blanche at Super-Toulon. Guide-books say that the best time of day to go up to the limestone crag of Faron is towards evening when the light plays its most dramatic role. At the top is the old fort, Tour Beaumont, next to which is the **Memorial to the Allied Landings in Provence**[1] in 1944. In the museum are models, documents and dioramas explaining the military operations. Outside again, the visitor is rewarded with impressive views in all directions. Other favourite goals for the excursionists of Toulon are the *plages* of Les Sablettes and Tamaris, where in the old days the naval officers and their wives used to live.

Between Toulon and Marseilles is a series of small seaside towns. All have pleasant sandy beaches and are a good deal cheaper than the resorts further east. They tend to be crowded with holiday-makers and week-enders from Marseilles. **Sanary** (which is Provençal for St Nazaire) is a fishing village which has now become a resort. Aldous Huxley used to live at Sanary, but then, there is hardly a town or hamlet along this whole coast which has not harboured some celebrated writer or painter since the end of the nineteenth century. Further on, **Bandol**, fairly elegant but not yet too commercialized, has an attractive sweep of beach, with a castle on the point and the island of Bendor in front of it. Bendor, a rocky deserted isle a few years ago, has been made into a Provençal village with tourist hotels, a congress centre, museums, an open-air theatre, yachting, regatta and subaqua amenities by the energy of Paul Ricard, whose *pastis* is drunk in every bar in the south. Frequent launches ply between Bandol and the island. Paul Ricard's energy has developed the Île des Embiez, offshore from Le Brusc, into a powerboat centre, and the motor race-track inland near Le Camp-du-Castelet, as well as the Mas Méjanes in the Camargue. Les Lecques is a resort which has expanded round its mile-long, sweeping bay of sand and safe bathing.

At the entrance to La Ciotat is the bathing resort of Ciotat-Plage and then if you keep on round the semicircular harbour you are brought up short by the dock-gates, for ever since the time of the Greeks this has been a shipyard. 'The City' has twenty-four thousand inhabitants and can build ships of fifty or sixty thousand tons.

Cassis is a very attractive little fishing port with three beaches,

1. Open all day between July 15 and August 15; closed during lunch for the rest of the year.

sheltered from the north by high limestone precipices. Many rich Marseillais have villas and flats in Cassis. It is famed for its rather heady white wine, greenish like the *vinho verde* of Portugal, which is locally held to be the right drink for washing down *bouillabaisse*. Formerly the town was known for its production of muscat wine and coral but abandoned these two luxury articles as unprofitable on account of the quantities it had to give away as 'presents' to a number of powerful people who were in a position to make themselves unpleasant if their hints were ignored. Now the Cassidiens have taken to the more prosaic occupations of quarrying and cement-making; the modern quarters and the docks of Marseilles are largely built of their white stone.

The coast on both sides is very rugged, and at twelve hundred feet, the cliffs of Cap Canaille, just east of the town, are the highest in France. To the west are the famous *calanques*, En Vau, Port Miou, Port Pin and the others. They are long creeks like miniature fjords, varying from a hundred and fifty to five hundred feet in width and framed by perpendicular cliffs. They can be visited with some exertion on foot and without any by hiring a motor-boat.

Between Cassis and the outskirts of Marseilles are the rugged limestone cliffs formed by the Massifs of Puget and Marseilleveyre. Marseilles itself is edging eastwards towards the *calanques* with the construction of an ambitious university complex at Luminy.

Chapter 15

Marseilles

❧

The Vieux Port – the Canebière – the Palais Longchamp –
the Château d'If – the Harbour – Martigues

Two thousand five hundred years ago Marseilles was the principal
Greek city in the Western Mediterranean, and it has a sentimental,
almost filial, interest for the natives of the British Isles, and indeed of
Scandinavia, since one of its explorers discovered them and put them
on the map. The Massiliot, Pytheas, was the first navigator to visit,
name and describe our remote northern islands in the fourth century
BC. Greek traders from Marseilles, using the Rhône corridor, pene-
trated to all parts of Gaul and it was, no doubt, through them that
our blue-painted forefathers made their first regular cultural and
commercial contacts with the Mediterranean world. It was not, as
we have always been told, the Phoenicians who used to sail to Corn-
wall to take on cargoes of tin, but those 'young, lighthearted masters
of the waves', the Greeks of Marseilles.

Ever since her foundation about 600 BC by colonists from Phocea
in Ionia, on the shores of Asia Minor, Marseilles has devoted herself
almost exclusively to commerce (although she has found herself
associated inescapably with *la gloire* ever since Rouget de l'Isle's
'Hymn of the Army of the Rhine' was misnamed *La Marseillaise*).
When the Romans came, she possessed counters and colonies from
Emporion in Catalonia all the way along the coast to Nice. After the
troubles of the Dark Ages her second period of wealth and power
came with the Crusades when she competed with the Genoese and
Venetians for the lucrative carrying trade, and established trading
posts all over Syria, Cyprus and Asia Minor. Marseilles suffered
greatly from the discovery of America and the opening of the sea
route to India, which transferred commercial primacy to the Atlantic
ports of Bordeaux, Nantes, La Rochelle and Le Havre. The city
entered upon its third period of prodigious prosperity with the conquest of Algiers and the suppression of the Barbary pirates in 1830,
and with the opening of the Suez Canal in 1869.

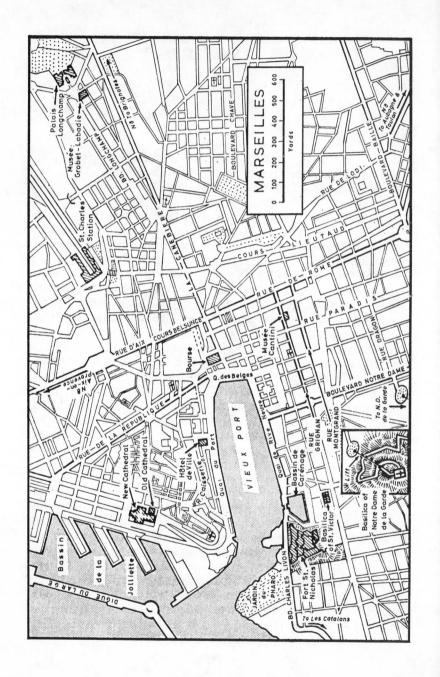

Today Marseilles is the greatest port of the Mediterranean and the third city of France (it having been recently overhauled by Lyons) – and much more typically a Mediterranean port than a French city. Even more than Nice, it is a city to stroll about in and watch the life and the people rather than to visit 'sights'. In fact, though it is by all odds the oldest city in France, it is practically devoid of antiquities or 'musts' of any sort for the church-and-museum enthusiast.

Greek, Roman, medieval and modern Marseilles has always centred round the Lacydon, now known as the **Vieux Port** – which is, one might say, the heart of the city. On the north it was bounded, until 1943, by a warren of narrow lanes known as the Quartier du Vieux Port. Like the Dublin slums, this was a once aristocratic district which had come down in the world, and amid the squalor and the stench one could find many an old house built by the ancient mercantile nobility of Marseilles, with a coat of arms over the sculptured door, a wrought-iron balcony and a fine staircase in the courtyard. The last real 'wide-open town' left in Europe, the water-front section, allotted as the red-light quarter by a decree of Louis-Philippe and luridly described in *Decline and Fall*, exists no more, for in 1943 the Germans, finding it impossible to control, gave its denizens twenty-four hours to move and dynamited the whole fetid quarter. Now the waterfront is lined by a row of modern apartment blocks, more hygienic and comfortable, no doubt, than the slums but looking dismally self-conscious and out of place here, under the scornful eye of Mansard's seventeenth-century Hôtel de Ville, standing in lonely dignity in the middle of them. One may, however, still walk through the narrow streets of the surviving and rather more reputable half of the Vieux Port, north of the Rue Caisserie. Only recently have the Greek origins of Marseilles come to light. In 1967 reconstruction work behind the Bourse revealed ramparts, quays and fortifications dating from the third and second centuries BC, thus some three hundred years after the foundation of Massilia. It has not yet been decided how these valuable finds are to be disposed of.

If the Greek remains are not available to the public, the Roman ones are. They are in the **Roman Docks Museum**[1] at 28 Place Vivaux, and came to light when reconstruction work was started after the demolition of the area by the Germans. The original jetty and *dolia* silos can be seen in the position they occupied two thousand years ago. A wreck retrieved by Jacques Cousteau, amphorae and a

1. All the museums of Marseilles mentioned in the next few pages close on Tuesdays and Friday mornings, as well as between 12 and 2.

model of the ancient city take one back to Marseilles' distant past

The **New Cathedral** is a vast Byzantine edifice built in the latter half of the nineteenth century. By its side nestles the little **Old Cathedral**, Romanesque in part, which is now converted into a museum of Christian antiquities. Except for 'La Spasme' in St Didier at Avignon, also the work of the Istrian, Francesco Laurana, the statues in the chapel of St Lazarus in the left transept are the oldest Renaissance sculptures in France – about 1480. Nearby is an attractive Della Robbia 'Entombment'.

The **Vieux Port**, until the middle of the last century the commercial harbour of Marseilles, is now only used by yachts, fishing boats and the little *balancelles* which bring the oranges from Majorca. At the end of it is the **Quai des Belges**, whence the vedettes leave for the Château d'If, the *calanques* and the basins of the harbour, and where the fishermen lay out their night's catch, patterned and sorted on the quayside to tempt the housewife's eye. The Quai is lined with cafés and restaurants which specialize in such local fish dishes as *bouillabaisse* (good but expensive and too much for one person alone) and *bourride*, both fish soups flavoured with saffron, and aïoli, which is salt cod with garlic mayonnaise. There are few pleasanter places to dine on a summer evening than at one of the restaurants looking over the Vieux Port, while the sun goes down and the lights come out one by one to be reflected by the little dancing waves.

The **Canebière**, which runs dead straight down to the Quai des Belges and the Vieux Port, is the main street of Marseilles, with broad pavements lined with shops, cafés and cinemas. Blond sailors from the lands which Pytheas discovered; sloe-eyed, gold-skinned students from Indo-China; Algerian carpet-sellers whose ancestors terrorized the merchants of Marseilles for a thousand years; wide-eyed Negroes from the lands far down in tropical Africa which the Massiliot sailor Euthymenes visited over two thousand years ago; white-uniformed cadets from an Italian training ship in the Vieux Port; lithe cat-like quadroon girls from Martinique; all rub shoulders in the Canebière. 'If Paris only had a Canebière it would be a little Marseilles,' boasts Marius, the typical Marseillais hero of so many French jokes. (Several derivations have been suggested for it by etymologists, such as *cannabis*, Latin for hemp, because the medieval rope-makers worked there, but all are agreed that it has nothing to do with cans of beer.) On the left is the enormous Bourse, the oldest in France, which adminsters the port and the great Marignane Airport, and just in front is the spot where King Alexander of Jugoslavia was shot dead by a Macedonian terrorist in 1934.

The Boulevard Longchamp to the left of the Canebière leads to the great Palais Longchamp, twin museums connected by a colonnade. Between them a magnificent fountain adorns the Château d'Eau, the outflow of the canal which brings the water of the River Durance to Marseilles. The building on the right is the Natural History Museum. That on the left is the **Musée des Beaux Arts**, which very well rewards a visit. The ground floor is mainly devoted to Provençal painters such as Monticelli, Ricard and Guigou. There are the only four surviving works by the Marseillaise, Françoise Duparc, who painted in the manner of Chardin and spent most of her working life in England. Three entire rooms are given up to the greatest artist Marseilles has produced, the seventeenth-century sculptor, painter and architect, Pierre Puget, who is so strangely little known outside Provence. His 'Faun' and his 'Louis XIV' reveal him as the French Bernini, while his design for a *place* for his native city would have given it one of the most magnificent squares in Europe had it ever been carried out. (One is sharply reminded of his contemporary, Wren, and the London which might have been but was not.)

The staircase landings are decorated with two enormous and rather impressive murals by Puvis de Chavannes, depicting Marseilles as a Greek Colony and as the Gateway to the East. In the main *salle*, as so often in provincial galleries, that versatile painter, Anon, shows up well, in his German incarnation in a 'Resurrection' and in his French in a portrait of King René of Provence. Nearly everything in this museum has a strong local flavour, even to Perugino's noble 'Family of the Madonna', for it includes, beside St Anne and St Joachim, the two Maries of Les Saintes-Maries-de-la-Mer. Look out also for Rubens's 'Boarhunt' and the Spaniard Antonio Pereda's 'Deposition from the Cross'. At the extreme left of the first floor is a room dedicated to Daumier, who was born in Marseilles although he did not live there. It consists of a collection of savage and brutal caricatures in bronze and charcoal of the supporters of his *bête noire*, Louis-Philippe. The end room on the right is devoted to such nineteenth-century painters as Courbet, Isabey, Millet, Corot and Daubigny, together with a few modern Provençals such as Seyssaud and Chabaud. The room immediately preceding it, Room C, contains what is perhaps the best picture in the whole gallery, a small Tiepolo of 'The Woman Taken in Adultery', but it is 'skied' among a lot of inferior French paintings and very easy to miss unless you are looking out for it.

Two very catholic collections of paintings, sculptures, furniture, tapestries, ceramics, musical instruments and iron-work of a number of periods and from a number of countries are to be found in the attractive little **Musée Grobet-Labadié**, close to the Palais Long-champ, and in the **Musée Cantini** in the Rue de Grignan. The latter occupies the seventeenth-century Hôtel de Montgrand which, with the collection, was left to the city by the sculptor Jules Cantini. It has a particularly good representation of Provençal faience, including examples of such artists as Louis Leroy, Fouchier and La Veuve Perrin of Marseilles, and Clérissy and Olerys, who introduced new polychrome designs from Spain into Moustiers. Its Provençal paintings include eleven Monticellis. On the first floor are works by such twentieth-century masters as Vuillard, Marquet and Dufy, and sculptures by Maillol and César.

The most conspicuous feature of Marseilles is the isolated limestone peak crowned by the **Basilica of Notre Dame de la Garde** in the southern part of the town. This landmark, watched for by innumerable eager-eyed sailors from far out to sea, affords a magnificent panorama over the city, the islands and the coast. Romanesque-Byzantine in style, the Basilica, like the Cathedral, the Bourse, the Palais Longchamp, the Préfecture, the Library and nearly all the other public buildings of Marseilles, was built during the Algiers-Suez boom of the Second Empire and is of equally little significance from the architectural point of view. The church and the crypt contain, however, thousands of sailors' ex-votos, which are of interest to students alike of marine painting and of modern primitives. The Boulevard Notre Dame leads up to it from the Quai de la Rive Neuve, as the south side of the Vieux Port is called. Motorists can either drive up the hill and park at the top or leave their car at the bottom and take the *ascenseur*.

The classic and well worth-while excursion for the traveller in Marseilles with a couple of hours to spare is to take one of the motor-boats which run from the Quai des Belges out to the Château d'If. It starts out down the Vieux Port, with the Hôtel de Ville and the new blocks on the right, and the Rive Neuve on the left. The bastioned, castellated building like a fortress, just behind the Bassin de Carénage on the left, is the Basilica of St Victor, the oldest church in Marseilles, which was founded in the fifth century by St Cassian. His old basilica was buried when the eleventh-century church was built above it and now forms the crypt, with catacombs from which all the best sarcophagi have been taken to the Borély Museum. According to a twelfth-century legend, St Lazarus and St Mary Magdalene sought refuge in these deserted grottoes when they came to Marseilles from Les Saintes Maries and swiftly made the town too hot to hold them by preaching in the Temple of Diana, where the Old Cathedral now stands. One is even shown here the tomb of the man who died twice.

Beyond St Victor is the great Fort St Nicolas, built by Louis XIV to keep the rebellious Marseillais in order. Beyond that again is the Park of the Pharo, athwart the mouth of the creek with a palace which once belonged to the Empress Eugénie and is now a medical school. Off Marseilles are a number of small islands. Among them is the **Château d'If**, equally celebrated in history as the prison of the Man in the Iron Mask and in fiction as that of Dumas's Count of Monte Cristo. Like the other islands near it, and indeed the neighbouring mainland, the little island, hardly more than an islet, is of snow-white limestone with very sparse vegetation. Francis I built the castle as part of the defences of Marseilles but it was never used in war, and soon afterwards a wall was built all along the rocks above the shore and the place converted into a state prison. Inside is a central court with storeys of cells around it. On some of the walls are carvings by the Huguenot prisoners concentrated here on the way to the galleys of Toulon. There is a memorial to the three thousand, five hundred Protestants condemned to the galleys between 1545 and 1750, and another to the leaders of the 1848 movement who died here. There is a horrifying black, windowless den like a fox's earth, where they used to put people who were not intended to come out alive. Very few lasted more than a few months, but the guide tells of a sailor who was put into this hole for striking an officer and achieved the record of still breathing that fetid air thirty years later – blind, deaf and reduced to a slobbering idiot. On the first floor one can visit the more spacious and airy cells, with views over the sea, occupied by such privileged prisoners as the Man in the Iron Mask, the young Mirabeau, put in by a *lettre de cachet* for running up debts of two hundred thousand livres to the tradesmen of Aix, and the temerarious Glandevès de Niozelles, who got six years for appearing before Louis XIV with his hat on.

On the return voyage the boat goes inshore for passengers to admire the Corniche Président J. F. Kennedy, which runs for four miles along the rocky shore past the Avenue du Prado and the Parc Borély, with its fine gardens and its **Archaeological Museum**. It includes the famous Egyptian collection of Clot Bey, and the recent Gaulish finds from Roquepertuse, a Celto-Ligurian necropolis near Velaux, between Aix and the Étang de Berre. Just inland from here, on the Boulevard Michelet, is Le Corbusier's seventeen-storey 'dwelling unit', *La Cité Radieuse* of 1952, which forms a landmark in the history of modern architecture.

Instead of turning back directly into the Vieux Port, the boat now steers left into the Bassin de la Joliette, sheltered from the sea by the long Digue du Large. There one can see the big packet-boats making ready to take off to Algiers and Tunis and Oran. (Commercial freight apart, nearly two million passengers pass through Marseilles in a year.) Begun in 1844, the Joliette was followed between 1866 and 1959 by half a dozen other new basins stretching away northwards right to L'Estaque, the mountain which Cézanne so often painted. L'Estaque is pierced by the four-mile-long tunnel of the Rove, through which ships can pass from Marseilles to the Étang de Berre, with its enormous oil refineries and storage tanks, and thence to the Rhône and a system of canals and connected waterways linking up with all parts of France and Central Europe. The largest oil port in Europe is at Lavéra at the other end of the Rhône Canal to the sharply contrasting fishing village of Martigues, still the 'Little Venice' which Ziem used to paint and its native son, Charles Maurras, wrote of so lovingly. We may yet see Marseilles doubling its historic role of gateway to Africa, the Levant and the Far East by becoming a southern Rotterdam, outstripping the mountain-bound Italian ports to capture the waterborne traffic of Central Europe.

Parts of old Martigues are still as attractive as when Félix Ziem, who came from Burgundy, first discovered the village in 1840 and put it on the artistic map. Nearly a century later, the light of 'amphibious' Martigues bewitched Augustus John who received there friends such as the poet Roy Campbell, the musician E. J. Moeran, and the practical joker Horace de Vere Cole. By 1939, John found Martigues a little too industrialized, and went to St Rémy-de-Provence instead. What he would have thought of the huge oil and industrial developments of Port-de-Fos, l'Estaque, and the Étang de Berre is not difficult to imagine. Martigues' **Musée des Beaux-Arts**[1] is of interest because one room is given over to paintings by Ziem. A second little museum, the Musée du Vieux Martigues, [1]includes a fourteenth-century wood-carving of the Virgin.

1. Open daily June–September; open on Thursdays, Sundays and public holidays out of season.

Chapter 16

Aix-en-Provence

The Cours Mirabeau – the Granet Museum – the Hôtels – the Museums – the Cathedral – the Pavilion of Cézanne

'At Aix, the air is healthy and food is plentiful; there is no need to fear the inhabitants, who are friendly and peaceful. Finally, as everyone knows, there are a great many wise people here.' Such is the picture of this happy city drawn in the Act of Foundation of the Royal University in 1413. For a hundred years Aix has been overshadowed by the prodigious growth of its neighbour, Marseilles, but it is still the seat of a University, an Archbishopric and a Court of Appeal. Even now *'Ais, la cieutá reino e coumtalo'*, the city of the kings and the counts, preserves all the prestige of the historic capital of Provence together with the reputation of being one of the most elegant and aristocratic of all French cities. Emile Henriot wrote that Aix reminded him at the same time of Rome and of Vicenza.

Aix, rather surprisingly, is pronounced exactly as it is spelt, Englishwise, like 'aches'. Like Aix-les-Bains and Charlemagne's capital of Aix-la-Chapelle, it derives its name from the Latin (accusative) *aquas*, 'the waters', for it began its history as a Roman watering place and is still famous not only for its twenty-one plashing fountains but also for the thermal establishment in the Cours Sextius where arthritics and people with bad circulation come to take the waters as they have done for two thousand years.

After the conquest of the native Salyans, whose *oppidum* was at nearby Entremont, the Consul Sextius established first a camp and then a town beside the thermal springs and named it after himself, Aquae Sextiae. Twenty years later, in 102 BC, the savage Teutons swept down from the shores of the Baltic, migrating with their wives and children in leather-curtained wagons, and were annihilated near Aix, at the foot of what is still known as the Montagne Ste Victoire, by the Roman general Marius. A hundred thousand Germans are said to have been slain and the same number taken prisoner. Their

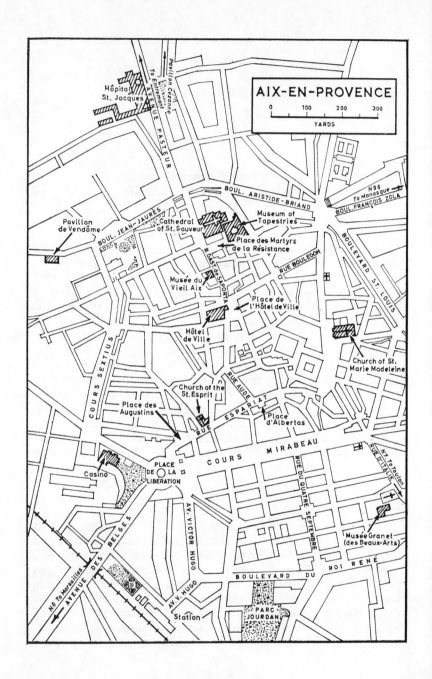

AIX-EN-PROVENCE

0   100   200   300
YARDS

Hôpital St. Jacques

Pavillon Cézanne

AVENUE PASTEUR

To Entremont

BOUL. ARISTIDE-BRIAND

N96 To Manosque

BOUL. FRANÇOIS ZOLA

Pavillon de Vendôme

BOUL. JEAN-JAURÈS

Cathedral of St. Sauveur

Museum of Tapestries

Place des Martyrs de la Résistance

RUE BOULEGON

BOULEVARD ST. LOUIS

Musée du Vieil Aix

R. GASTde SAPORTA

Place de l'Hôtel de Ville

Hôtel de Ville

Church of St. Marie Madeleine

COURS SEXTIUS

Church of the St. Esprit

RUE AUDE

RUE ESPARIAT

Place des Augustins

Place d'Albertas

RUE

Casino

PLACE DE LA LIBÉRATION

COURS MIRABEAU

RUE DU QUATRE SEPTEMBRE

N7 To Toulon

RUE D'ITALIE

AVENUE DES BELGES

N8 To Marseilles

AV. VICTOR HUGO

AV. V. Hugo

Station

Musée Granet (des Beaux-Arts)

BOULEVARD   DU   ROI RENÉ

PARC JOURDAN

wives strangled their children in the wagons and then killed themselves to avoid capture. Marius is a typical Marseillais name today, like Jack or Billy or Bobby. Most people think the name has survived two thousand years in honour of the Roman general. In fact, nobody was called Marius until Napoleon's time. He, infatuated with Roman antiquities, probably bequeathed Marius to the Marseillais. Moreover, Provençal experts maintain that the name is widespread only because it permits a masculination of the name of Mother of Christ whom the Catholic Marseillais have always venerated.

At one time the capital of the Second Gallia Narbonensis, Aix became overshadowed by Arles in the fourth century as by Marseilles in the nineteenth, but in the later Middle Ages both the Aragonese and the Angevin Counts of Provence held their courts there. The golden age of Provence, still remembered and seen through a romantic haze, was the reign of 'Good King René'. Provence was never a kingdom but he held the title because, in addition to being Count of Provence and Duke of Anjou, he was also the exiled King of Naples. Expelled from his southern kingdom by Alfonso of Aragon in 1442, he reigned at Aix until 1480. On terms of genial friendship with his subjects, he delighted in organizing such popular festivals as that of the Tarasque at Tarascon and the Fête-Dieu at Aix, and he restored the old games of chivalry. He is said, on authority which historians now dispute, to have painted and composed music and verse, to have been conversant with Latin, Greek and Hebrew, and to have had a knowledge of law, mathematics and geology. In short, he seems to have been a typical example of the cultivated Renaissance prince. If he was of a weak character and financially unscrupulous, at least *le bon Roi René* differed from the majority of contemporary rulers in that he had the welfare of his people at heart, allowed the Estates to carry through a number of beneficial reforms and furthered the economic progress of the country. Among his achievements were the encouragement of mulberries and silkworms, and the introduction of the muscat grape which brought so much prosperity to Provence, and also, it is said, of carnations, roses and peacocks. His domestic life was happier than might have been expected. He was only twelve when he married Isabella of Lorraine and he remained devoted to her for thirty-three years. Upon her death he married a girl of thirteen, Jeanne de Laval. His second marriage was as happy as his first, but when the Provençals talk of La Reine Jeanne, it is not Jeanne de Laval whom they mean but their beautiful Queen Jeanne of a hundred years earlier, who is said to have had her husband, Andrew of Hungary, strangled and who was in turn strangled by her cousin, Charles of Durazzo.

René died at Aix in 1480 at the age of seventy-two, and seventeen months later Provence was united to France on the death of his successor, Charles III. It retained, however, a large measure of autonomy, and for three centuries Aix was the seat of the provincial Estates, of a Parliament and of a Governor. In the sixteenth century Aix was racked by the Wars of Religion like the rest of the Midi, but the seventeenth and eighteenth centuries, when the city was thronged with the nobles of Provence, with counsellors, prelates and officials accompanied by their retinues, saw the construction of the great *hôtels* and the elegant streets, the squares and the fountains, which made Aix a model of urbanization.

The most characteristic quarter is that lying to the south of the Cours Mirabeau. The enormous **Place de la Libération**, with a spectacular three-basined fountain in the middle and the Casino at one side, may for the sake of convenience be regarded as the centre of the town. Through it runs the old highroad between Marseilles and Arles (a by-pass now siphons off much of the Routes Nationales 7 and 8 from the centre of the town), and not far along the Avenue Victor-Hugo are the railway station and the coach terminal. On the east side of the Place begins the famous **Cours Mirabeau**, named after the revolutionary orator who, though not born at Aix, lived there, was married and divorced there and was finally elected to the States General as deputy for the city. Constructed in the seventeenth century on the site of the old ramparts, it is a wide, straight boulevard shaded by four rows of towering plane trees, some of the most ancient in Provence, which, despite the great breadth of the Cours, meet overhead to form a cool green canopy, dappled by the sunlight playing on the upper leaves in patterns which change all the time as they flutter birdlike in the breeze. In addition to the Fontaine Grande in the Place de la Libération, which is visible from all down the Cours, the avenue has three other fountains. The first is the Fontaine des Neuf Canons. Further on, the Fontaine Chaude, a repulsive object overgrown with greenish moss, looks like an octopus with its tentacles cut off. As its name implies, it runs the warm thermal water of Aix and there is a superstition that one should dip one's fingers in it when one first arrives in the town. At the far end of the Cours is the Fontaine du Roi René, with a statue of the King holding a bunch of his famous muscat grapes.

The two sides of the Cours Mirabeau are strikingly different in character. The north side is lined with shops, restaurants and cafés; the south side with seventeenth- and eighteenth-century *hôtels* from which retail trade is almost entirely barred except for an occasional discreet *patisserie* selling *calissons*, the almond confections for which Aix is noted. (It is the world's greatest source of almond production.) Centring round the Fontaine des Quatre Dauphins (which are dolphins, of course, and not Dauphins), the sedate quarter behind this aristocratic façade remains almost exactly as it was built in the seventeenth century by Cardinal Mazarin, Archbishop of Aix and brother of the statesman, except for the great Lycée where little Emile Zola and little Paul Cézanne used to go to school, and later the musician, Darius Milhaud. The quarter takes its name from the handsome thirteenth-century church of St Jean de Malte, which has pictures by Mignard and Finsonius but nothing of the very first rank in it.

At the side of the church, facing the beautiful fourteenth-century belfry, is the old Priory of the Knights of Malta, dating from 1675. It now houses the **Musée Granet**[1], called after the Aix painter, a friend of Ingres, whose portrait of him, painted in Rome in 1807, hangs in the Museum. Granet himself contributed over five hundred pieces to the collection, and other Provençal connoisseurs were not behindhand. In the entrance hall devoted to archaeology are a very fine 'Persian Warrior' of the School of Pergamon and other Greek and Roman sculptures. Its particular pride is the unique collection of Celto-Ligurian sculptures from Entremont, the Salyan capital two miles outside Aix, most of which were excavated in the nineteenforties by M. Fernand Benoît. It is the most ancient collection of Gaulish sculptures known, and Greek and Etruscan influences are as strong as one would expect from the proximity of Marseilles. It includes masks of the dead, heads, bas-reliefs and torsos of warriors, from which all the details of their accoutrements can be discerned.

The Museum contains the most complete existing collection of Provençal faience from the ceramic factories of Moustiers, Marseilles, Avignon and Apt. Houdon is represented by busts of those two very dissimilar contemporaries, Cagliostro and the Bailli de Suffren. Among a number of primitives and other Dutch and Italian paintings are a Rembrandt self-portrait and a couple of Gabriel Metsus, but the main strength of the picture gallery lies in the French School, and particularly in the French Renaissance, François Clouet and the School of Fontainebleau. The seventeenth- and eighteenth-century portraitists, Rigaud, Largillière and Arnulphy, are each represented by several canvases and there is a self-portrait by Pierre Puget. For me, however, the entire gallery is dominated by
1. Closed on Tuesdays, and public holidays.

Ingres' great 'Jupiter and Thetis', painted in 1811.
Of the Provençal landscapists from before Cézanne's time, Emile
Loubon is represented by his most famous and dramatic large
Menons de Crau. There are numerous paintings by Guigou, Granet,
Grésy and J. A. Constantin, the first French painter to sketch from
nature.

Aix's most famous painter, Paul Cézanne, is virtually unrepre-
sented but there is a movement on foot to raise a fund and secure
some of his works. One may be permitted some scepticism as to its
results in view of the prices his paintings command at present, not
to mention the insurance premiums and security measures necessary
since the recent wave of picture thefts in the South of France. After
private collections in Villefranche and St Paul and the municipal
galleries in Menton and St Tropez, it was the turn, in July 1961, of
the Cézanne exhibition being held in the Pavillon de Vendôme here
in Aix. Despite police guards, burglars climbed in through a first-
floor window and stole about eight hundred thousand pounds' worth
of paintings, including the famous 'Cardplayers' lent by the Louvre.

The **Pavillon de Vendôme**,[1] set in a formal garden, was built in
1667 just outside the circuit of the boulevards as a summer house for
the Cardinal of Vendôme, the Governor of Provence and grandson
of Henri IV and Gabrielle d'Estrées. It later belonged to the Aix-
born painter, Jean Baptiste Van Loo, who died there in 1745 after
ornamenting several of the churches of the city with his pictures.
The façade is a perfect example of the seventeenth-century Provençal
style with Atlantes by Rambot supporting the balcony. (The attractive female head just below the Cardinal's coat of arms in the centre is
affectionately known to the Aixois as La Belle du Canet.) There is a
very fine double staircase in the interior.

The Pavillon de Vendôme is only one among the many magnificent
noblemen's houses for which Aix was and is famous. (One short
guide-book mentions no fewer than three dozen of them by name.)
Not all these *hôtels* are of first-class interest, of course, or for that
matter are open to the public, but several of the most worth-while
are the easier of access since they have been turned into public
buildings. For example, the Hôtel d'Espagnet, the house with the
enormous Atlantes in the Cours Mirabeau (No. 38) is now the
Rectorate of the University; the Hôtel de Boyer d'Eguilles of 1675, in
the Rue Esparait (No. 6), which is believed to have been designed by
Puget, is now the Museum of Natural History[2]; the Hôtel d'Estienne

1. Closed on Tuesdays.
2. Closed on Sunday mornings and Tuesdays.

Aix: Fontaine des Quatre Dauphins, in a quiet square surrounded
by 17th-century *hôtels*

The Benedictine Abbey of Montmajour

de St Jean in the Rue Gaston de Saporta, containing a beautiful little boudoir with a ceiling frescoed by Daret, is now the Musée de Vieil Aix[1]; the Hôtel de Châteaurenard next door, with a *trompe l'œil* staircase by the same artist, is the Bureaux de Bienfaisance; and the Hôtel Arbaud in the Rue du Quatre Septembre is the Musée Arbaud.[2] Its mixed collection of old books on Provence, ceramics, sculptures and paintings includes Puget's portrait of his mother, and a self-portrait by Granet.

To reach the most charming of all the delightful little squares of Aix take the Rue Espariat by the Fontaine des Augustins from the Place de la Libération. On the left is the church of the St Esprit, where Mirabeau was married in 1772 after cynically compromising the daughter of an opulent magnate of Aix. Further on is the Place d'Albertus, a completely unspoilt little square surrounded by grave eighteenth-century houses, with the inevitable fountain playing in the middle. Thence the Rue Aude leads north into the Place de l'Hôtel de Ville.

The two main buildings of this large (and, of course, fountain-centred) square are the Hôtel de Ville and the Post Office. Over the Post Office is a great sculpture by Chastel, who produced many works in Aix in the eighteenth century. It represents the River Rhône and the goddess Cybele, a reference to the fact that the building was at that time the corn market. The Aixois will swear to you that the foot of Cybele is so wonderfully carved that you can see the toes wriggle lazily in the sunlight and you are tempted to blow them a kiss. The **Hôtel de Ville** is a classical building begun in the late sixteenth century. At its entrance is a singularly beautiful wrought-iron grille. On the first floor and to the right it houses the library bequeathed in 1787 by the Marquis de Méjanes, which contains over three hundred thousand volumes, sixteen hundred manuscripts and four hundred incunabula. Among its most cherished treasures is King René's *Book of Hours*, once believed to be illuminated by himself. Next to the Hôtel de Ville rises a handsome clock-tower, dating from the beginning of the sixteenth century. A curious feature is the seventeenth-century 'Calendar', four wooden statues representing the Seasons, which revolve, emerge from their niche and take over from each other on sentry duty four times a year.

The Rue Saporta, running northwards, follows the line of the old Aurelian Way, which formed the main street of the Roman *castrum*. The former Hôtel d'Estienne de Saint Jean at No. 17 houses the

1. Closed on Tuesdays.
2. Closed on Wednesdays.

Musée du Vieil Aix,[1] created in 1933. It is, always excepting the Museon Arlaten at Arles, the most interesting of the many folklore museums in the South of France. It contains a number of prints and costumes and relics of the *Grand Siècle*. Among its more arresting exhibits are the so-called *velours Grégoire*, which are paintings on velvet by one Grégoire, an Aix painter who lived from 1751 to 1846. It seems that he was the first person to invent a method of painting on velvet and that the secret died with him. Another rather unexpected find, in the end room on the ground floor, is a picture of an Englishman, William Wilson, receiving honorary citizenship from the Municipality of Aix in 1790 as a reward for fourteen years of charitable work in the town. He must have been one of the earliest of the public-spirited English expatriates who afterwards became so common.

Unique in the Museum are two great collections of the model figures which played an important role in the religious rites of the *bon vieux temps*. There are a number of figures made to be drawn along the street in the popular procession of the Fête-Dieu, which took place for the last time in the winter of 1851. Even more striking is the collection of some eighty *santons* or figures for Christmas cribs. (Aubagne, near Marseilles, is still famous for the manufacture of *santons*.) About eighteen inches in height, they are articulated and mechanized so that they could play a series of animated tableaux before the Manger at the Nativity. They all represent characteristic Provençal types ranging from the gendarme to the chickenseller, the knifegrinder to the drunkard. Most of them have their own traditional names, such as Simoun and Bartolomieu.

Further on, the Place des Martyrs de la Résistance opens out on the right side of the Rue Saporta and at the end of it is the great eighteenth-century portal of the former Archbishop's Palace. The inner courtyard is the scene of the Music Festival which every July attracts music-lovers to Aix from all over Europe. (I met one old lady who had come especially from America for it.) On the first floor is a famous **Museum of Tapestries.**[2] It is built around the three series of eighteenth-century Beauvais tapestries which were discovered by chance among the rafters of the Palace in 1849. Nobody seems to know how they got there but it seems reasonable to suppose they were hidden at the time of the Revolution. The first series consists of six grotesques from the designs of Berain: the second, from designs by Batoire, of nine scenes from the story of Don Quixote:

1. Closed on Tuesdays.
2. Closed on Tuesdays.

and the third of four Russian Games, oddly so-called because the characters look more like Turks and gipsies, from designs by Leprince. There are also some pictures, including an 'Annunciation' by Puget and a couple of paintings by Jean Baptiste Van Loo, the Aixois member of that Dutch-descended dynasty of artists which we first encountered several chapters ago at Nice.

A little further on is the **Cathedral of St Sauveur**. It is a mixture of all styles from the fourth- or fifth-century baptistery down through the centuries to the flamboyant sixteenth-century Gothic of the tower and the façade. The right aisle was originally the nave of a Romanesque church which was incorporated in the Gothic cathedral when the latter was built. All the sculptures of the west front were destroyed in the Revolution except for the Virgin on the central pillar of the main door, who was saved because some quick-thinking art-lover promptly crowned her with the red cap of Liberty. The great doors were carved in the sixteenth century by Jean Guiramand of Toulon and depict the four major prophets below and the twelve sibyls above. To preserve them they are kept behind wooden shutters, as are several of the most valuable paintings in the Cathedral itself. The sacristan will unlock them for visitors and a *pourboire*. If he is not in the church, he is probably to be found in the little Gothic cloister off the right aisle.

Off the right aisle also is the Gallo-Roman baptistery with a pool for total immersion in the centre. It is surrounded by eight Roman columns, probably from the Temple of Apollo which once occupied this site. The whole is crowned by a rather incongruous sixteenth-century cupola. The interior of the Cathedral is a little museum. Round the Gothic nave and the Romanesque right aisle hang twenty-six magnificent Brussels tapestries. They trace the principal scenes and mysteries of the lives of Jesus and the Virgin, and it is melancholy to reflect that they were woven in 1511 for Canterbury Cathedral and hung there until they were sold under the Commonwealth. In 1656 they were bought in Paris by a canon of the chapter of Aix for a mere 1200 *écus*.

On the walls of the nave hang several pictures, of which much the most famous is Nicolas Froment's 'Burning Bush', symbolizing the virginity of Mary. It was executed for King René in 1475, and the two side panels embody portraits of the King and of his second wife, Jeanne de Laval, kneeling in prayer. The central panel is based on a text of Honorius of Autun: 'Moses saw a burning bush which the flame could not consume and in the middle of which God appeared to him. It was an image of the Holy Virgin, for she carries in her

the flame of the Holy Spirit without burning with the fire of con-
cupiscence.' Below, the Archangel Gabriel appears to Moses as he
watches his sheep. Above, the Virgin and Child are seated in the
midst of a burning 'bush', which is really a little copse with a number
of trunks supporting it. The Child holds a mirror which reflects both
Him and His Mother in it. It is a mystical prefiguration of the Incarnation. The castles in the background represent Beaucaire and
Tarascon as they were at the time. Like the doors of the Cathedral,
the picture is kept shuttered and has to be unlocked by the sacristan.

Other primitives hanging nearby include the central panel of a
fifteenth-century triptych of the Passion, showing the Arrest of
Christ and the Crowning with Thorns, and a wooden panel of the
same date depicting the Martyrdom of St Mitre, who stands with his
heels together, in a black cloak, holding his severed but still haloed
head to his chest. St Mitre, like St Victor of Marseilles, was a
Levantine martyr 'naturalized' when his relics were shipped to Provence. The Flemish inscription on Finsonius's seventeenth-century
'Incredulity of St Thomas' on the opposite wall betrays a certain
exasperation not uncommon among artists. Translated, it reads: 'By
the servants of Bacchus and the companions of Venus, painting is
here despised; whence the saying, "As beggarly as a painter," which
is repeated every day.' The altar of 1470 in St Catherine's chapel
may be the work of Francesco Laurana, whom King René is known
to have invited to his court. Among the other sculptures is one of St
Martha leading the Tarasque, on the right – a scene which alone
would have endeared the altar to René.

There are some other good pictures in the great **Church of Ste
Marie Madeleine**, just opposite the Palais de Justice, such as a 'St
Paul' by Rubens and an 'Annunciation' by J. B. Van Loo. The
greatest picture is at the end of the left aisle in the chapel of the
miraculous Virgin, Notre Dame de Grâce. It is the central panel of a
lovely 'Annunciation', with the Virgin, in a wonderful glowing robe
of gold brocade, receiving the astonishing news in an elaborate
Gothic church. (The side panels are copies, the originals being in
England and Belgium.) While the painting has been variously attributed to Colantonio, the master of Antonello da Messina, to an
unknown Burgundian and even to Albrecht Dürer, it is now believed
to be the work of Jean Chapus of Avignon. An attempt has been
made to connect this strange picture with the cult of satanism, or at
the very least with the evil eye, on the grounds that the feathers of
Gabriel's wings are those of an owl and the ray which emanates
from the hands of God passes over the head of a monkey – both of

them animals of ill omen. It is hard to believe that there is any substance in this.

From the Cathedral a road leads north out of the city past the Hospital of St Jacques, and nearby on the left, in the Avenue Paul Cézanne, is an unobtrusive little house surrounded by a garden, which served Paul Cézanne as a studio.[1] He lived and died at 23 Rue Boulegon in the city and used to come out here every day to paint. His studio was on the first floor, with a fine north light occupying the whole side of one room. There are none of his works here except one or two small drawings, but such intimate relics as his easel, his palette and various letters and photographs have been preserved. His hat, cap, beret, cape and coat hang on pegs in the corner. His knapsack, his purse, his clay pipe and the skulls which he loved to paint are all here. On the table are glasses and wine bottles, with their contents long evaporated but which were evidently left half-full as they were when he died. You can, if you should wish to, put your lips to a glass which has touched Cézanne's and never been rinsed since.

A friend of mine told me that, when painting at Aix a few years ago, he made a pilgrimage to Cézanne's studio. Finding the door open and nobody there, he walked in. He was upstairs in the studio when a voice from below asked who the devil was there and then somebody came stumping up the stairs. An angry, bearded, middle-aged Frenchman with a napkin wrapped round his head bawled him out roundly for his filthy bad manners in walking uninvited into other people's houses. Recognizing the Master (who had by then been dead some forty years), my friend mumbled an apology and beat a hasty retreat out of the house. I tell the story as it was told me. I cannot vouch for it, of course, nor yet for the sequel which my friend went on to tell me. It seemed that not long afterwards an American sculptress took a fancy to rent Cézanne's studio and approached the Municipality for the purpose. The Municipality refused. They did not say 'He would not have liked it' but 'He does not like it.' Nowadays, this place of pilgrimage is pleasantly and informally looked after and the custodian does not seem to mind if one wants to take photographs in the studio.

Though the Pavillon de Cézanne, as it is called, is within very easy walking distance, I would suggest this as an occasion for taking a taxi. Apart from the saving of time and trouble finding the place, the cabman will take you on afterwards for a drive up the hill, where a new housing estate now rises, and show you a fine view over the city,

1. Closed on Tuesdays and public holidays.

the mountains beyond towards Marseilles, and, most important of all, Cézanne's often-painted Montagne Ste Victoire, a strange limestone ridge which from here, end on, looks like a white pyramid. (It is very difficult to see from the city itself.) If you ask him, he will also take you for a drive along the Route du Tholonet, which Cézanne so loved to paint that it is now called the Route Cézanne. The truth is that all this country round Aix, whitish chalky soil and light-green dusty trees, relieved here and there by a red-tiled roof or a bluish-white cliff, is so saturated with Cézanne that it is almost impossible to see it except through the painter's eyes.

It would be agreeable to leave Cézanne with the idea that the family home of Jas de Bouffan in Aix, where he liked to paint, had been preserved in his honour. But no; it became the Fondation Vasarely in 1975, an interior design of clusters of hexagonal cells covered by strange cupolas, of black and white aluminium panels. Victor Vasarely calls the place 'an intellectual and cultural tool' for information, research and confrontation. It is mainly for the benefit of academics, architects, designers and sociologists, but the public can go in and see what is going on.

Some ten miles from Aix, embowered in deep, dark woods, is the **Château of Vauvenargues**, which is private property and not of much interest except that it was the home of the famous eighteenth-century author of the *Maximes*, the Marquis de Vauvenargues. The moralist who wrote that 'the greatest perfection of the soul is to be capable of pleasure' was surely in harmony with the spirit of eighteenth-century Aix. In 1958 Pablo Picasso bought the Château of Vauvenargues. Ownership of the property carries with it the title of Marquis; so that, somewhat paradoxically, the richest Communist in France became a Marquis also, although he never used the title.

When all is said and done, however, yet a third Marquis, Mirabeau, was the citizen of Aix who has left the most lasting mark on the world. It was while sitting one evening in the Cours which bears his name that I fell to musing idly on the course which human history might have taken had the city not elected this adventurer as its Deputy for the fateful States General of 1789. But for the eloquence of Mirabeau, there might well have been no French Revolution and without the French Revolution no rise of Nationalism. From that followed the grim, inevitable sequence: Bismarck and the Franco-Prussian War; the shooting at Sarajevo and the Kaiser's War; Hitler's War; and the atomic bomb as a grand finale. No doubt, however, the human race would have found some other means of making itself miserable even if Mirabeau had never existed and the voters of Aix had never elected him. In any case such gloomy, not to say controversial, speculations should have no place in a book such as this. It is no note on which to end a chapter which began with such an ideal picture of Aix as it was in the fifteenth century.

Chapter 17

Arles

✤

The Mistral – Hotels – the Cathedral – the Cloister – the Lapidary Museums – the Alyscamps – the Theatre and the Amphitheatre – the Réattu Museum – the Museon Arlaten

Were I asked to suggest a single base from which to explore Provence and the contiguous regions of Languedoc, I should have little hesitation in recommending Arles. I have in my mind someone who wants to be able to unpack his things, stow them on shelves and in cupboards and stay in one place for two or three weeks instead of submitting himself to a gruelling succession of what theatrical people call 'one night stands'. Arles is within easy reach of Aix, Avignon (two cities which richly merit sojourns in their own right), Nîmes, the Camargue, Les Baux, St Rémy, Tarascon, St Gilles and Aigues Mortes, which are all day or half-day trips. A car is not absolutely necessary, for, apart from the local bus and train services, there are agencies in the Boulevard des Lices, the principal promenade of the town, which run daily coach trips during the season to all these places and as far afield as the Cévennes. The city itself offers so much of interest that excursions need occupy no more than one day in every two. The alternate days can be agreeably spent sightseeing in Arles.

Spring is the best season to visit Rhodanian Provence. July and August can be very hot, the autumn is apt to be wet and stormy and in the winter the icy mistral can blow for days on end – three days, six days or nine days, according to the local tradition. The mistral or 'master wind' (from the Latin *magistralis*) is the north wind which blows with great force down the Rhône valley to the Mediterranean and, like the very similar *bora* of Trieste, owes its existence to the natural law that hot air rises and cold air sinks. When the warm Mediterranean air rises, cold air rushes down the funnel from the north to fill the vacuum. The mistral has been known to stop trains and once it even propelled an engineless train along the line from Arles to Port St Louis. In 1875 it was sufficiently powerful to blow down the bridge linking Beaucaire and Tarascon. Arles itself, straddling the Rhône though it does, nevertheless forms less of a funnel, as it is surrounded by wide flat expanses – on the west the salt marshes of the Camargue and on the east the pebbly plain of the Crau which, like the Maures, derives its name from the Greek. (The word κρανος, meaning 'stony', is to be found in Homer.) Both these plains are characterized by thick cypress hedges planted to break the force of the wind, which all the same sometimes breaks them instead and lays them flat across the road or railway line they are designed to defend. On January 3, 1786, records Arthur Young in his *Travels in France*, 'there was a mistral so furious, accompanied by so much snow, that flocks were carried four or five leagues from their pasturages . . . Five shepherds were taking eight hundred beasts to Marseilles; three of them and nearly all the sheep perished.'

Up to now, I have deliberately refrained from discussing the merits of hotels in this book. A traveller planning to spend several weeks on the Riviera will either make careful enquiries beforehand about prices and so forth among the multitude of hotels and *pensions* offering their hospitality or, more probably, go where his friends have been before him; if he is just spending one night in a town he will not need to be so particular and will pick one from the *Guide Michelin* or the appendix of this book or simply ask somebody which is the best. Having gone so far as to recommend a stay in Arles, however, I feel I can no longer shirk my responsibilities in this matter. The four-star hotel, the Jules César in the Lices, is comfortable, with good food, and is to be recommended for a meal or a night. It is on the main road, with plenty of parking space, and thereby saves all the time and trouble, which can be maddening when one arrives tired in a strange town, of hunting for one's hotel and, once one has found it, looking for somewhere to leave the car. It also offers an opportunity of seeing the lovely old costumes of Arles (now extremely rare except at big festivals), since the Jules César waitresses all wear them. But, let us face it, what is a mere fleabite on the budget for one night or for the enjoyment of a good luncheon can develop into an extravagance for an extended stay. One of the hardest economic lessons to learn is that if you keep adding molehill to molehill they will one day turn into a mountain.

For myself, I spent several weeks at the Mireille, a small two-star hotel (with a swimming pool) in the Place St Pierre across the bridge in Trinquetaille, at about a third of the price I would have paid at the Jules César and I never felt any desire to change from it. There are also a couple of three-star hotels in the Place du Forum, which can both be recommended. The Hôtel du Forum has been modernized

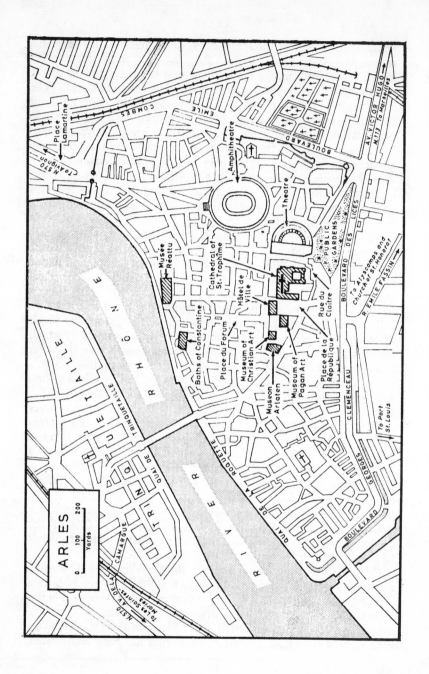

(or *touringisé*, as the French like to say) and some friends who stayed there told me that it is extremely comfortable. The Nord-Pinus, at right angles to it, is a place of an engaging eccentricity. It is, for example, the only hotel where I have ever barked my shin against a high-wheeler bicycle parked in the cloakroom. It is the favoured centre of the *afición* in Arles, which is proud of being the bullfighting capital of Provence. The visiting Spanish matadors always put up there and the bar is decorated with bulls' heads and other trophies of the arena. Ask Mme Bessière, the owner, to show you the precious *Livre d'Or* of the hotel. It spans the better part of a century, for on page one is the signature of Puvis de Chavannes and on page 393 that of Fernandel. Among the wartime guests were Odette and Peter Churchill, who lived 'underground', to use a singularly inapposite phrase, in an upstairs room, while German officers occupied the hotel beneath them and German troops paraded in the square.

The **Place du Forum** does not occupy the actual site of the ancient Forum, but the Corinthian columns and the fragment of a pediment built into the corner of the Nord-Pinus formed part of a temple abutting on it. The curious-looking railings in the square are in the form of the long tridents used by the *gardians*, the cattlemen of the Camargue, to control their bulls, and the bronze gentleman on the pedestal in the middle, with the walking-stick, the wideawake hat and the coat over his arm, who looks a little like Buffalo Bill, is Frédéric Mistral, the poet who founded the group called the Félibrige and devoted his life to the revival of the Provençal language and customs. If he succeeded only very partially in his romantic aim, he was at any rate the only writer in Provençal to win the Nobel Prize for Literature.

Vincent Van Gogh's '*Café du Soir*', with the tables outside it, was on the east side of the Place du Forum, where a furniture shop now stands. The corner of the Nord-Pinus just comes into the picture on the right. The more famous '*Café de Nuit*' stands in the Place Lamartine near the station and is called the Bar-Restaurant Alcazar. The billiard table is gone, the floor, the walls, the lamps and even the windows are changed. Only the clock still ticks away on the end wall just as the Dutchman painted it. He himself lived with Gauguin just across the square in a bistro called La Civette Arlésienne, which he painted as 'The Yellow House' and which was destroyed by a bomb in June 1944. The present Bar-Tabac Civette Arlésienne is about twenty-five feet behind the original one. (It figures in the background of 'The Yellow House'.) It was here that in December 1888,

Vincent cut off his ear, took it to *Maison de Tolérance Numéro Un*, gave it to a rather surprised lady named Rachel with the remark, *'Gardez cet objet précieusement,'* and walked out into the night. On the following day he was removed to the lunatic asylum at St Rémy.

Not far from the Place du Forum is the **Place de la République**, the principle square of Arles. On the north side is the Hôtel de Ville designed by Mansard, the architect who built the no less delightful Hôtel de Ville at Beaucaire. The statue on the sixteenth-century clock-tower is known locally as 'The Bronze Man' and actually represents Mars, although few Arlésiens are aware of the fact. (Fix it in your memory before you go out to St Rémy and you will realize how strongly the Renaissance architect has been influenced by the Roman mausoleum there.) The ground-floor hall, which serves as a passage and short cut between the Place de la République and the Place du Forum, is covered by a curious flattened arch which intrigues architects for technical reasons and laymen because it is also attractive to look at.

On the east side of the square is the **Cathedral of St Trophîme**, which might almost be described as the baptismal font of English Christianity, for it was on this spot that in 597 St Augustine was consecrated the first Bishop of England by St Virgil, Bishop of Arles. Little now remains of the old Carolingian building but it was in the existing Cathedral, then newly built, that the Emperor Frederic Barbarossa was crowned King of Arles in 1178. For Arles, now no more than a *sous-préfecture* of the Department of the Bouches-du-Rhône, was for centuries the capital of a kingdom which covered not only Provence but Burgundy and Dauphiné as well.

The great twelfth-century portal of St Trophîme is one of the finest flowers of Southern Romanesque. (To avoid getting tripped up in French guide-books, bear in mind that *romain* and *romaine* mean 'Roman', while *roman* and *romane* mean 'Romanesque'.) All the way round the façade, above the tall stone saints, runs a frieze which must have given a rather nervous shiver to many a passing sinner. On the left the procession of the saved (fully clothed, of course) advances to be handed by an angel into Abraham's bosom. On the right the damned who have been repulsed from the gates of Paradise are dragged (stark naked to show how wicked they are) in a chain-gang by a demon and thrust into the flames of Hell. The frieze is a ballet in stone which recalls those lovely Dancing Women of Ruvo, who dance for us still in the Naples Museum.

The dark, narrow nave, the highest in Provence, contains some Aubusson tapestries and a number of Gallo-Roman sarcophagi.

One of the best, in the left aisle, has been converted into a font and another, representing the crossing of the Red Sea, serves as an altar. The Rue du Cloître on the right of the Cathedral leads to the cloister,[1] famous for its medieval carvings. It was originally the residence of the canons of the Cathedral, whose dormitory, chapter-house and refectory open off it. It takes a long time to examine properly and I would recommend taking it right-handed. After an unnerving scene of knights and ladies being cast into Hell on the first capital, the corner pillar depicts the Temptation, the Baptism, the Last Supper, the Betrayal and the Washing of the Feet. The north and east galleries, with barrel vaulting, date from the twelfth century and the west and south, with ogival arches, from the fourteenth. The scenes are easy enough to follow for anyone who knows their Bible, although the scene of St Martha leading the Tarasque may prove a little baffling.

Opposite the great door of St Trophîme is the 'disaffected' church of St Anne, which contains the **Museum of Pagan Art**.[2] (The so-called Venus of Arles, found in the Theatre in 1651 and presented to the King, is in the Louvre and only a cast is here.) Arles possesses two of the greatest lapidary museums in Europe. The other is the **Museum of Christian Art**[1] in the old Jesuit College, which is exceeded in richness only by the Lateran Museum in Rome. The Pagan Museum displays Roman mosaics from Trinquetaille and pagan statues from the Theatre and from the great Cryptoporticus, once a granary and more recently an air-raid shelter, which lies under the Christian Museum itself. The huge U-shaped **Cryptoporticus** is visited from the Museum of Christian Art, and was built by the Romans as a storage place for the cereals milled at Barbegal in the Alpilles (where the remains of the Roman hydraulic mill can be seen). The flour was shipped to the port of Ostia for Rome's consumption by the Guild of Navigators of Arles. During the last war, the Cryptoporticus made a useful air-raid shelter. Both museums contain also a number of sarcophagi. They are well worth the effort of examining in detail for, instead of leaving the visitor to gape uncomprehendingly as he so often has to, the Direction of the two Museums has tacked on to every sarcophagus an exact description of what is represented on it. He will not only be able to understand the sculptures here but will take away a rich store of knowledge to

1. Open daily. It is possible to buy from any of the custodians a *carte d'entrée globale* which admits to the eight principal monuments and museums of Arles, excluding the Museon Arlaten, at a price below that of separate tickets.
2. Open daily.

less enterprising museums. He should not on any account miss the Hippolytus and Phaedra sarcophagus in the Pagan Museum.

Most of these sarcophagi come from the **Alyscamps**.[1] This was formerly a pagan necropolis on the Via Aurelia and on being taken over by the new religion became one of the most famous cemeteries in Christendom. All manner of rather odd legends attached themselves to it in the Middle Ages; as that Roland and the others of Charlemagne's peers killed by the Saracens were miraculously brought to Arles and buried here; and that corpses were floated down the Rhône in wooden coffins, each with its burial fee trustingly attached to it, like Charon's obol, to be fished out of the river by the boatsmen of Arles and buried in the Alyscamps. The word is generally believed to mean the Elysian Fields – *Les Champs Élysées* – although there is another school of philologists who would like to derive it from a wild flower called the alyssum and make it the Fields of Alyssum. At one time there were several thousands of sarcophagi in what was all through the Middle Ages the most desirable of all burial grounds, but in the sixteenth century, when classical art became the fashion, the city fathers of Arles fell into the habit of presenting the best of their carved sarcophagi to various potentates and collectors and to distinguished foreign visitors. (It is said that a whole boatful of them destined for Charles IX was so overloaded that it went to the bottom of the Rhône at Pont St Esprit.) Before it was entirely too late the last of the good sculptures were saved for the two museums of Arles and, as I have said, form the best collection outside Rome itself.

The cemetery, once nearly a mile long by half a mile wide, has been cut to ribbons by a railway, a rather smelly canal, a factory area and a housing estate; the surviving sarcophagi, mostly uncarved blocks of stone, have been lined up on either side of the last remaining alley. One or two of the chapels are left, out of nearly a score which once stood here, and at the end of the poplar-shaded lane is the ruined Romanesque Church of St Honorat, of which only the chancel and belfry remain. To conjure up the right kind of gentle, evocative melancholy in this desecrated place beyond the railway track and the canal is difficult; one needs to keep repeating to oneself its lovely name and trying to recall Paul Jean Toulet's lines:

> Dans Arles, où sont les Aliscams,
> Quand l'ombre est rouge, sous les roses,
>   Et clair le temps,

1. Open daily.

Prends garde à la douceur des choses,
Lorsque tu sens battre sans cause
Ton cœur trop lourd,

Et que se taisent les colombes:
Parle tout bas, si c'est d'amour,
Au bord des tombes.

Arles owed most of its ancient prosperity and importance to its geographical situation. When Marius dug a canal to the mouth of the Rhône near Fos it developed into a maritime as well as a river port, especially after Julius Caesar destroyed the power of Marseilles in 49 BC for siding with Pompey in the Civil War. It was also the site of the most southerly possible bridge over the Rhône and so carried the main traffic between Italy and Spain. It was an important centre of trade and industry, with shipyards at Trinquetaille; later it became a favourite residence of Constantine the Great and in AD 400, when the Prefect had been driven from Trier in the Rhineland by the German incursions, Honorius made it the capital of the three Gauls – France, Spain and Britain. The Emperor himself in a rescript of 418 wrote that 'Arles is so fortunately placed, its commerce is so active and merchants come in such numbers that all the products of the universe are channelled there; the riches of the Orient, perfumes of Arabia, delicacies of Assyria . . . are found in such abundance that one would believe them products of the country'. Alas, the city was very near the end of its prosperity. In 476 the Western Empire ceased to exist and Arles fell victim to a succession of rapacious barbarian conquerors.

The two greatest classical monuments of Arles are the **Theatre**[1] and the **Amphitheatre**.[1] There is not very much left of the former. First the triumphant Christians did their best to wreck it and mutilated most of the statues. Then it was used as a convenient source of material for building churches and in the twelfth century most of the seats were taken away to build the ramparts of the city. At one time it actually went by the name of 'the quarry'. By the seventeenth century it had so far disappeared from view that a convent was built on the site. There are only two columns left of the stage wall, but some twenty rows of seats survive and at the annual Festival at the beginning of July, open-air spectacles such as costume fêtes and folk dances, *farandoles provençales* and *pégoulades* are staged there. The Arena, one of the earliest in the Roman Empire, was built in 46BC. A mathematically-minded investigator has meas-

1. Open daily.

ured the kilometrage of the seats and reckoned that it could hold 23,435 people. That is a few hundred more than the great Plaza de Toros in Madrid. In the Middle Ages it became a fortress containing a church and a couple of hundred houses. Three towers erected in the thirteenth century are standing today. Like the Theatre it was used as a convenient quarry for building the walls but enough of it remains to be still serviceable as a bull-ring several times a year.

Near the banks of the Rhône are the **Baths of Constantine**, (the key is obtainable at Musée Réattu close by), built in alternate courses of brick and stone. They are the only visible portions of the imperial palace which once covered all this part of the town and was the setting of the famous Council of Arles in 314. Almost next door to the *Thermes* is the fifteenth-century **Priory of the Knights of Malta**, once the Mother House of the Langue de Provence. It is worth going behind it to look at the fortifications on the river side and the view up the wide bend of the Rhône, peaceful enough today but still scarred by the ruins of the bombed railway bridge. Look across the river also to the new Trinquetaille, built after the War to replace the suburb which was flattened by the Allied airmen in 1944. It is worth a visit for anyone interested in contemporary architecture and town-planning. The new church of St Pierre has some interesting abstract glass in the windows. There is a similar church in the bombed quarter on the right of the Tarascon road past the railway bridge.

The Priory itself now houses the **Musée Réattu**, so called after the local painter who lived there and whose daughters left it to the city. The first room contains some magnificent Brussels tapestries representing five of the seven wonders of the world. Notice how the Colosseum is opened up like an architectural section of a house or a ship to show the wild beasts fighting in the interior, and how the men are all in ancient Roman costumes while the women are in those of the seventeenth century. There is a Lurçat Room, with three tapestries and four ceramics. There is a female torso in wood by Zadkine, five bronzes by Bourdelle, and works by Henri Rousseau, Rouault, Vlaminck and Léger. In the photographic section work by Cecil Beaton, Man Ray and Dora Maar (known also as a painter) are shown. The paintings are on the whole second-rate. It is clear that Jacques Réattu's real talent lay in the direction of landscape, which he painted rather in the early manner of Corot, but he persisted in depicting classical, mythological and historical scenes. Unfortunately, he was as deplorable a figure painter as his uncle, Antoine Raspal, who also fills a good deal of wall-space here.

In recent years, the range of subjects displayed in the museum has

Above, Provençal-style bullfighting in the Roman arena at Arles; *below,* the other 'national' game of Provence, pétanque, at St Tropez

The cloister of St Trophîme, Arles

been expanded through the addition of a pre-Roman art section, while during the summer months temporary exhibitions are held there every year. For many, however, Musée Réattu has been elevated from its relative mediocrity by the acquisition in 1971 of fifty-seven small drawings by Pablo Picasso in addition to those already on show.

If the Musée Réattu is disappointing, the **Museon Arlaten**[1] is one of Europe's most fascinating collections of local ethnography. The first floor at least is as impossible to skip as a well-written and fact-packed book. There are over thirty rooms and I would advise you to allow yourself time for at least two visits. If you find yourself pressed, it would be better to cut out the second floor rather than have to hurry round the first. Frédéric Mistral founded the museum with the money he won for the Nobel Prize in 1896, buying the sixteenth-century Hôtel de Castellane-Laval for the purpose. He spent several years collecting for it and arranging it himself. Many of the labels on the exhibits are in the poet's own hand – for example, those of Room One, which is devoted to local medicinal and magical herbs and balms.

Most people have seen representations of the costumes of the women of Arles on the operatic stage or in such pictures as Van Gogh's '*Arlésienne*'. They are acknowledged to be among the most beautiful in Europe, and the first three rooms on the first floor are devoted to their evolution from the eighteenth century down to the First World War, when they began to die out. One life-size scene behind glass shows a dressmaker's workroom with a group of seamstresses making up various costumes. It is modelled in plaster and copied from a picture by Raspal of 1760 in the Musée Réattu. Exhibits in the third room show just how the hair is done and the head-dress constructed. The foundation is a bun on top of the head fixed with a comb. A piece of muslin is laid over it and a strip of velvet or brocade wound round it. Like the costumes, with their characteristic fichus, hard bodices and full skirts, these styles were alive and developing all the time, so that an expert looking at one can tell not only the period to within two or three decades, but the approximate age of the woman who wore it, for young, middle-aged and old women used slightly different styles.

Room Seven is devoted to the local furniture, which is in the tradition of Louis XV and of which the characteristic material is black walnut. Room Eight, of absorbing interest, is devoted to the religious customs, legends and superstitions of Provence. The most

1. The circular ticket does not admit; closed on Mondays in winter.

famous exhibit is *La Chevelure d'Or*, a long golden tress from a woman's head which was found in a tomb in the Church of St Vincent at Les Baux and secured by Mistral for his new museum. (A number of similar women's tresses adorn the Church of Santa Eulalia at Mérida, but nobody there could tell me the reason for them.) There is an old Tarasque which was once carried in procession at Tarascon in the days when the monster was renewed every year. Green, round, scaly and covered with spines, it has a black Picasso-type head equipped with red-and-white striped tusks incongruously like the 'squeakers' at a Christmas party. There is an interesting picture of the sacrificial Ox of Barjols. There are innumerable *santons*, Christmas cribs, ex-votos, holy pictures and pious objects of all sorts in wax, wood, glass, beads and terracotta, and local cakes and loaves in traditional shapes produced for the innumerable festivals. There are charms and talismans of every sort and for every purpose; among them are frogs, walnuts, seahorses, and sharks' teeth.

At this point a staircase leads to the second floor, which contains rooms dedicated to local paintings with a *folklorique* interest, to local arts and crafts and to a number of Van Gogh reproductions, including three out of the four versions of Langlois's famous bridge, which was demolished in 1926. Happily, an exact reproduction of it stands on the site.

Back on the first floor are two rooms with tableaux behind plate-glass representing typical Provençal customs in typical Provençal settings. The *Salle de la Visite à l'Accouchée* is a bedroom in an old house showing a visit to a new-born child. The mother is in bed and the neighbours bring the four traditional gifts of salt, bread, an egg and a match. May the baby be as wise as salt, as good as bread, as full as an egg and as straight as a match, is their significance. The *Salle Calendal* shows an elaborate party for a Christmas dinner in a well-to-do farmhouse of the Pays d'Arles, the great table groaning beneath the different kinds of food and the peasants all dressed in their Sunday best.

Two rooms are filled with relics and souvenirs of Frédéric Mistral and his fellow poets of the Félibrige. The penultimate room occupies itself with the Rhône, the lives of the fishermen and the boatmen and the technique of their craft. The last room of all is devoted to the life of the Camargue with a reproduction of a *gardian*'s hut, part of the wall of which has been cut away to show the interior. Nervous visitors have been known to shy away on catching sight of a bull's head peering out at them from among the reeds.

Chapter 18

The Camargue

❧

The Delta – Les Saintes-Maries-de-la-Mer – the Pilgrimage

Arles is the gateway to a strange region unlike anywhere else in
Europe, even the deltas of the Danube and the Guadalquivir. The
city itself is at the apex of a triangle composed in almost equal parts
of land and water, whose sides are the two main branches of the
Rhône delta and whose base is the sea. This triangle, known since
ancient times as the Camargue, consists of 185,000 acres of salt-
marsh and lagoon. At least, it did until very recently but in the course
of the last twenty years most of its northern half has been drained,
desalinated, irrigated and turned into ricefields, whose output of
120,000 tons a year just about covers the rice consumption of France.
The motorist drives between a succession of rectangular paddy-
fields, and in the early summer, with the thin, green blades of the rice
sprouting through the surface of the water, they look like flooded
tennis lawns.

The southern half, however, is still given over to herds of half-
wild bulls and horses. It is the haunt of many thousands of rare, shy
creatures 'of the wild. The last beavers left in Europe have their
lodges in the banks of the Little Rhône, and in recent years have
bred successfully and spread beyond the Camargue to some of the
Rhône's west-bank tributaries, especially the Gardon. The **Étang de
Vaccarès** is, I believe, the only European breeding ground of the
flamingo (endangered by the noise from low-flying aircraft), several
thousands of which rise into the air like a pink and white cloud when
a stranger approaches. Nearly forty thousand acres round the great
lagoon of the Étang de Vaccarès have been made into a nature
reserve, where wild creatures ranging from boars, polecats and
martens to egrets, ibis, avocets, cormorants and storks can live freely
and unmolested. There is a very good collection of the fauna of the
Camargue in the Musée Baroncelli[1] (named after the eccentric

1. Open daily between March 1 and October 31; afternoons only out of season.
Closed in November.

nobleman and poet who revitalized the traditions of the Camargue at the turn of the century) at Les Saintes-Maries-de-la-Mer. These are stuffed. Living ones may be seen in the Zoo at Pont de Gau two or three miles north of the village. To visit the *Réserve zoologique et botanique de la Camargue,* it is necessary to apply several days in advance to the Director of the Reserve, Rue Honoré-Nicolas, Arles, giving some good reason. Properly accredited naturalists and students can obtain permission to stay in the keepers' cottages in the Reserve.

The southern part of the Camargue is divided up into about thirty ranches, each centring round a *mas,* which is Provençal for a farm or country house and is derived, like *maison,* from the Low Latin *mansio.* Each ranch-owner has his *manade* or herd of black fighting bulls and of the stocky white Camargue horses, a breed which some have connected with the ponies of the Mongols and others with the barbs imported by the Saracens. Sturdy they have to be, for they spend their lives splashing in and out of the muddy ponds or fetlock-deep in the bogs of the Camargue. They are the only means of locomotion off the few roads, for walking in these marshes is out of the question. Apart from the watercourses and the ditches, they are full of dangerous quicksands and bogholes which the horses seem to avoid by instinct.

The five thousand bulls of the Camargue are not a remunerative proposition, for they are raised mainly for fighting. The *manadiers* breed them as a hobby, from local pride and for prestige. One of the largest ranches, for example, Méjanes near Albaron, belongs to M. Ricard of Marseilles, the millionaire distiller of *pastis.* (*Pastis* is the habitual *apéritif* of the Midi. It consists of 45° absinthe taken with ice and water in a long glass.) There is something or other going on at Méjanes every Sunday from April to October, perhaps *courses libres* or perhaps a branding. For the rest, the Syndicat d'Initiative in Arles (which is just on the right of the Cathedral) should be able to advise you as to what is happening in the Camargue on any particular day.

For the *mise à mort corridas* in Arles, Nîmes and the other cities bulls are imported from Spain and the matadors are mostly Spanish also. The local bulls are not killed. They are bred only for the Provençal *courses à la cocarde,* which can hardly offend the most tenderhearted zoophile. There is no record of any bull ever having been hurt in one of these romps. The animal has a rosette or cockade attached to its forehead by a string round its horns. It goes into the ring with a number of athletic young men in white shirts and white trousers, each of whom has a kind of metal talon in his right hand. The winner is the one who can first snatch the rosette from the bull's head. It is an exciting and dangerous sport, for a fighting bull can turn quicker than a polo pony and run faster than a racehorse from a standing start. Very often the *razeteur*, as he is called, has to make a flying leap over both the barrier and the corridor into the seats, with the horns a few inches behind him. This is known as the *coup de barrière*. The bull can, and often does, leap the barrier with the greatest of ease. The *razeteurs* do not take their name from the rosette which is their objective (and which is called a *cocarde*) but from the *razet* or half-circle in which they have to run to snatch it, rather like the arc a *banderillero* makes to plant his *banderillas*. They are all local amateurs who perform for the sport and for the money prizes offered to the first man who takes the *cocarde*. These *courses provençales* are very popular and take place in most of the villages in permanent or improvised rings. When the 'running' is over, the bulls are taken back to their *manade*. The other popular spectacle is the *ferrade* or branding, when the yearlings are separated from the rest and brought in to be thrown on their sides and branded.

After being branded with the owner's mark, the bulls are allowed to roam freely over their master's ranch, living on the saltwort and other halophilous plants which grow there. They are supervised by *gardians*, the herdsmen who are the aristocrats of the Camargue and who spend their lives in the saddle riding round with their long tridents or *ficherouns*, which I have seen turn a charging bull with a single jab in the muzzle. Their *cabanes* may be seen here and there dotted about the marshes. Each consists of a single-roomed white-washed cottage with a thatched roof and a cross mounted on the roof-top. It is longer than it is wide and one end is formed by a windowless apse. At the other end is the door. To look at one is as good as consulting a compass, for they all face in the same direction like cows in a storm. The apse backs north on to the mistral, while the end with the door faces the lee side, the south.

There are several establishments, such as the Mas de Cacharel, where visitors can enjoy a very good equestrian holiday, hiring horses and riding in parties with a *gardian* across the salt-caked solitudes. All manner of strange aquatic birds fly overhead; the sky-line is broken only by an occasional *cabane* or a clump of tamarisks; in the distance, perhaps, a black and white herd of bulls and horses is grazing on the *salicornes* and the *saladelles*. Be assured. The bulls only become dangerous when detached from their herd. In a group they are perfectly docile. I have walked among the fighting bulls grazing on a ranch near Salamanca. They would gaze at one in-quisitively until one approached within a few yards and then turn on their heel and canter slowly off like domestic cattle. The best season to stay in the Camargue is the spring, for then one avoids alike the mistrals of the winter, the tourists of the summer and the mos-quitoes of the autumn.

These *gardians* lead a lonely life out on the marshes between the sun and the wind. Their year is broken only by the two annual pilgrimages in May and October to **Les Saintes-Maries-de-la-Mer**, the village in the dunes between the sea and the lagoons at the south-west corner of the Camargue. Now, as the nearest seaside resort to Arles, it has become blanketed by summer villas, but the old houses still cluster round the high, fortified church which one sees riding like a galleon in full sail far across the marshlands. It is built like a castle. The windows are mere loopholes. A castellated promenade runs round the roof like a battlement. The *mâchicoulis* jutting out from the curved apse recalls the poop of a ship. The five-arched belfry stands out against the sky like topsails, and the weathercock at the top floats out in the wind like a pennant. One can well understand how the term 'nave' or *vaisseau* came to be applied to a church.

The church was designed as a place in which to take refuge when a Saracen sail appeared, and the population must, one would imagine, have been limited by the capacity of the church in a remote and desolate spot such as this, which lay wide open to the corsairs and remote from all aid. It is related that in the year 869 the Arch-bishop of Arles himself came down to the Villo de la Mar, as the village was then called, to look at the defences and was carried off by a sudden descent of the Saracens. A bargain was struck. The Archbishop was priced at a hundred and fifty swords, a hundred and fifty pounds of gold, a hundred and fifty slaves and a hundred and fifty cloaks. To the dismay of the Saracens their valuable prisoner died on them before the ransom was paid over. They dressed the corpse up in the archiepiscopal robes, tied it on a throne and talked to it, keeping it always at a discreet distance from the Arlésiens. The ransom was paid and the Saracens sailed away, to the great chagrin of everyone – but especially, no doubt, of the slaves.

Les Saintes-Maries-de-la-Mer, locally known as Les Saintes, or in Provençal as Li Santo, is closely bound up with the legends concern-ing the origins of Christianity in Provence, which relate that a boat without sails or oars was set adrift from the Holy Land and made a miraculous landfall at this spot. Its hallowed cargo consisted of St Mary Magdalene; St Mary Jacobé, the sister of the Virgin; St Mary

Salomé, the mother of James and John; St Lazarus the Resurrected; St Martha, his sister; St Maximin; St Sidonius, the man born blind; and Sara, their black servant. After landing, the saints separated to preach the Word in Provence. The legend sends Mary Magdalene to the Ste Baume, Lazarus to Marseilles, Maximin and Sidonius to Aix, and Martha to Tarascon. Only Mary Jacobé and Mary Salomé stayed on with Sara at the spot where they had landed. A pilgrimage grew up round their tomb and later on round that of Sara, the only one of the original passenger list who was not a saint. In spite of that handicap, she became the patroness of the gipsies, who found her dusky skin and humble station consonant with their own.

There are really three storeys to the church. The Romanesque nave is bare, austere and almost pitch-dark. (It was in front of the altar here that Mistral killed off his heroine, Mireille.) In a chapel on the roof over the apse, originally built as a watch-tower, is the reliquary containing the bones of the two Maries. In the crypt is the tomb of Sara the Egyptian. The church dates from the twelfth century but the crypt was constructed by King René after the discovery of the bones of the saints in 1448. It contains the reliquary of Sara, an altar made from a piece of a Roman sarcophagus, a Mithraic taurobolium (which led Baroncelli to believe that the place was originally a temple of Mithras) and a very curious statue of Sara, her face kissed and fingered so many thousands of times that the black has worn off and it is now piebald. It is dressed in innumerable layers of shawls and brocades, to which devotees pin photographs of their loved ones. Beside it is a glass case filled with more photographs and another with pieces of tawdry jewellery.

The spring pilgrimage is the great event of the year for the Romany, who flock in their thousands from far and near. Nowadays their caravans are all motorized and there is not a single horse-drawn *roulotte* to be seen among the hundreds assembled at Les Saintes. The pilgrimage begins on May 24 and the gipsies assemble the day before. The ones I talked to were all from France, although mostly Spanish by origin and many still speaking Spanish among themselves, but it is said that they come from all parts of Europe. It is reported that every three or four years they meet to elect a queen here, but they are very secretive about their affairs and very sparing of the truth if they are questioned. It is said also that the annual pilgrimage is a great time for weddings and that many young couples get married in this, the Romany Rome, by the simple rite of severing veins and mingling the blood, but here again the crowd of gipsies take care to keep the inquisitive at a distance from the ceremony, if it is so.

Nor do they welcome strangers to the all-night vigil which they keep in the little crypt on the eve of the festival, when they make their simple petitions to Sara. It is in any case crowded out with the gipsies and suffocating with the heat and the smell of burning candle-grease. I did not attempt to force my way in, but Mr Alan Houghton Brodrick quotes some of their supplications: 'O Sara, console me . . . O Sara, thanks for my necklace . . . Find me a lover . . . Help me recover my dog . . . I want a fine bay horse . . . Save him from death . . . O Sara, calm my heart.'

On the 24th the pilgrimage opens with a mass at ten o'clock and at half past three there is a service with a sermon interrupted perpetually by cries of *Salut aux Saintes!* Then the precentor sings a special hymn, '*Les Saintes des Provence*', while the packed congregation joins in the chorus. Excited cheers keep ringing out – *Vivent les Saintes Maries!* – for meanwhile the door of the chapel high over the altar has opened and the reliquary of the two saints is being slowly, inch by inch, lowered by three men above, on cords, which are decorated with bunches of flowers. First candles and then hands are stretched out to be the first to touch it as it descends. The reliquary is placed behind the altar, and the faithful go up to kiss it and rub some object such as a handkerchief against it, which is then taken home and kept as a *porte-bonheur* until the following year. I rubbed my car-keys and had my windscreen shatter itself into a thousand pieces a fortnight later.

Afterwards I went down into the crypt where the gipsies were parting the voluminous petticoats and embroidered robes to kiss the image of Sara and holding up their children to stroke the sad black face. There was still a stifling smell from the countless candles which had been burning all night. The crypt was like an oven, for the melted tallow lay inches deep on the floor, and little fires were blazing everywhere where fallen candles had set it alight.

In the evening the streets are crowded with *romanichel*, dark, wild and handsome. The women are all in their gaudiest colours, with flowers in their hair and long, flounced, polka-dot skirts in the Andalusian style. As they stride along, brown-skinned, earrings a-jingle, with their beautiful, erect carriage, swinging slightly from the hips, the conclusion already reached by the philologists seems obviously the right and inevitable one – that they are descended from a nomad tribe in Northern India who walked into Europe in the Middle Ages. Many of the men have brought their guitars, and flamenco dancing breaks out spontaneously in the streets. It is all done for their own pleasure and no one sends the hat round or tries to tell your fortune. It is said that the gipsies observe a kind of 'truce of God' which lasts as long as the reliquaries are down, and it was only once that I had gently to detach a small hand which had absent-mindedly found its way into my coat pocket.

Next day is the day of the pilgrimage itself. The proceedings open at ten o'clock with a high mass and a sermon in Provençal. Afterwards, at about eleven o'clock, the procession with the images of the saints starts off down to the shore. The cowboys – *la nacioun gardiano* – in broad-brimmed hats and black velvet jackets ride escort on their little horses, picturesque with flowing white manes and tails. Musicians play their *galoubets*, the three-holed flutes of Provence. Then come the two little pink and blue saints, standing side by side in a little blue boat and borne on the shoulders of stalwart gipsies. The rear is brought up by the Bishop and the local clergy. The crowds keep pace with the procession, running along the beach and the sea-wall, and scramble for places from which to watch the Benediction of the Sea (for those of the inhabitants who are not herdsmen are fishermen, and the blue Van Gogh boats are drawn up on the long, deserted strand beyond). When the procession has arrived at the traditional spot, the *gardians* ride their horses into the waves, the saints are taken to the water's edge and the Bishop blesses the sea.

In the afternoon there is another ceremony in the church, when the traditional address is pronounced, *Adieu aux Saintes*, and the reliquaries are drawn up once more into the chapel above the apse. Watch your pockets from now on, for the 'truce of God' is over.

The religious part of the festival is concluded and the following day is given over to *fêtes provençales*. At ten in the morning is a *ferrade* or branding, which is really an excuse for an exhibition of strength and skill, as the bull-calves are caught and thrown on their flanks to be branded. After that comes the *abrivado*, as it is called, when the bulls are led to the ring by a group of centaurs at full gallop through the sandy lanes between the tamarisks which serve as streets. In the afternoon is a *course libre* or *course à la cocarde* in the bullring. By the next day the gipsies and their caravans have vanished and gone their various ways until the following May.

Chapter 19

St Gilles and Aigues Mortes

✤

The Abbey of St Gilles – Aigues Mortes – the Tour Constance – Le Grau du Roi

Aigues Mortes, one of the few perfect examples surviving in Europe of a medieval fortified town, lay marooned and forgotten among the remote marshlands beyond the Little Rhône until the newly-built tourist road made access from Arles and Nîmes easier. It is physically, although not technically, in the Camargue, for the Camargue proper comprises only the delta between the two arms of the Rhône. There are alternative ways of reaching it from Arles. One is to take the Route Nationale 570 to Les Saintes-Maries, keep on past Albaron and turn right where a signpost says 'Sylvéréal'. The other is to take the main road (Route Nationale 572) to Montpellier and turn left at Aimargues on Route Nationale 579 before reaching Lunel.

St Gilles, where St Giles or Aegidius is buried, had thirty thousand inhabitants in the twelfth century and now has less than ten thousand. It was one of the most famous places of pilgrimage during the Middle Ages and also an important staging post on the great road to Santiago de Compostela. In addition to enjoying lavish favours from the Counts of Toulouse, whose dynasty took its name from St Gilles, it was a prosperous river port, which imported exotic products from the Levant and in turn exported pilgrims and crusaders. St Gilles played a dramatic part in the outbreak of the Albigensian War, for it was here that in 1208 a squire of Count Raymond VI of Toulouse slew Pierre de Castelnau, the Papal Legate – a crime which provided Innocent III with the immediate pretext for excommunicating Raymond and launching the Crusade against the Albigensians. In the following year the Count made his submission, naked to the waist, in front of the doors of the Abbey Church of St Gilles and was whipped into the church with rods, laid vigorously (we may be sure) across his bare shoulders by the new Legate. So great was the crowd of people who came to see their ruler flogged that he could not go out by the way he had come in but had to go through the crypt past the tombs of the murdered Legate.

During the Wars of Religion the church was twice destroyed by the Protestants (who for good measure threw the monks down the well), and the interior is without interest. Very fortunately the Catholic army arrived a few days before the Duc de Rohan, who was then knocking down the church for the second time, was able to get around to the west front. It is a masterpiece of medieval sculpture rivalled only by St Trophîme. There are three doorways, linked by a colonnade and richly adorned with sculptures of the life of Christ. Nearly all the scenes are taken from the Gospel, except for a few from the Old Testament such as Balaam on his ass cursing the Hebrews. (Other animals represented are bears, lions, camels, monkeys and, if you can call it an animal, a centaur.) A close inspection shows that the sculptures are the work of different schools. The central portal, which is the earliest, was carved by sculptors from Toulouse at the end of the twelfth century, while the other two, postdating the Crusader conquest, were by Northern artists from the Île de France. The statues of the Apostles, which are later still, seem to have been the work of local artisans.

The crypt is the same size as the church above and is in fact an underground church, one of the earliest in France to be built with ogival vaulting. Here is the tomb of St Giles, Hermit and Thaumaturge, to which the pilgrims used to flock. To get into the crypt ring the bell on the gate near the right-hand side of the façade. Behind the church are the ruins of the original chancel, including the northern bell-tower, which contains a remarkable spiral staircase known as Le Vis de St Gilles. To gain entry, you must apply to the Syndicat d'Initiative in the Maison Romane, across the Place de l'Eglise.

As you drive across the endless melancholy marshes, a walled city rises like a mirage on the flat horizon. It is **Aigues Mortes**, the city of the Dead Waters, which was built by St Louis in the thirteenth century. At that time France possessed no port, indeed no seaboard, of her own on the Mediterranean, and St Louis, who was meditating the Seventh Crusade, decided to remedy the deficiency. This strip of coast was in the territory of a local Benedictine abbey with the delightful name of Psalmody (one of four 'salt' abbeys, now vanished, which acquired their wealth by harvesting the brine that crystallized itself under the sun and mistral of the Camargue), from which the King negotiated its purchase in 1240.

He attracted settlers to this forlorn spot by promises of tax-exemptions and built the Tour de Constance to protect them from marauders. The town was laid out, like all the new towns of the period, in a chequerboard pattern with straight streets meeting at right angles. It is in the form of a quadrilateral, almost of a rectangle. Basins were dug outside the walls, and canals made to connect them with the sea, which was more accessible then than it is now. In 1248, the King with thirty thousand crusaders and pilgrims set sail in a fleet chartered from the Genoese and after a voyage of twenty-three days cast anchor off Cyprus. Such was the pace of ocean travel in the Middle Ages.

St Louis was to set sail from Aigues Mortes a second time in 1270, when he was already old and ailing. From this second crusade he never returned. When he died of the plague in Tunis, it was left to his son, Philip the Bold, to build the fortifications of Aigues Mortes. They are generally considered to be a model of medieval military architecture comparable only with those of Carcassonne. If less elaborate, Aigues Mortes has the advantage that it is 'all of a piece', built continuously between 1272 and 1300 as a homogeneous whole. Nor has it been extensively and rather fancifully restored like Carcassonne. It is in almost perfect preservation except that the moat has been filled in, thereby detracting from the apparent height of the walls.

The traveller coming from Aimargues passes the Tour Carbonnière blocking the road which was the only approach to the city before the marshes on either side of the causeway were drained. On the west, south and east the waters of the lagoons and the harbour lapped at the walls of the city. Aigues Mortes could only be attacked from the north. The Porte de la Gardette, on the north side, was therefore the strongest of the five gates of the city. All of them were defended by twin towers, two *mâchicoulis*, two iron doors and two portcullises, but the Porte de la Gardette had a drawbridge in addition. Ready to enfilade attackers from the right was the great Tour de Constance, detached from the walls and formerly surrounded by a moat.

We would do best to leave our car in the shade of the trees outside the Porte de la Gardette and enter the old city on foot. The centre of the town, the Place St Louis, lies right ahead, but in fact there is nothing much to see in Aigues Mortes except the fortifications. Once inside the gate we turn sharp right through the Place d'Armes to the *châtelet*, where we take tickets for the **Tour de Constance**,[1] which is reached by a bridge across what is left of the moat. It was

1. Open daily.

called after Constance, the daughter of Louis VI of France and wife of Raymond V of Toulouse, suzerain of Psalmody, who had built a watch-tower on the site a hundred years earlier and given it her name.

The Tour de Constance is a majestic circular keep, which until the time of Philip the Bold was the sole defence of Aigues Mortes. It is ninety feet high and sixty feet in diameter. The two storeys each consist of a single large vaulted room. Stairs, dungeons and the so-called Oratory of St Louis are contained in the eighteen-foot thickness of the walls. The bridge across the water leads directly into the Salles des Gardes and above it is the Salle des Chevaliers. Above that again is a flat terrace with a turret which once served as a lighthouse.

The Tour de Constance saw very little active service and, like the Château d'If, was used mainly as a political prison, first for the Templars of Beaucaire after the suppression of their Order, then for state prisoners of high rank and lastly for Huguenots. There is a moving picture by Michel Leenhardt in the hall of the Medical School at Montpellier showing Huguenot women prisoners on the roof of Constance's Tower, and it is a place still revered by the Protestants of the South on account of the sufferings and the constancy of their coreligionists. Their particular heroine was one Marie Durand who carved the words '*Au ciel. Résistez*', which may still be seen in the Salle des Chevaliers. She had been thirty-seven years in the Tower when the Prince de Beauvau, Governor of Languedoc, came on a tour of inspection and, impressed by her frail physique and indomitable spirit, released her with a dozen of her companions from the prison which she had entered as a child of eight. A number of captives have carved their names on the walls and preceded them by the letter W, which in this place of lamentation and living death means not *Vive* but *Vae Victis*.

The same guardian who lets visitors into the Tower will open the door leading on to the ramparts. The circuit of the walls, with their five gates, their five posterns and their five towers, takes about three-quarters of an hour. (Actually, anyone who does not want to study the fortifications in detail can get a very adequate bird's-eye view from the roof of the Tour de Constance.) At the end of the round press a bell in the wall on the right for the custodian to come and unlock the door.

The population of Aigues Mortes has shrunk from fifteen thousand in the Middle Ages to just over four thousand today, for its brief prosperity as a port declined rapidly when the sea receded and despite all efforts the canals became silted up in the middle of the fourteenth century. The annexation of Marseilles by France and, later on, the building of Sète finally sealed its doom. Nowadays, Aigues Mortes is dependent for its livelihood on the great saltpans which chequer the coast and the lagoons. A quarter of a million tons of salt a year are produced on the flat lands between Aigues Mortes and Les Saintes Maries.

Three or four miles away, at the mouth of the Grande Roubine, is the gay little fishing port of **Le Grau-du-Roi**. It is now a rapidly growing seaside resort with miles of sandy beach stretching in both directions. Next door, on one side, is La Grande Motte, first of the new tourist complexes in the Languedoc-Roussillon development programme, about which more will be said in Chapter 25. On the other side, is the new Port Camargue for yachtsmen, and beyond are the extensive beaches and dunes of Pointe de l'Espiguette, creeping up to the margin of the Camargue itself. The original nucleus of Le Grau-du-Roi is hemmed in. (*Grau* is a Provençal word meaning an estuary or river mouth, the equivalent of the Catalan *grao* which we meet in Grao de Valencia and Grao de Castellón.) Le Grau being the nearest *plage* to Nîmes, as Les Saintes-Maries is to Arles, a number of villas are naturally springing up, but the channel itself, which is the spinal column of the village, is full of life, lined always with gaily-coloured fishing boats. Of all the ports on the French Mediterranean, except perhaps Martigues, Le Grau is the one which has best preserved its character of a fishing village. From here one can drive along the coast to Montpellier by way of Carnon and Palavas-les-Flots.

Chapter 20

Les Baux and St Rémy

❧

*The Abbey of Montmajour – Daudet's Mill – Les Baux – Glanum –
Les Antiques – St Rémy*

Often in Arles I used to walk up in the evening to the ancient church
of La Major, behind the Arènes, for the sake of the view across the
plain of the Crau to the Alpilles, a range of jagged, bare hills which
look like mountains in miniature. It is the view which Van Gogh
painted with the blue cart in the foreground. The Pays d'Arles is as
inseparable from Van Gogh as the country further east is from
Cézanne. For those who cannot read Mistral this crazy Dutchman,
with his passion for light, is the great poet of Provence.

All this region was once waterlogged and when the early monks of
Montmajour wished to go to Arles they had to take a flat-bottomed
boat or one of the rafts of inflated bladders which the Rhône boatmen have used from immemorial times. Their original function was
to look after the cemetery and after that to drain the marshes and
ponds which stretched from Arles to the foot of the Alpilles and as
far north as Tarascon. After many fruitless attempts the work was
successfully carried out in the middle of the seventeenth century by a
Dutch engineer called Van Ens. He himself fell a victim to the
Revocation of the Edict of Nantes and had to return to his native
Amsterdam but he left behind him many broad acres of rich corn-
land where before had been only swamp. Now much of it is converted
into rice-fields and flooded once more.

The first little hill, once an island like Ely, which rises out of the
fens is crowned by the ruins of Montmajour. (According to the pious
legend, St Trophîme was sent by St Peter himself to evangelize the
Province, became the first Bishop of Arles and lived here in Montmajour, but in historic fact the first bishop recorded in Gaul was St
Marcian, who was Bishop of Arles in 254. St Trophîme must be
regarded as a figure of myth.) The Benedictine **Abbey of Montmajour,**[1] founded in the tenth century by a pious lady named
1. Open daily.

Teucinda, at one time owned a number of priories all over Provence and enjoyed great wealth. It has no relics to attract pilgrims, but its great 'draw' was a *pardon* every year on the Day of the Invention of the True Cross, when as many as a hundred thousand people would come to have their sins forgiven.

After the Revolution, when it was sold as national property, part of it was pulled down and the stones carted away as building material. The enormous chapterhouse and monks' quarters, built by Pierre Mignard in the eighteenth century, are half-demolished and are now used to shelter a flock of sheep, but the high medieval donjon still towers above the great Romanesque church. Both these have been restored and put in order by the Beaux Arts. The church consists of a single wide nave and a transept. Some of the medieval tombs survive. Near the main door, in the nave, is the entrance to the crypt, partly built up and partly hewn out of the rock, which is in the shape of a cross with a central chapel and others at the end of the arms. The light enters by way of slit-windows in the ambulatory, unique in the South of France, which surrounds it. The cloister is one of the finest in Provence and on the capitals of the columns we encounter again the camels, bears and other animals which adorn St Gilles. Notice the curious carving of the mistral puffing out its cheeks in the act of efflation.

Do not miss one of those graceful little rural Romanesque chapels in which Provence abounds; Chapelle Ste Croix stands alone in an open field, once a cemetery, a short way down the road from the abbey. An apse clings to each side of the Greek cruciform building which is topped by a campanile. The key to the chapel can be asked for at the abbey.

Beyond Montmajour is **Fontvieille**. Turn right at the crossroads in the town along an avenue of pine trees and you will see Alphonse Daudet's famous windmill on a low hill to the left. Put into working order with its sails restored, it is now a little museum containing relics of the novelist and early editions of his works. Upstairs is a kind of compass marked with the vernacular names of the thirty-two winds which blast Provence. It is only for literary purposes that *Lettres de Mon Moulin* was datelined from the mill. Actually the book was written in Paris, and on the rare occasions when Daudet visited Fontvieille he stayed in comfort with friends in the town. The Musée du Moulin is open every day.

The white road winds on into the Alpilles, and on a spur to the right rise the ruined village and castle of **Les Baux**, which in the Middle Ages was the seat of one of the most ancient and powerful feudal houses in Provence. The Seigneurs of Les Baux claimed descent from Balthasar, one of the Three Kings, and did not hesitate to adopt the Star of Bethlehem as their coat of arms. They were lords of more than seventy towns and villages between the Alps and the sea, including the Principality of Orange. They took a prominent part in the Neapolitan campaigns of the Angevins and founded the Balsha dynasty of Scutari which ruled for several generations over Northern Albania. (The Latin form of their name was de Balcio. In Provençal *baou* means 'a rock' – plural *baoussé*; whence 'Les Baux'.)

In the thirteenth century Les Baux was celebrated for its Courts of Love and was a favourite meeting place for troubadours from all the South. In the next century, alas, it became little less than a bandit's nest, when Raymond de Turenne, Viscount of Les Baux, used to raid the countryside with his men, kidnapping whom he could for ransom. Those from whom no ransom could be expected were pushed over the castle cliff into the abyss beneath, while Raymond watched their anguish and laughed until he cried. (One feels he missed a great deal of pleasure by living before the invention of the movie camera.) In the end this pest, who had so well earned himself the name of 'The Scourge of Provence', was cornered near Tarascon by the combined armies of the King of France, the Pope and the Count of Provence and drowned while trying to escape across the Rhône.

When the dynasty died out in the fifteenth century, Les Baux was incorporated into Provence. King René gave it to his wife, Jeanne de Laval, who often resided there. (The elegant Renaissance Pavillon de la Reine Jeanne down in the valley, on the property of a farm called the Mas de la Fontaine, which admits visitors in return for a modest tip, dates, however, from 1581, a hundred years after Queen Jeanne de Laval and two hundred after Queen Jeanne des Baux of Naples). Under the influence of the Manville family, who ruled Les Baux for the King, the place became a stronghold of the Protestants and a supporter of every rebellion which broke out, until in 1632 Louis XIII, or rather his minister Cardinal de Richelieu, lost patience, demolished the castle and the ramparts at the expense of the inhabitants and fined them a hundred thousand livres on top of it. It was the end of Les Baux. The 'eagles' nest', as Richelieu called it, had been finally destroyed. The empty title of Les Baux was upgraded to a Marquisate and given to Prince Hercules of Monaco. His descendant, Prince Rainier, has bestowed it upon his son, whose official style is Marquis des Baux. Nowadays the name of Les Baux, the mere whisper of which spread terror over Provence six hundred years ago, is familiar to millions of people in five continents who have never consciously heard of it, for it has been given to bauxite, a mineral whose first discovery here in 1822 has given rise to the vast aluminium industry of the present day.

Les Baux stands on a perpendicular-sided plateau jutting out from the southern flank of the Alpilles. The village itself, which once had four thousand inhabitants, now has only three hundred. It had already become largely deserted when it was sold as national property at the time of the Revolution. Like Montmajour, it was used as a stone quarry. A few houses are still lived in and those who are afraid neither of spooks nor of breaking their ankle among the ruins can stay at either Hôtel Reine Jeanne or Hôtel Bautezar and wander about the ghost-town in the moonlight. (There is another hotel, the Baumanière, down in the valley whose restaurant, gourmets may care to know, is one of the half-dozen or so restaurants in France honoured with top starring in the exacting *Guide Michelin*.) A few ruinous Renaissance mansions lift empty window-sockets to the sky, such as the Hôtel des Porcelets, now a youth hostel, and the Hôtel des Manvilles. Attached to the latter is an oratory carved with the Protestant text *Post Tenebras Lux* and the date 1571. Most of the remaining houses are little more than holes in the ground where the cellars and foundations were hollowed out, the walls themselves having been pulled down and carted away.

The Romanesque **Church of St Vincent** is one of the few buildings left from the Middle Ages. There are some interesting tombs inside and the chapels of the Manville family and of the Confraternities of Shepherds and of Winegrowers. Transhumance is the system still practised, by which the sheep are driven up to the high pastures of the Alps at the beginning of the summer and driven down again to the lowlands in October, and it is believed by some authorities that the Lords of Les Baux, who are first recorded here in a document of 975, may have been originally transhumant sheepfarmers from the Alps. Certainly sheep-raising was once the principal activity of the Alpilles and the Crau. Every Christmas since the Confraternity of Shepherds was founded in the sixteenth century a curious midnight mass has been celebrated for them in St Vincent. An 'angel' hidden behind the altar announces the Nativity to the assembled shepherds, muffled in their great cloaks. Preceded by drums and fifes, they lead a little beribboned cart up to the altar. Illuminated by candles, it is drawn by a ram and bears a newborn lamb as an offering to the newborn Saviour. Such is the *fête de pâtrage* which has taken place with its traditional ceremonial every Christmas for four hundred years, but it looks as if its end is very near now. Of all the shepherds who formerly watched their sheep on the hills of Les Baux only one solitary ancient is now left to present the lamb.

The narrow Rue du Trencat, hewn out of the rock in Roman times, leads up to the fourteenth-century Tour de Brau, which contains a lapidary museum and, rather enterprisingly, a non-stop magic-lantern show, lasting a quarter of an hour and consisting of photographs of Les Baux with interpolated explanations. There one buys a ticket to walk up to the castle, which stands on higher ground on the far edge of the plateau. Its destruction was conscientiously carried out but it still presents a curious Petra-like aspect, since much of it was hewn out of the solid rock and so could not be demolished. There are square rooms in the cliffs like empty cisterns, and staircases which begin and end in nothingness. From the castle there is a short cut down to the Place Fortin and luncheon by way of a path leading downhill to the left.

On the topmost crest of Les Baux are the remains of the donjon, with a splendid view over the Crau, the Camargue and, on a clear day, as far as Aigues Mortes. Below it drops the sheer cliff from which the sadist Raymond de Turenne made his 'useless' prisoners walk the plank. The view from the eastern valley is one of the most impressive which can be obtained of Les Baux. When one comes down, as I have done, from St Rémy in the evening, the sun, sinking behind Les Baux, shines through the gaping windows of the donjon, which seems to form part of the cliff-top, and the black figures walking on the crest are magnified far beyond their real size, so that for a moment one catches oneself imagining that the tyrants of Les Baux are condemned for all time to walk their battlements at sundown.

From here the St Rémy road winds across the crest of the Alpilles and dips to a little grassy plateau called **Les Antiques**. On the right of the road is a signpost marked 'Glanum' and on the left an arch and a cenotaph which are two of the finest Roman monuments in France. **Glanum** was first a Gallo-Greek and later a Gallo-Roman town, nestling in what one would have imagined to be a quite indefensible situation in a pocket of the Alpilles, which rise sharply in cliffs and gorges at the back of it. About a tenth of it has been excavated since the work began in 1921. There is a custodian in the shed at the entrance to the barbed-wire enclosure, three or four hundred yards off the main road, who sells tickets and lets visitors into the ruins.[1]

1. Open daily.

The town was built by native Gauls on the site of an older Gaulish sanctuary whose remains have been uncovered to the south of the classical remains at the entrance to one of the ravines of the Alpilles. The builders were, however, strongly influenced by the Greeks from neighbouring Marseilles and there are several Greek-style houses, with columns, peristyles and courtyards, among those already excavated. Dating from the second or third century BC, they are the only Greek dwelling-houses so far discovered in Gaul. The Massiliots never made any attempt to enlarge their territory or subjugate the native tribes and for the sake of their trade and their caravans they took care to keep on good terms with them. It is probable that they used Glanum both as a commercial centre and staging post and as a 'hill station' during the hot weather. Later on, it became gradually Romanized. The ruins are divided by a wide street; the buildings on the near side of this street are mainly Hellenistic and those on the far side Roman, with the characteristic baths and gymnasium of a Roman town. Glanum was destroyed by a German incursion as early as the third century and was never rebuilt.

The arch beside the road is the oldest in the South of France and probably adorned the entrance to the city. Dating from about 20 BC, it is sculptured with garlands of fruit and flowers, notably oaks and acorns, and with two groups showing prisoners chained to a tree. Beside it is the so-called Mausoleum, or more correctly cenotaph, which is so perfectly preserved that it is hard not to believe that it was erected two or three centuries ago. The square base is covered with bas-reliefs, scenes of war and the chase, and above it are four rounded openings between Corinthian columns. Round the frieze above runs the inscription 'Sextius, Lucius, Marcus, sons of Caius Julius, to their parents'. The two statues are enclosed in a circular colonnade on the second storey. The whole was once crowned by a stone pine-cone. It is the only thing missing to mar the completeness of the 'Mausoleum'.

A little further on, on the right, is the entrance to the former **Priory of St Paul-de-Mausole**, now the mental home where Van Gogh was immured after cutting off his ear – the tragic painter whose last letter to his brother Theo, just before he committed suicide two months after his release in May 1890, concluded with the words: 'Misery will never end.' There is a miniature Romanesque church, complete with apses, transept and side-chapels; on the right is an attractive Romanesque cloister. The Asylum Garden which Van Gogh painted is still there and, if you can find anyone to show it to you, you can also see Van Gogh's cell, now hung with reproductions of his works, and a bronze bust of him stands in the drive that leads to the church and cloister. Dr Albert Schweitzer was interned here during the 1914–18 war, on account of his Alsatian origin which made him a German at that time.

The little town of **St Rémy**, called after St Remigius, the Bishop of Rheims who baptized Clovis, lies at the base of the foothills. An important centre of the grain and seed industry, it is surrounded by market gardens where they grow *primeurs*, which are early vegetables and fruits, for the markets of Paris and London. St Rémy was the birthplace of the sixteenth-century astrologer and prophet, Nostradamus, whose *Centuries* are still reprinted and studied today and whose tomb may be seen in the Church of St Laurent at Salon in the Crau, and also of Joseph Roumanille, one of the seven founders of the Félibrige. Mistral himself was born in the nearby village of Maillane, lived there, died there and is buried there beneath a reproduction of the Pavillon de la Reine Jeanne at Les Baux. Gounod came to live in St Rémy in 1863, when he was collaborating with Mistral on his opera *Mireille*. Gertrude Stein spent the year 1922 here writing.

On the left of St Martin, the great church opposite the Place de la République as you come into the town from Arles and Tarascon, the Rue Carnot leads to the chestnut-shaded Place Favier, with a museum of local folklore in the Renaissance Hôtel Mistral de Mondragon.[1] The custodian there will take you across to another old aristocratic house, the **Hôtel de Sade**, which houses the finds from Glanum.[1] The de Sades were an ancient local family, whose members included not only the husband of Petrarch's Laura but the author of *Justine* and *Juliette*. The famous Marquis who gave his name to Raymond de Turenne's besetting vice may never have come to St Rémy, but his château was at Lacoste, a few miles to the east in the Luberon hills, to which he fled after scandalous affairs in Paris. The de Sade family owned other domains in Provence – at Saumane, Bonnieux, Oppède, Eyguières and Mazan. At Lacoste, the Château de Sade is being slowly renovated by the present owner.

Do not tackle the museum if you are in a hurry to get on to the next place, for the guide is very conscientious, assumes you are a brother archaeologist or you would not have come there, and takes you round each case, explaining everything in detail. The collection, which contains some good Roman portrait busts, is of particular interest since the crude technique of many of the sculptures betrays native Gaulish workmanship, but nearly all of them are quite

1. Closed on Tuesdays in summer; open at weekends at other times.

obviously taken from Greek and sometimes even Etruscan models (for example, the acroterium with the bust of Valetudo). Overwhelmed by Rome, one is only too apt to forget the civilizing influence of the Greeks in Southern Gaul. They are credited by a first-generation Gallo-Roman writer with introducing not only the plough but even the olive, for two thousand years the mainspring of the economy and the characteristic tree of Provence.

Chapter 21

Beaucaire and Tarascon

❧

Beaucaire Castle – the Fair – the Tarasque – Tarascon Castle

> From Beaucaire to Tarascon,
> There is only one bridge, but a long one!

ran the old song. And again:

> Between Beaucaire and Tarascon,
> Neither lambs nor sheep graze.

The lively imagination of the Provençals was early caught by the dramatic situation of these two strongholds, which for centuries faced each other across the swiftly flowing Rhône. One was in Languedoc and the other in Provence, for this stretch of the river was long a frontier. In the old days the masters of the river boats used to give their helmsmen orders by saying not 'Port!' and 'Starboard!' but 'Kingdom!' and 'Empire!' according to which bank they were to steer for.

The great **Castle of Beaucaire**[1] was built on a steep rock overlooking the river by Raymond VI, Count of Toulouse. The fortifications were demolished by Richelieu at the same time as he destroyed Les Baux and so many other Southern castles. The donjon still crowns the rock, however, and one can walk up through the pine-shaded promenade and thence climb a narrow staircase in the wall to the curious triangular platform at the top. The Castle of Beaucaire was the scene of that loveliest of all medieval romances, *Aucassin et Nicolette*.

In 1217 Raymond VI also instituted the greatest fair in Western Europe, which raised Beaucaire to the eminence of Leipzig and Nijni Novgorod and which survived until the building of the railways in the middle of the last century. Every July some three hundred thousand strangers from all over the Mediterranean and even from

1. Open daily.

beyond it flooded into the little river port. The city fathers offered a fat sheep to the first ship to arrive, which thereafter hung the fleece Jason-like at its masthead for the duration of the Fair. All the houses were crammed with merchants and their goods; the streets were a babel of tongues; cargoes of furs, tin and amber came floating down the river from the North; and seven or eight hundred gaily-beflagged ships lay moored off the quays. There were schooners which had sailed all the way from England, and Mistral in his *Poème du Rhône* writes of '*les goélettes anglaises et du Havre-du-Grâce*,' which lay alongside the Aleppo brigantines and the black *trabuchi* from the Adriatic.

The fairground itself occupied the large flat expanse between the cliff of the Castle and the river, which is today a peaceful meadow shaded by enormous plane trees. A theatre and a bull-ring have now been built in Le Pré, as it is called, for Beaucaire, at one time the Catholic rival of Protestant Nîmes, now challenges it once more for the title of the tauromachic capital of Languedoc.

Stendhal has described the Fair, which he visited early in the last century, in his *Mémoires d'un Touriste*. Each avenue in this fantastic wooden town of booths and stalls was devoted to a different country or corporation. Thus they were allotted to the merchants of Marseilles, who sold soap, oils and drugs; the traders in Morocco leather; the turbaned Turks who sold carpets and pipes; the red-fezzed Greeks who dealt in sweetmeats; the Persians with their precious attar of roses; the jewellers; the spicers; the pastrycooks; the vendors of onions and garlic; of oranges and lemons; of figs, dried raisins and the dates which were packed in *massapans* or narrow wooden boxes with frilly paper exactly as they are today; of toys and dolls; of pottery from Moustiers and Marseilles; of perfumes from Grasse; of doves, parrots and other cage-birds; of kerchiefs; of cloth; of Indian shawls; of silks from China; of coral necklaces and cameo brooches from Naples; of swords and knives from Toledo; of holy images; of saddlery; of ropes and cords; of dried fish from the Atlantic Ocean; of sugar; of coffee; of brooms from the Comtat; of wicker baskets; of hats; of shoes; of horses and mules, and a hundred other things beside. Scattered among them were Venetian ballad-singers; tumblers and acrobats; quack physicians and toothpullers; long-bearded fortune-tellers modelled on Nostradamus; jugglers; sword-swallowers and fire-eaters; dwarfs and bearded ladies; tattoo artists; waxworks proprietors; leaders of performing bears, dogs and monkeys – and everywhere, of course, the gipsies.

Tarascon, on the opposite bank of the river, is best known to the outside world as the home of *Tartarin de Tarascon*, a book which considerably annoyed the Tarasconnais. They were no more ridiculous than people anywhere else, they complained – no doubt with justice. If Alphonse Daudet is the most unpopular figure in the history of Tarascon, King René, seen through a rosy veil five centuries old, is certainly the best loved. He it was who completed the building of the Castle and made it his favourite place of residence and he it was who in 1469, organized the great Festival of the Tarasque which rendered the town famous – until the exasperating Daudet came long to spoil everything and turn the place into a joke.

The Tarasque is a part of the curious legend of St Martha of Bethany, who is said to have landed at Les Saintes with Lazarus and the three Maries and to have wandered thence up to Tarascon, at that time called Nerluc. She found the little town terrorized by the Tarasque, an amphibious dragon which used to come up out of the Rhône and carry off the washerwomen. (It kept one of them seven years in its cave and made her act as wet-nurse to its child, the little Drac.) It had devoured eight young men out of sixteen who set out to fight it. The bravest knights of the Province had been defeated by the Tarasque, but the saint subdued it with the aid of holy water and a cross. She fashioned her girdle into a halter and led the monster three times round the ramparts and then back to the Rhône with strict orders to stay there until the end of time. It plunged in, returned to its lair and has never, so far as is known, been seen again. St Martha lived on in Tarascon, of which she had naturally become the most popular citizen, and left her bones there. Her tomb in the church just opposite the Castle became a place of pilgrimage like so many others in the Midi.

The **Church of Ste Marthe** was badly bombed in 1944 but it has now been restored. The attractive Gothic interior contains some good pictures by Provençal artists, and in particular a 'St Francis' by Carle Van Loo. The tomb of the saint herself is in the crypt. A singularly beautiful piece of sculpture shows her lying draped on a bier. It is seventeenth-century Genoese work and beneath it is the fifth-century sarcophagus of the saint herself. On the right of the stairs leading down to the crypt, notice the Renaissance tomb of Jean de Cossa, King René's seneschal, who completed the building of the Castle. It is by Francesco Laurana, the Istrian sculptor whom René patronized.

Just to the north of Ste Marthe is a shanty bearing outside it the rather startling invitation: *Ici Visitez la Tarasque!* It is the stable of the papier-mâché monster which is pushed in procession through the streets every year on the last Sunday in June – a final vestigial remnant of the great festival of the old days. Until the end of the last century there were two processions a year when the Tarasque was carried (not pushed) by eight men inside it, symbolic of the eight young men it had eaten, and another eight outside, symbolic of their eight comrades who had escaped, while the people sang the festival song:

Lagadigadéu! La Tarasco!
Lagadigadéu! La Tarasco du Castel!

In the first procession, on the second Sunday after Easter, the furious beast used to swing its scaly tail from side to side, knocking over anyone within reach; in the second, on St Martha's Day, it was led, as tame as a kitten, on a halter by a virgin. Now there is only one procession a year, the *Fête de la Tarasque*, when the dragon is pushed on wheels by eight men who steer it by its fixed tail. The guardian shows you the piece of string which shakes its gloomy head and opens and shuts its mouth. The poor beast is getting shabby and moth-eaten by now. In its grand days it was renewed every year (we have seen one of the old ones at Arles) but the present one bears the date 1840.

I know of nothing in Provence which quite so vividly recalls the best of the Middle Ages as the **Castle of Tarascon**. It is incomparable for its satisfying lines and proportions, its superb situation, perched on a rock projecting into the great river, and for its wonderful preservation. It has hardly needed to be restored at all. Where it has been restored, the restorations are obvious and no attempt has been made to fake them. After the death of King René, who divided his time between Aix and Tarascon, it became for dreary centuries a prison, until the Beaux Arts rescued it and took it in hand in 1926. There has long been talk of making it into a museum of chivalry. At present it is open to the public and the guardian takes parties round every hour – on the hour – except, of course, at twelve and one.[1]

The *logis seigneurial* is a quadrilateral fortress with towers at the corners, square on the river and round facing the town, crowned with castellations on the roof-platform. It is everybody's idea of a medieval castle. There is an interior court which was used for a variety of purposes. Troubadours, minstrels, jugglers and miracle-players used to perform there, watched by King René and his queen from an elegant loggia on the first floor, which led out of the queen's

1. Closed on Tuesdays.

chamber. The loggia is now destroyed but is apparently to be restored. The *cour d'honneur* was also the parade ground and the adjacent chapel has a window opening on to the court so that the men-at-arms could hear mass therefrom. Upstairs is a series of magnificent rooms, which it would be tedious to try and enumerate. Do not miss the great banqueting hall, which has an open fireplace for roasting and a narrow flue which leads to the roof a hundred feet above. Finally one finds oneself on the great roof-terrace from which in 1794 the partisans of Robespierre were thrown into the Rhône a hundred and fifty feet below.

Not only is the Castle of Tarascon one of the most impressive in France by any standards but, unlike so many of them, it is lent a peculiarly human touch by the *graffiti* scratched on the walls, with all the time in the world at their disposal, by the captured English seamen confined here in the eighteenth century. Among the prisoners who have striven to attain immortality with a blunt knife are Samuel Abigail of Great Yarmouth; Edward Wright of Stockton, *The Marie*, 1793; J. Prossington of Cork, 1793; and Charles Morgan of Newport in Monmouthshire. The one who has vouchsafed the most information about his adventures is 'John Wallters (*sic*) Taken in the Constantine Privateer of Bristol on the 19th Day of February Landed on the Island of Minorca the 9th Day of March Brought to Toulon the 28th Brought to the Castel Tenth Day of April 1747.'

In the Salon du Roi on the second floor, on the wall to the left of the door, is a pathetic little poem:

> Here be three Davids in one Mess
> Prisoners we are in Distress
> By the French we was caught
> And to this prison we was brought.

Perhaps the 'three Davids' were three Taffies; perhaps again they were the three sailors whose names are carved at the side of the doggerel and two of whom were called David: David Siday, London, 1778, David Haworth and Isaac Richer, sailing mate of the *Zephyr*, taken August 25, 1778. They were indeed 'in one Mess', poor devils, however one likes to take the word.

Chapter 22

Avignon

✤

The Pont St Bénézet – the Palace of the Popes – the Calvet Museum – Villeneuve Church – the Charterhouse – the Hospice

The ancient city of Avignon is known to every child in France as the scene of something that almost certainly never happened there.

> Sur le pont d'Avignon
> L'on y dansait, l'on y dansait.
> Sur le pont d'Avignon
> L'on y dansait tout en ronde.

A part at least of the old bridge of St Bénézet still breasts the swiftly flowing current of the Rhône but, designed as it was for packhorse traffic, it is obviously far too narrow for people to dance in a circle on it. The bridge, linking Avignon with Villeneuve-lès-Avignon, straddled the green, reedy island of La Barthelasse, which bisects the Rhône and provides flat surfaces eminently suitable for dancing. We know that in Petrarch's time the citizens used to go in the summer to the pleasure gardens on the island to eat fried fish and to wash them down with the heady wines of the Côtes du Rhône. It may be taken as certain that they danced there also in the shade of the arches of the bridge – *sous le pont d'Avignon.*

A local legend runs that in the twelfth century a shepherd lad from the Vivarais, named Bénézet, was told in a vision to build a bridge and taken by an angel to Avignon, was laughed at by the city authorities, won them over by performing a miracle and built the bridge which was to bring so much prosperity to the town. Stone bridges were few and far between in the Middle Ages (even Arles possessed only a bridge of boats) and they had a semi-religious character. The Pope himself bore the proud title of *Pontifex Maximus,* the Supreme Bridge-builder. The usual method of crossing a river was by means of a ferry, which was a long, tedious, expensive and occasionally hazardous business, especially when one had a large train of mules or packhorses. To avoid this waste of time the Beau-

172

caire merchants were only too willing to pay a toll to the city for the use of its bridge. The money-spinning Bénézet was very properly made a saint, if not by the Church at least by the grateful Avignonnais. The greater part of the bridge has been carried away by floods but several arches still jut out into the Rhône from the Avignon end. On one of the piers is the Chapel of St Nicolas, which consists of two superimposed chapels, the lower one Romanesque and the upper one Gothic.

Avignon is entirely surrounded by ramparts, into which the bridge runs. They were built in the fourteenth century by Pope Innocent VI and restored in the nineteenth by the famous architect Viollet-le-Duc. They are certainly impressive but, like those of Aigues Mortes, would be more so had they not lost so much of their height by the filling in of the moat which formerly surrounded them.

To understand how a Pope of Rome could fortify a city here in the middle of France, it is necessary to delve some way into the peculiar history of the Comtat Venaissin, of which Avignon was the principal town. Although surrounded by French territory, it did not itself become part of France until the Revolution. In the fourteenth century Avignon was the dramatic setting both for 'the Babylonian Captivity', as the Italians called it, and for the Great Schism. In the thirteenth century the Comtat Venaissin had been ceded to the Papacy as part of the spoils, the *spolia opima*, of the Albigensian Crusade, for it had belonged to the vanquished Count of Toulouse. The city-republic of Avignon itself did not form part of the territory transferred, as it owed allegiance to the Count of Provence.

In the meantime the anarchy to which the factious barons had reduced Rome was making it (or indeed anywhere else in Italy, ravaged as it was by the endless wars of Guelfs and Ghibellines) impossible as the seat of the Papacy. Such at least was the opinion of Bertrand de Got, Archbishop of Bordeaux, when he was elected to succeed Pope Boniface VIII in 1305. Remembering that he fortunately possessed a little territory on the banks of the Rhône, he moved the Papal Court thither, lock, stock and barrel. Carpentras was actually the capital of the Comtat, but on account of its river communications Clement V, as he now was, preferred to make his headquarters in the enclave of Avignon, where he lived in the Dominican convent. His successor, John XXII, who had been up to then Bishop of Avignon, decided to remain on in the Bishop's Palace, which was just south of the Cathedral on the Rocher des Doms. He was followed by yet a third Frenchman, Benedict XII, the first Pope who showed that he regarded Avignon as anything more than a temporary refuge by rebuilding the Palace on a scale befitting a Pope but in the austere style of his own Cistercian Order. His art-loving successor, Clement VI, who was accustomed to the great Gothic buildings of the North, erected the New Palace in a more ornate style than that of Benedict's Old Palace, from which it is separated by the Great Courtyard. The whole ensemble covered fifteen thousand square yards and it is not to be wondered at that the historian Froissart described it as 'the finest and the strongest house in the world'. It is a fortress outside and a palace inside.

In 1348 Clement VI seized the opportunity of adding Avignon to his possessions in the Comtat when the beautiful Jeanne des Baux, Countess of Provence, who was then a girl of twenty, came to pay homage for her Neapolitan realm and to defend herself against the accusation of complicity in the strangulation of her husband, Andrew of Hungary. It seems clear that a mutually profitable bargain was struck. The Queen was absolved by the Pope of connivance in the crime and sold him the city of Avignon for the knockdown price of eighty thousand ducats. Jeanne left Avignon without a stain on her character, while the Vicar of Christ was henceforth master in his own house and no longer the guest of his own vassal.

The fourteenth century was the gorgeous period of Avignon when the wealth of the Church, derived from innumerable dues and perquisites ranging from the sale of bulls, pardons, dispensations and indulgences to the fees of the pleaders in the Papal Tribunal, was flooding into the town, and cardinals, prelates and secretaries were building themselves palatial homes. Excited crowds would jostle to receive the Papal blessing and to see him when he rode abroad on his white mule, or to gape at such spectacles as Queen Jeanne, in a flowered robe and a blue mantle, landing from the galley which had brought her from Naples, mounting her white palfrey and riding up to the Palace with eight cardinals in attendance.

The city was famous alike for its luxury and gaiety, for its religious processions and festivals and for its crime and immorality. The Popes not only made Avignon a place of refuge for heretics and Jews but extended their tolerance to criminals and escaped gaol-birds from neighbouring countries. The latter found a ready-made prey not only in the gullible pilgrims but in the merchants who, with their pockets filled with gold, crossed the Rhône by the Pont St Bénézet on their way to or from Beaucaire and paused to spend some of it in a haunt of vice and pleasure whose reputation ranked second only to that of Venice. Petrarch, who was a familiar of the Papal Court for many years, described Avignon as 'an abode of sorrows, the shame of mankind, a sink of vice . . . a sewer where all the filth of the universe has gathered. There God is held in contempt, money is worshipped, and the laws of God and man are trampled underfoot. Everything there breathes a lie; the air, the earth, the houses and above all the bedrooms.'

In 1377 St Catherine of Siena persuaded Gregory XI to return to Rome. Avignon, which had been the seat of seven Popes, now became the seat of two Antipopes when a faction of the Cardinals, who preferred the fleshpots of Avignon, elected a Pope of their own. The Great Schism had begun which was to result in the spectacle of rival Popes hurling anathemas and excommunications at each other between Rome and Avignon. The Antipope Benedict XIII was finally expelled after a five-year siege and retired to carry on the battle in his native Spain in 1403. Thereafter the Comtat Venaissin was governed by Papal Legates appointed from Rome until its annexation to France at the Revolution, when it suffered severely from mob violence, both as regards lives and architecture. It is partly for this reason that it lacks the abundance of ancient buildings which one would expect to find in a city with such an illustrious past. The cloister of the Cathedral, the Franciscan and Dominican convents, the Town Hall and the Priory of the Knights were among the casualties. An order even went out to demolish the Papal Palace itself. As it was, the building was pillaged, damaged and converted first into a prison and then into a barracks. A barracks it remained until 1906, when the Beaux Arts managed to eject the soldiery and begin the long slow work of restoration. Not before it was time either, for it is said that the ingenious soldiers, not content with using the frescoes as targets, had fashioned a special knife for chipping away bits of them, which they sold to tourists and dealers in the town.

The Palace lies on the southern slopes of the **Rocher des Doms**, a great bluff overlooking the Rhône which was first a Ligurian and later a Roman stronghold. It is now a public garden with a little lake, pine trees on crutches bent double by the mistral, and a lovely view over the Rhône to Villeneuve. The **Cathedral**, between the Rocher des Doms and the Palace, dates from the twelfth century, but the frescoes by Simone Martini which once adorned it are in very poor condition, and were transferred to the Papal Palace in 1962 along with the original sketches which came to light when the frescoes were removed. It contains the elaborate tomb of John XXII and an archiepiscopal throne in white marble. Its exterior, unfortunately, has been ruined by an enormous gilt Madonna mounted on the top of the belfry in the nineteenth century, which makes an eyesore of the noblest site in Avignon.

The exterior of the **Palace** is one of the most imposing medieval monuments in Europe. Some of its towers are a hundred and fifty feet high and its walls are not so very much lower. The windows are mostly set in ogival recesses which run almost the full height of the Palace and carry the eye vertically up to the roof. They also give the building a curiously Islamic aspect. To realize what the interior was like in the days of its glory, it is necessary for the imagination to put the frescoes and the tapestries back on the bare walls, to replace the furniture and the statues and to re-people it with cardinals, princes, prelates, ambassadors, advocates and soldiers of the Guard. To add to its air of nudity, the Palace has been in a chronic state of being restored for several decades, which means that a part of it is always invisible. Happily, the very attractive frescoes of hunting and fishing, hawking and bird-nesting, which decorate La Chambre du Cerf in the Tour de la Garde-Robe have had their restoration completed. They are French work, quite different from the contemporary Italian frescoes in the Chapel of St Martial, with a green background of leafy trees and were probably modelled on Flemish tapestries.

Visitors enter by the door in the middle of the façade of the New Palace, leading into the Great Court. Here they are marshalled for conducted tours by the custodians.[1] It is also the scene of a Festival of Dramatic Art every July. On the right is the flamboyant New Palace of Clement VI and on the left the severe and chaste Old Palace of Benedict XII, centring round a cloister from which the tour starts.

The guide takes groups in person through the vast labyrinth of rooms, chapels, oratories, courts and corridors (and there is a guide-book in 90 per cent intelligible English on sale) so that it would be a waste of time to describe it all room by room. It is better to mention the highlights to look out for as the guide comes to them – such as the five Gobelin tapestries in the great Salle des Festins or Banqueting Hall; just off the Salle, the Oratory of St Martial in the Tour St Jean, with charming frescoes by Matteo Giovanetti da Viterbo, a contemporary of Giotto; the great chimney in the Kitchen Tower nearby; the beautiful vaulted Galerie du Conclave which led to the Conclave, so-called because the cardinals were locked up there *cum clave* and had their food ration reduced every day until they had

1. Daily with visits on the hour except noon and one o'clock, as at Tarascon. In July and August visits are half-hourly. Son et lumière on Monday, Thursday and Saturday evenings in August and September.

The Camargue: *above*, a gardian and his horse;
below, a rice-plantation

Mass and weight. *Above,* the ramparts of Aigues Mortes, 13th century: *below,* supporting pillars in Le Corbusier's block at Marseilles, 1949

elected a new Pope; the enormous Salle de la Grande Audience or Palais des Grandes Causes, which was the seat of the Papal Tribunal, known as the Rota from the circular table at the far end of the hall, round which its members sat; and above it the Clementine Chapel, whose ground measurements, though not its height, are those of the nave of Amiens Cathedral. At the top of the Great Staircase, which leads from Clement's Chapel down into the Great Court, is the Indulgence Window, from which the Popes used to give their blessing to the pilgrims below.

It is difficult to believe that this gigantic palace was built in twenty years, especially in view of the striking difference between the plain, Cistercian-Gothic of Benedict XII (1334–1342) and the rich flamboyant Gothic of his successor (1342–1352). It would be hard to look at a window or door in the Palace and be in doubt as to which decade to place it in – or even a ceiling, for Benedict's are flat, while those of Clement have ogival vaulting.

Just in front of the Palace is a good example of an ornate seventeenth-century palace, built in 1616 by the Legate, Cardinal Borghese, whose family emblems of the eagles and the dragons, familiar to all visitors to Rome, adorn the façade. Formerly the Mint, it is now the Conservatory of Music. Other palaces are the arboreally ornamented Hôtel du Roure and the eighteenth-century Hôtel de Villeneuve-Martignan, which is now the **Musée Calvet**.[1] The latter is built round a garden or inner court inhabited by posturing peacocks, where an inscription recalls that Stendhal used to like to repose in it. It is said that in this courtyard the brothers Montgolfier first experimented with their hot-air balloon in 1782.

The collection of French paintings is particularly rich in the works of the eighteenth-century masters, Hubert Robert and Joseph Vernet of Avignon. It includes several of the classic views of Avignon and of the Fontaine de Vaucluse before the days of the paper mill, but the best of the landscapes is an Italian one by Corot – of the 'right' period. The pride of the Museum, however, is the collection of primitives of the École d'Avignon, of whom Nicolas Froment, Enguerrand Charonton and Jean Chapus are the best-known masters. Look well at the portrait of the young Cardinal of Luxembourg, who died when he was only nineteen, and at the 'St Siffrein', which is believed to be by Froment himself. Although a number of Italian painters and sculptors came to work for the Popes and the Legates, the Avignon School is much more markedly under Flemish and Burgundian influences than the contemporary School of Nice.

1. Open daily except Tuesdays.

The Museum contains some good classical sculpture and a beautiful 'Head of a Boy' by Desiderio da Settignano. The world-famous collection of wrought iron and locksmiths' work amounts to six thousand pieces of which only a few are on show.

On the top floor to the left is the collection of modern pictures presented in 1947 by M. Joseph Rignault. It contains three early Dufys and two early Matisses, which are interesting as showing the development of their respective styles. In addition, examples of the works of Renoir, Seurat, Toulouse-Lautrec, Vuillard, Marquet, Utrillo, Vlaminck, Rouault, Soutine and Berthe Morisot make a remarkable collection of modern art. The revelation of the room, however, consists in the five Daumiers. It amazes one to think that he should have been regarded for so long as a mere draughtsman and caricaturist when one looks at the 'Notre Dame de Paris' and 'The Departure of the Mountebanks'. The other three pictures here, a mythological scene, a drinking scene and a self-portrait, are also Daumier at his very best.

An annexe of the Musée Calvet, in the chapel of the old Jesuit College in the Rue de la République, is devoted to the **Lapidary Museum**,[1] which contains a number of Roman mosaics and sarcophagi, and sculptures ranging from Gaulish to Renaissance. The two star pieces are the 'Venus of Pourrières', which has acquired a curious patina from being so long buried in ferruginous clay, and the so-called 'Tarasque of Noves', a sculpture from the La Tène Period (Second Iron Age) representing a lion gripping two bearded Gauls with its claws. There are several lovely Florentine bas-reliefs.

Of the surviving sculptures in the churches of Avignon the most striking by far is the reredos showing the Bearing of the Cross in the fourteenth-century Church of St Didier, just off the Rue de la République. By Francesco Laurana, the Istrian, it is one of the earliest Renaissance sculptures in France. It is known as '*Notre Dame de la Spasme*' on account of the realistic expression of anguish on the Virgin's face. St Pierre, St Agricol and St Symphorien contain a number of eighteenth-century altarpieces by Nicolas Mignard and the Parrocels of Avignon.

On the right bank of the Rhône lies **Villeneuve-lès-Avignon**. (*Lès* with a *grave* accent means 'near' in French geographical names.) It is dominated by the great **Fort of St André**,[1] which the French kings built to watch their neighbours at the other end of the bridge. The fort is a splendid piece of medieval military architecture, with its rotund twin towers flanking the only gate. The view from the ram-

1. Closed on Tuesdays.

parts is the 'classic' one of Avignon, which Corot and many others have painted, looking across the island and the river. The best time to see it is the evening or the late afternoon when the sun is setting on the great walls and reflected by the windows of the Palace.

Villeneuve was originally a high-class residential suburb of Avignon, where the cardinals, finding little room to build in the city itself on a scale worthy of the princes of the Church and doubtless not sorry to be away from prying Papal eyes, erected their palaces on the other bank of the Rhône. Once there were fifteen of these 'liveries', as they were called, but only two or three are left in the sleepy little town.

The road from Avignon brings one first to the dominant sight of Villeneuve, the tall, well-preserved **Tower of Philippe le Bel**,[1] standing on a rock from which it dominates Avignon and the Rhône. Built in the late thirteenth century, and added to in the fourteenth, it does not have much of intrinsic interest, other than some dilapidated fifteenth-century frescoes. It is worth going to the top for the view of Villeneuve, Avignon, the Plain of Avignon and Mont Ventoux on the horizon, almost the view, one could imagine, that Enguerrand Quarton had when he painted the *Couronnement de la Vierge* in 1453–54, and which we shall visit shortly.

The main road leads to the **Church of Notre Dame**, built by Cardinal Arnaud de Via, who was a nephew of John XXII. It contains some good pictures by the Mignards of Avignon and by Philippe de Champaigne, but its main treasure is a fourteenth-century polychrome ivory Madonna in the sacristy, which follows the curve of the elephant's tusk. (There is a bell on the left of the choir to summon the sacristan.)

The only problem about luncheon in Villeneuve-lès-Avignon is whether one has francs enough in one's wallet, for just behind the church is Le Prieuré, a hotel where one can eat out of doors in a flower garden rather like that of an English country house. The first entry in its *Livre d'Or*, dated September 27, 1947, reads 'Wallis Windsor' and the one beneath it 'Edward, Duke of Windsor'. In 1976, the *Guide Michelin* said the *à la carte* meals cost from 80 to 125 francs. At least once in their lives, anyone with a few pounds to spare should have a meal and a bottle of Châteauneuf-du-Pape 1926 at Le Prieuré. (Châteauneuf-du-Pape itself is a few miles north of Avignon. There is nothing much to see except the ruins of a castle, but there is a three-star hotel in case anyone wants to be able to boast that he has stayed in Châteauneuf-du-Pape and drunk Châteauneuf-

1. Closed on Tuesdays.

du-Pape in Châteauneuf-du-Pape.) Avignon seems to specialize in these good hotel-restaurants with rather exotic dishes such as Le Prieuré's speciality, *Sole au plat Pétrarque*. The restaurant of the excellent Hôtel de l'Europe in the Place Crillon, which was the eighteenth-century Hôtel Graveson, has the only hotel menu I have ever seen which includes bird's-nest soup and palm-tree heart as a matter of course.

Coming back to the café, turn north at the cross-roads along the Rue de la République. On the left are the Hôtel de Conti at No. 45 and the Palace of Cardinal Thury at 53. On the right at No. 60 is the **Chartreuse du Val de Bénédiction**,[1] founded by Innocent VI in 1356. One of the largest Charter-houses in France, it is like a small village with streets and cottages and, of course, rooms, courts and cloisters galore. Do not on any account miss the frescoes in the Chapel of Innocent VI by the same Matteo Giovanetti da Viterbo who painted the Oratory of St Martial in the Papal Palace. If he is not exactly a Giotto, he displays a great feeling for form and line, notably in the portrait of Innocent VI, the Visitation and the Virgin at the Crucifixion. Innocent's own tomb has been removed to the Hospice, after being at one period used as a rabbit-hutch by squatters in the Chartreuse.

To reach the Hospice return to the cross-roads and go straight ahead. Formerly a seventeenth-century palace, it is now the **Musée Municipal of Villeneuve**[2] and most visitors to Avignon skip it altogether unless they are aware beforehand that in Quarton or Charonton's 'Coronation of the Virgin' it contains one of the finest primitives ever painted in France and certainly the masterpiece of the School of Avignon. If it were in the Louvre or the National Gallery it would be famous as one of the world's great pictures. Enguerrand Charonton, actually a Northerner born in Laon in 1410, painted it for the Abbé de Montagnac of the Chartreuse in 1453. The best light to see it by is between four and five in the afternoon.

The bottom eighth of the picture, like a sort of wainscoting, depicts Hell, where little white figures, slender and spindly like mantises, walk amid the flames with the devils. This part of the picture is all vertical lines, red, white and black. The two-eighths above, in contrast, is horizontal. It shows the green expanse of Earth with broad plains and white cities, all designed to carry the beholder's eye up to Christ nailed on a cross which rises on a low hill in the centre. The lonely white figure of St Bruno, founder of the Car-

1. Guided visits each half-hour except at lunch time; closed on Tuesdays.
2. Closed on Tuesdays.

thusian Order, kneels in adoration of the Crucified.

The remaining five-eighths of the picture depicts Heaven. The eye is skilfully directed to the central figure of the Virgin, crowned and robed in red and gold brocade. Above her is the Trinity, the white Dove with wings outspread, and the Father and Son both in crimson robes which dominate the colour scheme of the picture. Below, the blue mantle of the Virgin spills over on to a white cloud. On either side the Trinity is flanked by worshippers, all ranged in a rigid hierarchy. At the top are angels; then below, in order, prophets, saints, popes and emperors down to ordinary mortals at the bottom. Behind, against a gold background, sing little red cherubim and seraphim with crossed wings. The picture is designed to express a double theme, the cult of the Madonna and the Triumph of the Church.

Chapter 23

Orange

❧

The Triumphal Arch – the Theatre – the Museum

Some seventeen miles north of Avignon lies the little city of Orange, which has two claims to fame. Firstly, it possesses the third largest Roman triumphal arch in existence and the best preserved Roman theatre in Europe. Secondly, the name of this town of fewer than twenty-six thousand people is borne today by the Dutch royal house, a district in Gelderland, a political party in Ireland, a county in California, a river and a country in South Africa, and a town in New Jersey. Only to the fruit can Orange lay no claim to have given its name. The orange was brought from Asia by the Arabs to Spain and thence introduced into France by way of Nice. Its name is derived from the Arabic word *narandji*, which is the Spanish *naranja*.

The town of Orange, on the other hand, takes its name from the Cavarian city of Arausio, which after the Roman conquest was settled with a colony of veterans of the Second Legion. It became the seat of a bishopric as early as the fourth century and its wealth and population (the latter was four times that of the present day) are attested by the remains of its public buildings. It possessed temples, baths, a circus, a theatre, an amphitheatre, a triumphal arch and a gymnasium or stadium a thousand feet long. Many centuries later, in 1622, Prince Maurice of Nassau, its ruler, decided to fortify the city and to erect a strong castle on the Capitol Hill. Unfortunately he used the surviving Roman buildings as a convenient stone quarry. The theatre and the arch alone survive because they were incorporated in the fortification scheme. (Orange has its two great monuments still standing, but otherwise it is much easier to grasp the layout of a small Roman city at **Vaison-la-Romaine**, a few miles to the north-east, for there the picturesque little medieval town was built outside, and not on top of, the ancient one so that it has been possible to lay bare the foundations of the ancient capital of the Vocones, later a Roman colony.)

The **arch** had already been turned into a donjon called the Château de l'Arc. It was somewhat knocked about in the process but, though the west side is almost wholly restored, the north face is one of the best preserved of such monuments in existence. The arch commemorates Julius Caesar's victories over the Gauls and over the Massiliot fleet. The reliefs show combats with the Gauls, captive chiefs with their names carved on their shields, and trophies of war. The naval victory over the Greeks is recorded in the upper right section of the north side, where such nautical symbols as anchors, prows and ropes may be descried.

The **theatre**[1] owes its preservation to the fact that Maurice of Nassau used it as a section of his city wall. It is the only Roman theatre in Europe of which the façade remains standing. A hundred and twenty feet high by three hundred feet long, it is an immensely impressive sight as one comes into the Place Mounet. Well may Louis XIV have described it as 'the finest wall in my kingdom'. It is the only Roman theatre also to preserve the square stone blocks which carried the masts supporting the awnings. They may be seen near the top of the outer façade in two rows. The lower ones are solid in order to support the bases of the masts, while the upper ones are pierced each with a circular aperture to hold the masts in place. On the analogy of other Roman theatres the square in front was probably occupied by a large garden and a covered portico.

The dimensions of the theatre are the same as those of Arles, but it is easier than at Arles to visualize what it must once have been. The ten-foot statue of Augustus has been replaced in its niche in the middle of the great interior stage wall, which once held three tiers of niches, statues and columns. There are remains of a frieze of centaurs, and of columns of granite, breccia and *rosso affricano*, standing out against the rusty brown and reddish sandstone. The seats, which hold about ten thousand people, are hewn out of the slopes of the Capitol Hill. At the side of the theatre the foundations of a temple, the largest so far found in Gaul, have been laid bare. It probably stood on one end of the great sports ground. Stairs led up from it to the Capitol, which was at that time crowned with temples and porticoes. It must have formed an ensemble rarely to be matched outside Rome itself.

In the square opposite the theatre is a curious little museum – but indeed it is no more curious than the history of the town itself, which was for centuries a tiny enclave enclosed in the hardly-larger Comtat Venaissin like the yolk in a wren's egg. It was as though Monaco were to be embedded in the middle of Luxembourg.

1. Open daily; between Easter and October 31 open all day.

When in 1229 the Count Venaissin was ceded to the Papacy, the Seigneurie of Orange was excluded from the arrangement. It passed by marriage from the Des Baux to the Chalon family and thence in 1559 to the heir of Philibert de Chalon, who happened to be none other than William the Silent, Prince of Nassau, Stadtholder of the United Provinces and founder of the Dutch Republic. Orange thus became united with the Netherlands and even, for a few years during the reign of William III, with England also. The Principality was finally ceded to France by the Treaty of Utrecht in 1713. The Dutch dynasty were allowed to retain the name of the House of Orange, however, and Queen Juliana of the Netherlands paid an official visit to the city in 1952. There is a square named after her on the Colline St Eutrope where the Capitol used to be.

The little **Municipal Museum**[1] in the Place Mounet, to which your theatre ticket will also admit you, contains a roomful of portraits of the House of Orange-Nassau; Roman remains, including some unique marble fragments of a cadastral plan or survey of the city; and a roomful of paintings by the late Sir Frank Brangwyn, R.A. Orange is indeed a city of surprises.

1. Open daily; between Easter and October 31 open all day.

Chapter 24

Nîmes

❧

The Amphitheatre – the Maison Carrée – the Museums – the Garden of the Fountain – the Pont du Gard – Uzès

Nîmes resembles Aix in that it is built not on a river but beside a spring. In this case, however, it is not a thermal spring but a *source vauclusienne*, which gushes in full force out of the rock at the foot of the Mont Cavalier and for that reason inspired a superstitious awe among the ancient Gauls. In the eighteenth century the spot was tamed and terraced into an elaborate formal garden, the Jardin de la Fontaine, where it takes a great effort of the imagination to conjure up Nemausus, the ancient Celtic genius of the spring. Possibly on account of the sacred character of the *source*, the settlement of Nemausus became the capital of a Belgic tribe who rejoiced in the name of the Arecomic Volcians. Their territory was roughly conterminous with what is now Mediterranean Languedoc.

After Octavius's victory over Antony a number of veterans of the Egyptian campaign settled, or returned, here and gave Colonia Augusta Nemausensis its exotic crest or symbol of a crocodile chained to a palm tree. In the Jardin de la Fontaine there is an actual palm tree growing in the middle of a lawn and at its foot crouches a crocodile in the form of a bed of flowers. It is an amusing and effective conceit.

On the evidence of its monuments the South of Gaul was truly a little Rome, as Ausonius called Arles. It is little short of a miracle that so much has survived practically intact in this relatively small area on the Lower Rhône. It is difficult to think of any group of Roman buildings in Italy so well preserved of their kind as the Arena and the Temple at Nîmes, the Theatre at Orange, the Triumphal Arches at Orange and St Rémy, the Mausoleum at St Rémy and the Aqueduct at Pont du Gard. It would be the easiest thing in the world to visit all seven of them in a single day. They are all within a few miles of each other in a region which has been continuously subjected first to barbarian invasion and then to bitter civil strife. Nor

NIMES

were there those endless centuries of dry, drifting sand and a total absence of any construction such as have saved the great theatres of Leptis and Sabratha in Africa. These edifices have always stood boldly above ground, and people here needed building material quite as badly as they did in Italy.

Les Arènes,[1] the great amphitheatre at Nîmes, is practically a replica of that at Arles. If it is slightly smaller (it is in point of size twentieth among the seventy surviving amphitheatres) it is in a better state of preservation. That preservation it owes to the fact that as early as the Visigothic period it had been converted into a fortress and so never became a quarry like the Colosseum. During the later Middle Ages it was the headquarters of a militia of young knights called the *Milites Castri Arenarum*, whose officers lived in the amphitheatre itself. Three walled-up arcades pierced with little windows, on the east side facing the Palais de Justice, mark their quarters. A church was built in the arena and dedicated to St Martin, the soldier-saint. After Nîmes was united to France in 1229, the amphitheatre became a slum where two thousand people lived in a hundred and fifty houses. When it was cleared in 1809, twenty feet of debris had to be removed before the floor of the arena was reached.

Horse and chariot races took place in the arena but the main spectacle, no doubt, was gladiatorial combat, man against man or man against beast. Several times a year the arena is still put to its original use, as I have seen myself at one of the great bullfights which take place every Whitsun. The gladiators were three of the greatest *espadas* in Spain, Antonio Ordoñez, Gregorio Sanchez and Jaime Ostos. Long before the fight began I had to pay sixty francs for the last ticket left on the black market. The great arena was packed right up to the broken skyline of the 'attic', where people jostled each other for standing room, careless of the sixty-foot drop below them. Someone was perched precariously on every projecting piece of masonry – and had been perched there since early that morning. The ancient building was again being used for the purpose it was meant for after an interval of fifteen hundred years. Something of the old atmosphere came back as twenty thousand people held their breath so that the arena was deathly silent for several seconds and then suddenly exploded into a deafening roar.

The **Maison Carrée**, so called because it is oblong, is a Roman

1. A global ticket, obtainable at any of the Roman monuments, allows entry to all the others – Arènes, Maison Carrée, Temple de Diane, Tour Magne, which are open daily. Between July 1 and August 30, the Syndicat d'Initiative, 6 Rue Auguste, organizes guided tours of Nîmes daily except Saturdays and Sundays.

temple built in the purest Hellenic style by Agrippa, the son-in-law of Augustus. It was dedicated to his two sons, Caius and Lucius, 'the Princes of Youth', and presumably consecrated to Jupiter, Juno and Minerva, if the traditional name of 'Capitol', applied to it until the sixteenth century, be correct. Not only is it, most people would consider, the most beautiful and the best preserved Roman temple in existence but it can challenge any of the lovely temples of Hellas and Magna Grecia. (Of few Roman works of art indeed can it be claimed that they rival their Greek originals.) Its preservation is the more (or perhaps, on second thoughts, the less) remarkable inasmuch as it has throughout twenty centuries been in continuous daily use – as the city assembly place, as the town hall, as a private house, as a stable, as a church and for the last hundred and fifty years as a museum. In 1576 the Duchess of Uzès tried to buy it for a family tomb, and a century later Colbert had the idea of dismantling it stone by stone and transporting it to Versailles.

The Capitol was the centre of the city, facing on to the forum from which all the trunk roads started. Nîmes owed a great part of its prosperity to its position as a road centre. From it a number of roads fanned out to Central France and the Atlantic coast, and from it the Via Domitia started on its long dusty way to Spain.

The temple stands on a raised stylobate, and a flight of stairs leads up to the peristyle, which is supported by fluted Ionic columns with double acanthus capitals. The cella is enclosed, the intervals between the columns being walled up. Along the entablature runs a decorative frieze of stylized foliage. All this has hardly suffered at all from the centuries although a number of monkish accretions naturally had to be removed both within and without when the Augustinians were ejected at the Revolution and the place became first a store for the city archives and finally a museum.

The cella contains an archaeological collection,[1] small but select, of antique works of art found in Nîmes. In the centre of the room is a great mosaic of eighteen panels. Several of the exhibits were found among the Roman buildings of the Fountain, such as the bronze head and the statue of Apollo. The two best-known pieces are the 'Venus of Nîmes' and the Frieze of the Eagles, which formerly adorned Hadrian's Basilica of Plotina.

Frankly, I did not find very much in the other museums of Nîmes which cannot be seen as well or better elsewhere. As though to show how opinions differ, the *Guide Bleu* says that a visit to the town requires an entire day, while the *Michelin Guide* puts it at two hours

1. Open daily.

and a half. I was going to have said two hours myself. The paradox is that Nîmes is a 'must' in a way that even Arles is not, for the simple reason that it contains two masterpieces of classical architecture unique in Europe, which no traveller, hurrying however hard to the Riviera, should miss if he has never seen them. When he has seen them, he has seen almost everything. Arles, on the other hand, with nothing quite so star-spangled as these two, cannot be properly appreciated in less than two or three days. When you have admired the Maison Carrée and marvelled at the Arena, there is little else to do in Nîmes except to take a stroll in the Garden of the Fountain, whereas at Arles, St Trophîme and its cloister alone require two or three hours, as does the Museon Arlaten.

Nîmes was the headquarters and capital of the Huguenots, and the **Cathedral** was twice ruined in the Wars of Religion, the first time when the Huguenots massacred the local Catholics in 1567 and the second in 1621. It has been largely rebuilt in the nineteenth century. Of the Romanesque frieze on the façade only the eight scenes from Genesis on the left are original. The others are later copies. True, the **Castellum**, which received water channelled over the Pont du Gard and distributed it round Roman Nîmes, is an archaeological curiosity, for the only other Roman water-tower in Europe is at Pompeii.

Beside the Cathedral, in the former Bishop's Palace, is the **Musée du Vieux Nîmes**,[1] which contains costumes, furniture, pottery and examples of the fine stuffs – cloth, wool and silk – for which Nîmes has always been famous. Two rooms are devoted to bulls, one to Spanish bullfights and the other to the bulls of the Camargue, with examples of the *gardians'* tridents, of their curious cage-like stirrups and of the rosettes, their attachments and the comb-like claws used to snatch them in the bull-running.

The **Archaeological Museum**[2] contains a spirited Gallo-Roman mosaic of Bellerophon, mounted on Pegasus, killing the Chimera. The first floor contains a well-arranged and well-lit collection devoted to the daily life of a Gallo-Roman household – toilet articles, toys, games, cooking utensils, writing materials, glass scent bottles and so forth. In the central hall of the **Musée des Beaux Arts**[3] is a magnificent Gallo-Roman mosaic found in 1883 under the market-place and believed to represent the Marriage of Admetus. The gallery also includes some Watteaus, Lancrets and Bouchers, and Rodin's busts of Clemenceau and Dalou.

The ruined **Temple of Diana** is almost all that is left of the Roman

1. Closed on Saturdays and on Sunday mornings.
2. Open daily.   3. Closed on Tuesdays.

installations round the Fountain, where once were a nympheum, baths and a theatre. On the summit of Mont Cavalier, which rises behind the Fountain, is the **Tour Magne**. While nobody seems to know its origin or its purpose, everyone is agreed that it is the oldest Roman monument in Gaul. It may have been a watch-tower, a fort, a tomb or a 'trophy' like the one at La Turbie. A staircase of a hundred and forty steps leads up to a platform for the benefit of those who wish to enjoy the view from the top, which is ninety feet high and was once thirty feet higher. They say that on a clear day one can see the Pyrenees.

From the foot of the Mont Cavalier the Fountain gushes forth into a deep basin of brilliantly clear blue water with green foliage beneath it. Fat goldfish flock to be fed with bits of bread, and swans glide graciously among them. From here the water is led into various other basins. There are terraces and balustrades and urns and statues everywhere in the gardens, which were created in the eighteenth century by one Mareschal, Chief Military Engineer of Languedoc. His original grandiose scheme included not only the laying out of the Garden but the planting and terracing of the Mont Cavalier above, right up to the Tour Magne on the summit. After the work had been going on for ten years instead of the stipulated three, the alarmed citizens cut off funds for the project, so that only the Garden and the first terrace were actually completed.

The Fountain of Nemausus soon proved inadequate as a supply of water for the growing city, and in 19 BC Agrippa built a thirty-mile-long aqueduct to bring water from the springs of the Eure near Uzès across the *garrigues*. The *garrigues*, characteristic of Languedoc, are low, cave-pitted limestone hills, with very thin soil – a typical carstic formation. They were formerly covered with holm-oaks and Aleppo pines, but wood was needed to build the cities and, when they were built, to heat them during the winter, so that the *garrigues* are now reduced by deforestation to sparse scrub-oak, box, juniper, cistus, gorse and aromatic plants such as thyme, lavender and rosemary. The rivers carve deep gorges in the limestone and over one such, the Gard or Gardon, Agrippa's aqueduct had to be carried. The problem was solved by building the great bridge which is now called the Pont du Gard.

Artists, archaeologists and engineers alike have acknowledged the **Pont du Gard** to be one of the outstanding sights of France, with its golden stones standing out against the sky, spanning the river and disappearing into the woods on either side. Below, the blue waters of the Gard bear bathers and oarsmen, for the people of Nîmes and

Avignon are very fond of this beauty spot as an object for an excursion or a picnic. There are two hotels and extensive camping grounds beneath the pine trees. The best view is from two or three hundred yards upstream on the right bank, near the entrance to the Château de St Privat.

The bridge consists of three tiers of arches; the lower two match each other, while the upper one is composed of thirty-five smaller arches, roughly three to every one of the supporting arches. Along the top, which is a hundred and sixty-six feet high and nine hundred feet long, runs the water channel and people who are not afraid of heights can walk along it. To reach it, take the path marked with red arrows which winds up the wooded hill on the east bank. Having walked across to the west bank, one climbs down by a spiral staircase and another red-marked path, which brings one out near the road bridge.

The enormous stones of the aqueduct, some of which weigh six tons, are fitted together without mortar or cement, and it is indeed a tribute to the Roman engineers that the Pont du Gard has not collapsed before now. At the beginning of the sixteenth century the supporting piers of the second tier of arches were half cut away to enable packhorses to cross, and when these were restored the eighteenth-century engineers tacked on a road bridge to the Pont itself, so that today it is continually shaken by all the motor traffic which passes between Nîmes and Uzès.

The historic city of **Uzès** is only ten miles from the Pont du Gard and, if one has time, it is well worth visiting the 'Premier Duchy of France'. It is a brave sight to approach on a fine summer's day, as it stands on a little hill with its towers stabbing the sky and the red and white standard of the Duke flying from the highest one. Narrow, arcaded streets and old noblemen's *hôtels* cluster round the château. The **Duché**, as it is called, is open daily to visitors. It still centres round an eleventh-century donjon and is particularly worth a visit for the sake of its magnificent Renaissance façade, said to have been built for the first Duke by Philibert Delorme in 1563. The twelfth-century **Fenestrelle**, the circular, many-windowed, six-storied campanile of St Theodorit's Cathedral, is unique in France, although of a type not uncommon in North Italy.

The painter Nicolas Froment, so-called 'of Avignon', was in fact a native of Uzès, and Racine spent a couple of years here as a young man studying theology with his uncle, the vicar-general, whose house still stands in the village of St Maximin, south-east of Uzès. Racine's farewell to the fat-living, Philistine little city was:

Adieu, ville d'Uzès, ville de bonne chère,
Où vivraient vingt traiteurs, où mourrait un libraire.

Antiques of an entirely different sort are contained – a little un-expectedly, perhaps – in the **Museon di Rodo** (the museum of the wheel) at 5 Avenue Maréchal-Foch. Open daily between Easter and the end of October, and on Sundays and public holidays at other times, it houses forty and more vintage cars, velocipedes (dating from 1860) and working models of the old PLM railway's rolling stock, as well as old posters.

Avignon. *Above,* the Palais des Papes; *below,* remains of the Pont d'Avignon

La Maison Carée at Nîmes

Chapter 25

Montpellier

❧

*The Place de la Comédie – Hôtels – the Fabre Museum – the Peyrou –
the Botanical Gardens – the Medical School – Maguelone – La
Côte Vermeille – the Languedoc-Roussillon scheme*

Montpellier is sometimes described as 'the Oxford of France'. Even
if the Sorbonne may be reckoned to have a prior claim to that title,
Montpellier is surely the Cambridge of France. (After all, one talks
of 'Oxford and Cambridge' just as one talks of 'Eton and Harrow'
without any particular intention of pronouncing on their respective
merits.) Its university dates from the thirteenth century and, out of a
total population of a hundred and ninety-six thousand, now accounts
for twelve thousand. Of that number a tenth are foreign and overseas
students. This is essentially a city of youth.

The centre of Montpellier is the Place de la Comédie, which takes
its name from the theatre occupying one side of it, though it might
equally well be called the Place de la Comédie Humaine. There one
can sit by the hour at a pavement table outside one of the cafés,
admire the eighteenth-century Fountain of the Three Graces in the
middle (in an oval-shaped piece of ground called locally *l'œuf*), and
watch the multi-coloured youths and maidens assembled here in
search of learning – Europeans, Africans, Arabs, Indians, Indo-
Chinese, North Americans, South Americans – all doing very much
the same thing as oneself, as they gossip and chatter in various
tongues over cups of coffee and glasses of beer. One may also go on
to wonder whether such a meeting-place as Montpellier may not be
a more valuable force for world peace and unity than many more
expensive and elaborate agencies.

On the north the Place de la Comédie opens out into the wide
straight Esplanade, three-quarters of a mile long and shaded by four
rows of plane trees. It follows the line of the ramparts demolished by
Louis XIII after the capture of the city in 1622 and is bordered on
the right by some very attractive gardens with a lake, which beautify
the dusty site of the former Champ de Mars or parade ground.

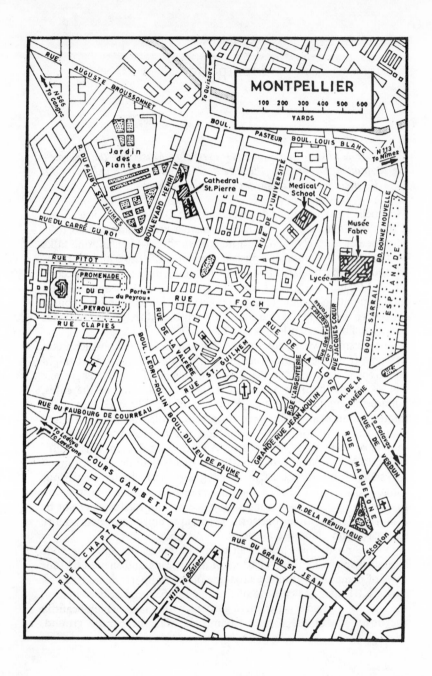

Beyond them again stood the citadel built by Louis XIII at the same time as he pulled down the city walls to keep the rebellious Protestant population in check. (Toulouse, Carcassonne and Beaucaire were practically the only Catholic cities in Languedoc.) It has now become the Lycée. On the west side is the old city of Montpellier, for centuries the capital of Lower Languedoc. This is the region which stretches from the Rhône down past Narbonne between the Cévennes and the sea. Toulouse is the capital of Upper Languedoc.

Languedoc must be unique among geographical entities in being called after its language instead of the other way round. In the Middle Ages Northern France spoke the *langue d'oïl* in which a 'yes' was *oïl*, while Southern France spoke the *langue d'oc*, in which a 'yes' was *oc*. The *langue d'oc* was the language in which the troubadours wrote and sang. It was spoken at the Hohenstaufen court in Palermo, and Dante himself seriously considered writing *The Divine Comedy* in it. (The adjectival form of *langue d'oc* is *occitanien*, and the epithet is applied not only to the language but to the people of Languedoc.) With the unification of France from the North the *langue d'oïl* became the official language, while the *langue d'oc* broke up into a number of dialects such as Provençal, Niçois and Limousin in France, and Catalan, Mallorquin and Valencian in Spain. Frédéric Mistral and the poets of the Félibrige made a noble effort to revive it as a literary tongue, and it still survives as an official language in the little Catalan Republic of Andorra.

Montpellier grew up as a stage on the Roman Via Domitia which led from Nîmes to Narbonne and the Pyrenees, and later on the great pilgrim route from St Gilles to Santiago de Compostela. From the tenth century onwards it was a rich centre for the import of spices from the Levant, but its commerce withered and died when Marseilles was annexed to France in the fifteenth century. The spice-merchants, however, had been long exploring the therapeutic properties of their exotic wares; some of them studied the works of Galen and Hippocrates, and as far back as the year 1000 they had begun to train pupils in medical science. They were greatly helped, of course, by their contacts with the Arabs and Jews with whom they were accustomed to trade. Early in the thirteenth century the masters grouped themselves into a *Universitas Medicorum*, the precursor of the famous Medical School where centuries later François Rabelais came from his native Touraine, and Michel Nostradamus the astrologer from Provence, to study the healing art and where both learnt many things besides. Faculties of Arts and Law were soon added, and in 1289 a bull of Nicholas IV recognized the University of

Montpellier, the third oldest in France after Paris and Toulouse. When it ceased to be a commercial city Montpellier became primarily a centre of learning, and such it has remained until the recent resurgence of its commercial life. Wine has been its major concern through the centuries, but now metallurgic, pharmaceutical and textile industries have come to the fore, and Montpellier is altogether a strategically-placed trading centre.

There are no medieval churches in the town, except for the restored nave of the Cathedral, for they were all destroyed in the sixteenth-century Wars of Religion, which raged as bitterly here as anywhere in the Midi. (In compensation there is an interesting modern church, noted for its stained glass and its mosaics, **St Thérèse de l'Enfant Jésus** in the Avenue d'Assas in the north-western suburbs. Follow the Rue Pitot or the Rue du Carré du Roi between the Peyrou and the Jardin des Plantes.) Architecturally speaking, Montpellier is a creation of the *Grand Siècle*. After peace was restored in 1622, the number of noblemen's *hôtels* soon came to rival Aix, for it was about this time that the seat of the States-General was definitely transferred here from Pézenas. The States-General was composed of twenty-two prelates, the same number of barons and forty-four deputies from the towns. Most of these grandees naturally felt it incumbent upon them to build luxurious houses in Montpellier.

The *hôtels* of Montpellier do not, generally speaking, present the same attraction to the casual stroller as those of Aix or Pézenas, for many of them resemble Arab palaces in presenting a blank wall to the street. Through the main door one passes through a vaulted passage to the central courtyard and only then sees the façade itself, which probably screens a great frescoed staircase, filling the far side of this inner patio. Streets particularly noted for their *hôtels* are the Rue de l'Argenterie, near the Hôtel St Côme (Nos. 3 and 8), the Rue de Valfère (Nos. 5 and 6), the Rue Jacques Cœur (Nos. 4 and 16) and the Rue de Cannau (Nos. 1, 3, 6 and 8). No. 8, the Hôtel Deydé, is the work of the noted architect d'Aviler and is typical of the new style he introduced when he returned to his native Montpellier in 1691.

Italian influence was paramount in the Montpellier *hôtels* of the seventeenth century and many of them bore a close family resemblance to the palaces of Rome and Genoa. Columns, pilasters and entablatures were all the vogue. Elaborate stucco decorations framed allegorical paintings by such local artists as Antoine Ranc and Jean de Troy. With the arrival of d'Aviler the classical orders disappeared and gave place to flattened arches (called after him *davilertes*) and a lighter, looser style. The Hôtel Deydé is one of the earliest examples of the new look. Typical of the older style is the handsome Hôtel St Côme in a little square just west of the Grande Rue Jean Moulin. Built for the College of Surgeons and now the Chamber of Commerce, it is easy of access, as is the Hôtel Richer-Belleval, now the Hôtel de Ville. In fact, these *hôtels* are not as a rule difficult to get into in return for a tip to the concierge, for they are mostly broken up into offices and apartments.

The **Hôtel de Lunaret** at No. 5 Rue des Trésoriers de France is particularly well worth a visit, with a façade of two superimposed colonnades facing its inner courtyard. There is a splendid staircase with a ceiling by Jean de Troy, showing the Discovery of Truth by Justice. It has been made into the Archaeological Museum.[1] It contains, in addition to its archaeological collections, examples of local folklore and, surprisingly enough, the well-known double portrait of Gabrielle d'Estrées and her sister, of the School of Fontainebleau.

The great pride and glory of Montpellier is the **Musée Fabre**,[2] which is reckoned by French connoisseurs to be not only the best picture-gallery in the Midi but to rank second only to the Musée des Beaux Arts at Lille among French provincial galleries. It is very easy to find, for a short distance along the Boulevard Sarrail, which borders the Esplanade, a sign points up the Rue Montpelliéret saying 'Musée Fabre'. The Museum occupies the former Hôtel de Massilian, where Moliére played a season in 1655.

Its origins are decidedly romantic. The painter, François Xavier Fabre, a pupil of David, was in Rome when the French Revolution broke out and very prudently decided to remain there. In Rome he had the good fortune to succeed the deceased Italian poet Alfieri in the favours of the Countess of Albany, widow of Charles James Stuart, whom the Jacobites styled Charles III of England. Together with the quasi-royal lady of Alfieri's heart he inherited also his valuable collection of pictures and books. The poet had bequeathed everything to the Countess, and she in due course left it to Fabre. He returned to Montpellier after the Restoration and in 1825 presented his great collection to his native city. Other munificent gifts and bequests, notably those of Valedau, Bruyas and Bazille, were added from time to time. The rich Albany and Alfieri libraries, which Fabre also presented to Montpellier, are in the Bibliothèque de la Ville next door on the corner of the Boulevard Sarrail.

1. Visits on Saturday afternoons by prior arrangement with the Société Archéologique, 11 Rue Rondelet.
2. Closed on Mondays and on public holidays.

In this magnificent museum the contents of the ground floor consist mainly of sculpture, although *salles* are devoted to the works of Fabre himself and of Alexandre Cabanel, like him a native of Montpellier. There is a whole roomful of Houdons, including the famous marble statues of Summer and Winter (better known to the French as *La Frileuse*, which means both 'the shivering girl' and 'the head shawl' she is wearing). His marble and terracotta busts include heads of Voltaire, Jean Jacques Rousseau and Benjamin Franklin. In cases surrounding sculptures by Maillol, Bourdelle and Despiau is an entire menagerie of little bronze animals by Barye.

The first room one comes to on mounting the stairs is devoted to modern painting. Utrillo and Othon Friesz are particularly well represented. There is an interesting early Matisse and an attractive self-portrait by Berthe Morisot. For me the outstanding picture in the room is a gouache by Caillebotte, 'Portrait of Madame X'. Next to the modern room is the Salle de Bazille, which contains eight pictures by Frédéric Bazille, a young man from Montpellier (born in the Hôtel Perier, 11 Grand-Rue Jean Moulin, the most delightful of old Montpellier's streets), who was a friend of the Impressionists and who figures among them in the *Jeu de Paume*. He was killed in the Franco-Prussian War at the early age of twenty-nine. While there are signs in two or three of the pictures here (for example, 'The Negress with the Peonies', the 'View of Castelnau' and 'The Toilet') that he might well have become a lesser Manet or at least a Tissot, there is little real evidence to show that a genius in his prime was carried off by a German bullet – such as might easily have been the case if Paul Cézanne had not hidden ignominiously under the bed when they came to fetch him and take him off to the War.

The gallery following contains the superb collection of Alfred Bruyas, a wealthy and discriminating patron as well as a personal friend of the best painters of his time. This red-bearded narcissist seems to have had a curious passion for being painted. (He once had himself depicted by Verdier as Christ, wearing a crown of thorns.) There are seventeen portraits of him in the Musée Fabre. Seven of them hang on the walls of the Galerie Bruyas, one by Delacroix, two by Glaize and four by Courbet, who represents him as an odd cross between Garibaldi and D. H. Lawrence. Undoubtedly the thirteen Courbets and the eight Delacroix are the highlights of the collection, if not indeed of the whole museum. There is Courbet's famous self-portrait, 'The Man with the Pipe', and the brilliantly-lit portrait of Baudelaire. There is, above all, that gayest of pictures, 'The Meeting', or *'Bonjour, Monsieur Courbet'*, in which Courbet, with his beard jutting like a battering-ram, his great staff in his hand and his painting gear strapped to his back, is walking along a country road when he meets – whom in the world but Alfred Bruyas? Other masterpieces in a room crammed with them are Delacroix's 'Mulattress', Ingres's 'Stratonice', one of his last works, a very unidealized portrait of Byron, painted 'warts and all' by Géricault, and a 'Portrait of Monsieur Joubert' by J. L. David, curiously modern in technique.

From the nineteenth-century French painters we move backwards to a large and crowded room of eighteenth-century French painters. (Thinking it over, I suppose I must have always done the Museum backwards on the several occasions when I have been there by starting with the moderns, going through the nineteenth and eighteenth centuries and finishing with the primitives.) Few of the pictures in this room are of the first water, but just by the door is Madame Vigée-Lebrun's portrait of the young Grand Duchess Elizabeth Alexievna, which seems to stand out all the more triumphantly and with all the greater integrity in comparison with the ten sickly Greuzes which jostle the Vernets and the Natoires on the crowded walls. Of a breathtaking simplicity, it shows a slim fair girl dressed in cool whites and greys and leaning against a red cushion, the only touch of vivid colour in the picture. Notice how exquisitely and with what careful art the lines of the silk shawl and the dress are arranged.

From here we move into the Galerie Fabre proper, which consists mostly of Italian pictures from the Alfieri Collection. They tend, naturally enough, to reflect the taste of Alfieri's time, which is not that of ours – Carlo Dolci, Salvator Rosa, Guercino, Guido Reni and the like. But there is a resplendent 'Mystic Marriage of St Catherine' by Paolo Veronese, a singularly sadistic 'Massacre at Hippo' by Palma Giovane and a delightful picture of the Lombard School, where Leda, with uplifted finger, seems to be reminding the Swan that he had promised to behave himself like a gentleman. I was nostalgically pleased to come on a Florentine picture still labelled *École d'Amico di Sandro*, a shadowy painter whom Bernard Berenson created and then himself destroyed in the nineteen-twenties. (The Florentine wits of the time, I remember, were busy inventing painters with names like Amico d'Ignoto and Amico de Nessuno.) The French pictures include a portrait of Fontenelle by Rigaud and a self-portrait by Largillière. On the whole, however, if I were told I could take away one picture from the Galerie Fabre to live with, it would not be any of the French or Italians but a delightful Zurbarán on the left-hand wall of the vestibule. Across the canvas trips a gay, pert little St Agatha, carrying her breasts, the symbols of her martyrdom, on a dish in front of her for all the world like a waitress told to bring two halves of lemon.

On the left of the vestibule a series of small rooms contain the Valedau Bequest of 1836. Consisting mainly of Flemish, Dutch and German paintings, it includes a couple of Breughels and nine Teniers. The British School is represented by four works. Three of them are by Richard Parkes Bonington, that astonishing young man who practically never painted a bad picture in his short life and seems to be represented in half the picture-galleries of France as well as of England. And yet he died when he was even younger than Bazille! The fourth of the English quartet is indeed a shock to come upon unexpectedly in remote Montpellier. Familiar in reproduction since one's childhood, it had never occurred to one to wonder where the original was. It is here – Sir Joshua Reynolds's 'Infant Samuel in Prayer', no less.

In the autumn of 1970, the Musée Fabre was raided and thieves got away with sixteen paintings, all of which were recovered undamaged three weeks later.

From the north-west side of the Place de la Comédie the main artery of the town, the Rue de la Loge, where the Grande Loge des Marchands once stood, runs up to the Place des Martyrs de la Résistance. Thence the Rue Foch leads at an angle to finish at the **Porte du Peyrou**, the great Triumphal Arch erected by d'Aviler in 1691 to celebrate the triumphs of Louis XIV. The bas-reliefs represent his victories over the English and the Austrians, the capture of Namur, the cutting of the Canal des Deux Mers and that worst of all his blunders, the Revocation of the Edict of Nantes. Outside is the entrance to the Peyrou, a wide, raised promenade crowning the highest point of Montpellier. Begun by d'Aviler, it was finally completed by Jean Antoine Giral only in 1776. In the centre rises an enormous equestrian statue of Louis XIV. The Peyrou ends in an ornamental basin and Giral's handsome *château d'eau*, a hexagonal building supported by Corinthian columns. It admirably solves the aesthetic problem of bringing the water supply into the town, for it is the terminal of a long aqueduct modelled on the Pont du Gard. It is said that from the raised terrace or belvedere behind the *château d'eau* one can on a clear morning see both Mont Ventoux, the nearest peak of the Alpine system, and the Canigou, the easternmost bulwark of the Pyrenees.

On the north side of the Promenade du Peyrou is the oldest botanical garden in France, the **Jardin des Plantes**[1] created by a decree of Henri IV in 1593 and enlarged in the nineteenth century. One of the most important scientific gardens in Southern Europe, it contains a number of rare and acclimatized trees and plants. Even if one is not oneself a botanist, there are delightful shady walks and corners to stroll in, in the cool of a summer's evening. The part behind the orangery known as La Montagne reproduces the flora of the *garrigues* of Languedoc. Near the orangery also a marble plaque bears the Latin inscription *Placandis Narcissae Manibus*. It is said that in the mid-eighteenth century the English poet Edward Young brought his consumptive daughter Narcissa to Montpellier in the vain hope that the change of climate might save her life. She continued in her decline, however, and, when she died, was buried in the beautiful garden she loved. It was a hundred years later that three romantic young students formed a habit of meeting at this deliciously melancholy spot. Their names were Paul Valéry, André Gide and Pierre Louys.

In front of the Gardens, on the Boulevard Henri IV, is the only surviving bastion of the medieval ramparts. It bears a modern inscription, written in the medieval *langue d'oc*, commemorating the birth here in 1208 of King Jayme I of Aragon – which was a more important event than it might at first appear. Montpellier had for centuries been ruled by a local feudal dynasty, the Guilhems, until the Lordship passed to Aragon in 1204 by the marriage of the last Guilhem heiress, Marie, to King Pedro of Aragon. The story goes that he deserted her two years later and she retired to the country. The consuls of Montpellier, understandably worried about the succession, plotted to reconcile the royal pair. They caught the King in a good humour after a successful hunting party. He readily agreed to meet his wife and, touched by her sadness, took her on the crupper of his horse, while the people danced round them for joy. Sure enough, a son, this same Jayme, was born to them a year later and the succession was secured. Up to our own times the happy event has been celebrated every year in Montpellier by the *danse du chevalet*, when white-clad dancers, wearing plumed and beribboned hats, danced round a man on a hobby-horse.

The people of Montpellier had better reason to dance round their king than they knew, for it was only the fact that Montpellier was an

1. Open daily; the glasshouses and orangerie are closed on Saturday afternoons and Sundays. Guided visits can be arranged through the Director, 5 Rue Auguste-Broussonet.

Aragonese possession which saved it from the horrors of the Albigensian Crusade, shortly to ravage Languedoc. When in 1262 Aragon was divided between the sons of Jayme I, the Seigneurie of Montpellier became part of the Kingdom of Majorca, and such it remained until Jayme III, hard pressed for cash, sold it to King Philip of France in 1349 for 120,000 gold crowns. Thenceforth, like the rest of Languedoc, it remained an integral part of France.

A little further down the Boulevard Henri IV is the famous **Medical School**, which in the Middle Ages was the Abbey of St Benedict. Later, it was the Archbishop's Palace and, under the Revolution, a political prison. The library possesses over three hundred thousand books, theses and periodicals. Of its six hundred and twenty-four manuscripts, many date from the eighth and ninth centuries. On the first floor is the Musée Atger, a collection of over three hundred drawings collected by Xavier Atger and bequeathed to the University in 1833. They are mainly the work of Southern artists such as Puget, who also has two sculptures, Mignard, the Parrocels, Rigaud, Bourdon, Vernet and Van Loo. Arrangements to see round can be made with the caretaker.

Next door to the Medical School is the **Cathedral**. Its characteristic feature is the pair of curious, conical, semi-detached turrets which form its porch. Only one is medieval. The other was destroyed by the Protestants in 1567, and its fall brought down the façade of the Cathedral with it. There is nothing of much interest in the interior. The Cathedral was originally the chapel of St Benedict's Abbey and was raised to its present rank when the See was transferred to Montpellier from Maguelone in 1536. Montpellier is spreading its urban tentacles out into the *garrigue*, and absorbing villages which once led an independent existence. One such is Castelnau which appears in one of Frédéric Bazille's chief paintings in the Musée Fabre. A whole new town of thirty thousand inhabitants has risen at Montpellier-la-Paillade on the banks of the Mosson river.

Of excursions out of Montpellier there are many, and the one to Maguelone, some eight miles away among lagoons and sandpits, is well worth-while.

Maguelone, in the Middle Ages the port of Montpellier, was a bishopric as far back as the third century, but it never fully recovered from its destruction by Charles Martel. Bishop Arnaud rebuilt and fortified the Cathedral in 1030. In the twelfth century the Pope himself sought refuge here from his enemies and raised it to the rank of a major basilica. But Maguelone was very exposed and insecure, and its inhabitants gradually melted away to Montpellier. The end came in 1633 when Louis XIII, to drive out the Protestant population, demolished the fortifications and pulled down the remaining houses.

Today only the Romanesque **Cathedral** stands in a park of pine trees on the little hill crowning the peninsula, which was the property of the Fabrège family of Montpellier. They restored the Cathedral in the nineteenth century; since the death of Mlle Fabrège the diocese of Montpellier has acquired and maintains it. The custodian lives just opposite the façade, and the church is open every day. The building is as much a fortress as a church, with enormously thick walls pierced rather haphazardly by loop-holes and crowned by machicolations. The single-arched nave, where a Pope once used to say mass, is of impressive proportions and there are recesses for stalls which once held seventy-two canons.

Maguelone was formerly an islet but now a spit of sand and tamarisks carries a bad road to the tunny-fishing village of Palavas two or three miles away. This is the only way by which Maguelone can be approached. Near the entrance to Palavas, turn right through a rather desolate-looking camping site, and continue on the rough track for about two-and-a-half miles. Palavas-les-Flots is the seaside resort of Montpellier at the mouth of the little River Lez, which cuts it in two. Further north along the coast is the growing *plage* of Carnon, and beyond that the road leads on between the sea and the sand-dunes to Le Grau-du-Roi, Aigues Mortes and so on to Arles.

The whole coast from the mouth of the Rhône down as far as Collioure, which has now been labelled for touristic purposes *La Côte Dorée* and *La Côte Vermeille*, is a hundred-and-forty-mile stretch of sandy beach. The flat coastal plain is broken only by small hills at Sète and Agde. Behind the shore stretches a long series of shallow, brackish lagoons or *étangs* left behind by the receding sea, so that sometimes the beaches are little more than sandspits – or *barres*, as they are locally known. They have been formed, mostly within historic times, by the quantities of silt brought down by the Rhône and washed inshore by the south-westerly currents. There are a score of little, newly-built, whitewashed seaside resorts on this coast, each very much like the other. They are fairly inexpensive, for the accommodation is simple (they consist mainly of summer villas belonging to residents of the neighbouring towns together with a few pensions) but nearly all, with such few exceptions as La Tamarissière near Agde, suffer from a lack of shade. Nevertheless, they offer distinct possibilities for people who simply want sun and sand

and sea and to get right away from the sound of their own language for a while. I knew some people who spent a very happy holiday, for example, at Canet-Plage near Perpignan in the days when the Languedoc-Roussillon coast was still almost *terra incognita*.

Now, the transformation of this coast is in full swing. In 1963, the French government decided to create six holiday 'units', first bringing fresh water, improving road communications, and draining stagnant lagoons which had had more than their fair share of mosquitoes for centuries. At the same time, a vast programme of anti-mosquito spraying took place, and although naturalists are not entirely happy about the balance of nature in consequence, at least the ordinary visitor to Languedoc in summer is little troubled by *moustiques*.

Of the six *unités* originally planned, one, l'Embouchure de l'Aude, has been abandoned, at least for the present. The other five are La Grande-Motte (which embraces Port Camargue, Grau-du-Roi, Carnon and Palavas, the last three of which have been long established); Le Cap d'Agde (with Sète, and Bassin de Thau and Marseillan which lie a little inland); Gruissan (with Valréas, St Pierre-sur-Mer and Narbonne-Plage); Leucate-Barcarès, the largest of the units; and St Cyprien (with Canet-Plage and Argelès). Before their development could be started, a trunk route through Bas-Languedoc had to be made to relieve the historic, slow highway through the town centres, Route Nationale 113. Autoroute 9 is now complete. Access roads to the coast are being created or improved, and pure water has been brought to this parched region by tapping the Rhône and other rivers.

First to be catered for have been the yachtsmen. Eight thousand moorings in safe harbours, and all the necessary appurtenances, have been provided, though the landlubber, looking on, may be allowed to wonder when all those boats bobbing at their moorings actually leave harbour and go sailing.

Architects and aesthetes have already levelled criticism – inevitably so – but at least they cannot deny the architectural variety which imposes a distinct character to each unit. **La Grande-Motte**'s pyramidal, ziggurat-like suntrap buildings have been much photographed, for this was the first complex to be started. Many people find the place pretentious, its layout of harbours, villas, apartments, hotels, restaurants and shops emanating a cold, soulless persona. They prefer **Cap d'Agde**, perhaps, where there is more colour, charm and a human scale of things. Cap d'Agde has been fortunate in that its site is more interesting than most along this flat coast; both its cliffs and beach are volcanic. Now, the yacht harbours, hotels, motels, nautels, flats, and an amphitheatrical naturist colony (to rival the one on Île du Levant, and one at Port-Leucate, the Village Aphrodite), crowd down to the sea's edge and make the old coastline and lagoons unrecognizable.

At **Le Barcarès** is the unexpected sight of the liner *Lydia* anchored on the sands, functioning as a casino and night-club, and adjoining a three-star hotel.

St Cyprien, in addition to its holiday installations that include two eighteen-hole golf courses, tennis courts, swimming pool, riding establishment and country club, boasts a Maillol statue, *La Baigneuse à la draperie*, at the beach end of the wide Avenue Maillol. Moreover, the town hall contains some modern paintings by François Desnoyers, the influential founder of the 'Montpellier-Sète Group'. He has presented the new town with more of his works, and these are on show in a newly-created museum.

Gruissan, an enchanting old circular village with a ruined keep rising at its centre, three parts lapped by the lagoon, has been left intact, but is surrounded, a little incongruously, by pleasure-craft.

Cynics may see all this as a way of tempting tourists from less expensive Spain, as pandering to France's affluent middle-class and her *jeunesse dorée* craving novelty, and as a bait for foreign capital. This 'French Florida', say its opponents, is only a modern kind of colonial exploitation. It remains a hard fact, however, that if this coast had been left to its own fragmented and unbridled devices, it would have become an ugly, uncontrolled rash of shacks, shanties and pestilential lagoons filling with garbage.

This ambitious Languedoc-Roussillon scheme is more than just the development of the potentials of a tourist area. It seeks to re-fashion the whole environment that, for so long having lacked ecological balance, is to be made more fully productive through reforestation, diversification of agriculture, green belts and nature reserves. It is too early to judge whether the natural elements of the scheme will prove successful. For that, we shall have to wait for trees to reach maturity in this shadeless strip of land.

The development plan may in due course direct its attention inland. For the present, ancient Languedoc survives in its oceans of vineyards in the plains, its cereals, forests and Nature Reserve in the Cévennes foothills, its medieval villages and Romanesque churches, the tranquil towpaths of the Canal du Midi, the bony landscapes of eroded limestone ridges that await the patient traveller.

Lawrence Durrell, a resident of Languedoc, has conjured the

essence of the inland region in four lines of poetry:

> The horizon like some keystone between soil and air
> Halves out all earth in quiet satisfaction,
> In tones of dust or biscuit, particularly kind to
> Loaves of the sunburnt soil the plough turned back . . .

Chapter 26

Béziers

❧

Pézenas – Sète – Agde – Béziers – Ensérune

In Languedoc travellers are fewer than in Provence, and most of them are not dallying but hurrying through to or from Spain. The existence of comfortable hotels, therefore, cannot be taken for granted as easily as it can in Provence. They exist, however, in Montpellier and Perpignan, and my advice to a traveller who values his ease and does not mind a difference of a few francs on his bill is to reserve a room in the Grand Hôtel at Perpignan or the Métropole at Montpellier; to make sure of striking Narbonne when the Cathedral and the Museum are open (which in summer is every day up to six, except, of course, for the two hours of *déjeuner* from twelve to two); and to lunch at Béziers in one of the several good small restaurants in the Allées Paul Riquet, the principal boulevard of the town.

There are alternative ways from Montpellier to Béziers. The inland route runs through **Pézenas**, a town which is surprisingly little known for all that it lies on the main old road to Spain and is possibly unique in Southern France. (There are seventy-seven buildings classified by the Beaux Arts.) The entire old quarter of the little town has been petrified by time, and the clock has stopped dead in the days of Louis Seize. The town houses of the Occitanian lords, which range in date from the fourteenth to the seventeenth century, remain as they were built and lived in, with their sculptured doors, wrought-iron balconies, courtyards and staircases intact. The Syndicat d'Initiative, justifying the name for once, has provided an itinerary of the main sights, starting from the Place du 14 Juillet (just off the main road, with parking for cars), numbered to correspond with the guide which it has brought out and distributes free. Near the Maison des Consuls is the **Musée de Vulliod-Saint-Germain**[1], with local archives going back to the tenth century and a room dedicated to Molière who, attracted by the gay and cultured society of this little local Aix, spent several winters here. He lived in the house of Gély

1. Closed on Tuesdays and Fridays.

the barber in the square in front of the Maison des Consuls, where the Estates of Languedoc used to meet in the days when Pézenas was once the co-capital with Montpellier. In Gély's barber shop he could study at his leisure the aristocrats whom he put into his plays. His patron, Prince Armand de Bourbon-Conti, was the Governor of Languedoc, and Molière staged his comedies in the Hôtel Alphonce, which one can visit today. It cannot be said that any of these *hôtels* are very remarkable in themselves but the number of them in so small a place, their homogeneity (for they are all built of the same grey stone) and the absence of any additions or alterations since the eighteenth century lends Pézenas a peculiar character of its own. It had already been discovered by cinema directors as a setting for historical films of the Ancien Régime and the Revolution.

The other road to Béziers leads down to **Sète**, the second port of the French Mediterranean. It is a bustling harbour town, built originally in the seventeenth century as the eastern terminal of Paul Riquet's Canal du Midi or Canal des Deux Mers, which connects the Atlantic with the Mediterranean. Riquet cut a canal through the sandbar which separated the Étang de Thau from the sea, and the *ville neuve* of Sète is built on several islands, divided by unexpected pieces of water where ships moor practically in the streets. It is the port through which the Hérault exports a great part of its enormous output of six hundred million litres of wine a year. (Since a litre corresponds to a large bottle, that is quite a lot of wine.) In fact, the main liquid to pass through the port is hydrocarbon, for industrial expansion is taking place to the east of the town, taking in Balaruc and Frontignan. The Bassin Nouveau can take large vessels, and lines run from Sète to Africa and the Far East. The Vieux Port is the most colourful and lively part of the town, for it is the harbour reserved for the fishing boats and on the quays the fishermen sort out their catch. Sète is the biggest fishing port on the Mediterranean and most of the fish eaten on the Côte d'Azur, especially the sardines, the mackerel and the tunny, is caught there. Bouzigues and Marseillan on the Étang de Thau are famous for their beds of oysters and mussels – excellent with the local white wine of Frontignan.

Sète is the birthplace of Paul Valéry, and his well-known poem, *Le Cimetière Marin*, is written about the cemetery here in Sète on the slopes of Mont St Clair, where he himself is buried. On his tomb is carved a couplet from *Le Cimetière Marin*:

> O récompense après une pensée
> Qu'un long regard sur le calme des dieux!

The Pont du Gard, one of the finest and highest Roman aqueducts in existence

Carcassonne

In 1970 the **Musée Paul Valéry**[1] was moved from Place Victor Hugo to a modern building just north of Valéry's *Cimetière Marin* (actually, the Cimetière St Charles), and looking out to sea. It contains a room devoted to the poet, with original manuscripts, rare editions, drawings and photographs. There is a good bust of him by Renée Vautier-Amyot in the Musée Fabre at Montpellier. In addition, the museum has a good collection of etchings by Cézanne, Bazille, Manet and Renoir, as well as a wide range of paintings, from Courbet and Monticelli to the modern Provençal artists, Ambrogiani and Baboulène.

August is the month when the Languedoc jousting tourneys take place. On the Feast of St Louis, Sète makes merry with a joust on the Grand Canal; at Palavas, they joust on the sea by both day and night, with fireworks to enhance the fun. Agde, too, puts on these antique water-jousts which had their origin in the sixteenth century. Eight men row each boat. On a platform at the stern, a jouster tries to topple his adversary on the other boat into the sea with a long lance which he aims at the other man's shield.

Southwards from Sète the road runs beside a seven-mile beach of sand as far as **Agde** (which rhymes with Magda). One of the first colonies founded by the Greeks of Marseilles, Agathé, as it was then called – the Good Place – is one of the oldest towns in France. Its main feature is the Cathedral, a fortified building of the twelfth century, complete with crenellations, *mâchicoulis* and a square donjon-like tower constructed, like the neighbouring buildings, of a black basaltic lava which makes it look even more sinister. It comes from the extinct volcano of Mont St Loup, at whose foot Agde is built. The round hole in the roof of the nave, where a chandelier now hangs, was designed for times of siege so that the defenders on the roof could communicate with the refugees huddled inside and haul up food and ammunition. Catholics and Protestants alike took refuge here during the Wars of Religion.

The Cathedral abuts on the Quai du Chapitre, where boats moor in the River Hérault and where one can almost forget the grim, black, turreted castle of a cathedral on its peaceful tree-shaded banks. In the old quarter is a little regional museum, the Musée Agathois,[2] of the personal kind so often found in France, for it was founded in 1935 by its present curator. It specializes in the local costume, and in particular the *sarret*, the traditional head-dress of the Agathoises. From Agde two roads lead to the sea; the one down the right bank of the Hérault to La Tamarissière with its camping grounds under

1. Closed on Tuesdays.   2. Ring the bell.

the pines, and the other down the left bank to the sandy beaches of Le Grau d'Agde.

Béziers should ideally be approached from Narbonne and not from Montpellier, for the traveller from the south comes quite suddenly upon the fortified Cathedral of St Nazaire, which crowns a perpendicular bluff overlooking the River Orb. Of this impressive and magnificent sight the voyager coming from the north sees nothing. There is an almost equally striking view from the terrace of the Cathedral itself, looking over the soft vineyard country rolling unbroken out to the low hills on the horizon, green in the summer, gold and red in the autumn and gnarled and naked in the winter. Béziers is the second city of the Hérault, which produces fifteen per cent of the total wine production of France. On Friday afternoons you may watch the wine-sales in the Allées Riquet, the growers all neatly dressed in their best black broadcloth suits.

The Gothic **Cathedral** dates from the end of the thirteenth century and must be visited if only for the seven lovely stained-glass windows at its east end. The list of Bishops of Béziers in a chapel off the right transept is worthy of study for anyone interested in history. From 1576 to 1659 the bishopric seems to have been practically hereditary, held by five bishops of the de Bonzi family. (There is a portrait by Domenichino of one of them, Cardinal Jean de Bonzi, in the Musée Fabre at Montpellier – the tough, shrewd, down-to-earth face one would expect.) Even more revealing is the thirteenth-century portion of the record, which reflects the Albigensian troubles of the period. In 1212 there were no fewer than three Bishops of Béziers, while in the fifth decade two others are mysteriously listed as 'R . . . . 1242. P . . . . 1245'.

It was in 1209 that the Massacre of Béziers took place when the Catholics killed the entire population, and Arnald Amalric, the Legate, reported to the Pope that 'nearly twenty thousand of the citizens were put to the sword, regardless of age and sex'. The Albigenses were a religious sect so heretical that it is only by stretching language that they can be called Christians at all. They were practically a rival religion. For them everything centred round the problem of evil. They reconciled the existence of an almighty and all-merciful God with the miserable state of humanity as they saw it in actual fact to be only by supposing that the world was created not by Him but by the Devil. However reasonable this hypothesis may be it can hardly be called a Christian one. They rejected the Eucharist and all other sacraments except laying on of hands, the Old Testament, images, churches, worship and even the symbol of the Cross itself, although they had no name for themselves except simply 'Christians'. They believed the world which Satan had made after his expulsion from Heaven was, in fact, purgatory. Their opponents used to harry them and burn them alive to show them just how wrong they were.

The Cathars, to use the correct word, stemmed originally from the third-century gnostics of Alexandria but, moving across into Asia, where they became known as Manicheans from their prophet Manes, their doctrines became blended with Zoroastrian Dualism and the eternal struggle between the two principles of Light and Darkness. They were almost as near to being Parsees as Christians. Moving westwards through Armenia under the name of Paulicians, through the Balkans as Bogomils, and through Lombardy as Patarenes, they made a large number of converts in Languedoc, where they were known as Albigensians. They enjoyed the protection of the local feudal lords, notably the young Raymond Roger Trencavel, Viscount of Carcassonne and Béziers, and his powerful overlord, Count Raymond VI of Toulouse.

In 1208 the Pope proclaimed a crusade against them and in the following year his Crusaders attacked Béziers, for Raymond Roger Trencavel had made himself a marked man. Summoned to suppress his heretics, he had answered defiantly: 'I offer a city, a roof, a refuge, a loaf of bread and my sword to all the outcast men who will soon be wandering through the country, without a city, nor a roof, nor a refuge, nor bread.' His brave and generous words were to cost his people dear. Béziers was taken by storm. The unarmed population, half Catholic and half Albigensian, sought refuge in the churches. 'How shall we distinguish between the Catholics and the heretics?' asked the soldiers. 'Kill them all. God will know his own,' replied the genocidal Abbot of Cîteaux, Legate of the Pope. Even if Caesarius of Heisterbach's story be apocryphal, it represents the ferocious spirit of the Crusade. There is no record of a single man, woman or child, Catholic or Albigensian, escaping with their life from Béziers. Seven thousand were said by a contemporary historian of the Crusade to have been slaughtered in the Church of the Madeleine alone, where the present-day market is, on that fateful July 22, 1209.

The great Cours Paul Riquet, named after the son of Béziers who built the Canal du Midi and the port of Sète in the seventeenth century, is five hundred yards long, with four rows of plane trees and an esplanade in the middle, like the Ramblas of Barcelona and Tarragona, and it is the first reminder that we are very soon approaching Catalonia.

211

There are two small museums near the Cathedral. The Musée des Beaux Arts,[1] Place de la Révolution, contains Greek vases, a portrait by Hans Holbein the Younger, another portrait by Roger van der Weyden, and some paintings of the Italian and Dutch schools. There are also portraits by Delacroix and Géricault and a small Goya. To see Goyas one must take the road inland to Castres, whose museum contains half a dozen (including the largest picture the master ever painted, 'The Council of the Philippines'). From Castres the road leads on to Albi, famous alike for its great fortified cathedral and its Museum of Toulouse-Lautrec.

The Musée du Vieux Biterrois,[2] 7 Rue Massol, is the regional folklore museum, with a special section on winegrowing. This museum's importance has grown because of additions to its marine archaeology collection. Most of the objects on view come from wrecks which have been explored off Cap d'Agde, a veritable graveyard for ships in olden days on account of the 'Greek wind' – *le grec* or *le marin* – which dashed them on the rocks. Many Greek, Roman and Etruscan amphorae, anchors, copper and lead ingots, as well as various articles found in the wreck of an eighteenth-century warship, can be seen.

Under the same roof is the Historical Museum which contains the Mouret Collection of vases dating from between the ninth and third centuries BC from Ensérune, ten miles outside Béziers.

On the summit of the hill of Ensérune (from which one is sometimes rewarded with a handsome view of the sea, the Cévennes and the Canigou – even though Ensérune rises less than four hundred feet) are the remains of the only reasonably complete pre-Roman settlement in France. Archaeological research shows the site to have been occupied since the sixth century BC, possibly longer. In the third century BC, this *oppidum* had a population of some 8,000 to 10,000. The **National Museum of Ensérune**[3] houses the arms, jewels, coins and ceramics (from Neolithic to Greek times) found close by. In one room the different types of tombs and their contents have been reconstructed.

1. Closed on Mondays, Sunday mornings, January 1, over Easter and Whitsun July 14, November 1, 2 and 11.
2. Closed on Mondays and public holidays.
3. Open daily between Easter and September 30; closed on Tuesdays during the rest of the year.

Chapter 27

Narbonne

ᴪ

The Cathedral – the Art Museum – the Archaeological Museum –
Montagne de la Clape – Abbey of Fontfroide – Minèrve

Not far from Béziers is Narbonne, which gave its name to the Roman province of Gallia Narbonensis and rivalled Lyons for the position of the first city of Roman Gaul. The barbarians did their work thoroughly. Nothing remains of its forum, its theatre and its arena, its temples, baths and palaces, except broken stones in museums. Of Roman Narbonne there exists only the single arch of a bridge, now built over with shops and houses like old London Bridge, which can be seen from the Cours Mirabeau spanning the Robine Canal. Before the gulf became silted up to form a lagoon, Narbonne was a flourishing port, and the troubadour Bertrand de Bar sang of 'the great ships with iron nails and the galleys laden with riches which create the wealth of the inhabitants of the good city'.

The Duke-Bishops of Narbonne were among the richest and most powerful prelates of France and bore such great names as Lorraine, d'Amboise, Beauvau and Crillon. They were ex-officio Presidents of the States General of Langudoc; their palace is said to have served as a model for the Palaces of the Popes at Avignon; and their **Cathedral**, had it ever been completed, would have ranked with the great Gothic fanes of Northern France. The foundation stone was sent from Rome by a former Archbishop of Narbonne, Pope Clement IV, but only the choir was actually built. Its height of a hundred and twenty feet is exceeded in all France by Amiens and Beauvais alone. This remarkable building towers above flat Narbonne like a fortress. Unfortunately its magnificent east end, with its wealth of pinnacles and flying buttresses, is masked by houses and can only be seen from neighbouring roof-tops and upper windows. It is best appreciated, believe it or not, from a picture postcard.

The interior, with its soaring vaults, must be as high as it is long and glows with lovely stained glass ranging in date from the thirteenth to the sixteenth century. There are some impressive tombs, notably the macabre monument of Cardinal Briçonnet. Below are the bones of dismembered skeletons, above are cowled monks and at the top cherubim alternate with death's heads. Most decidedly we are drawing ever nearer to Spain on our southward journey. In the first chapel of the right aisle is a remarkable group from Bavaria representing the Burial of Christ and dating from the beginning of the sixteenth century. It consists of nine life-sized figures in painted terracotta – Jesus, the three Marys, St John, two bearers and two flanking warriors. The sixteenth-century tapestries on the walls of the Cathedral add to the general atmosphere of subdued splendour. There are others in the Treasury to be seen by anyone clever enough to find the elusive sacristan who keeps the key.

Near the Cathedral is the Archbishop's Palace – or rather Palaces, for there is an Old Palace and a New Palace, not to mention Viollet-le-Duc's nineteenth-century Hôtel de Ville. In the New Palace were the state apartments of the Archbishops of Narbonne, now the **Musée d'Art et d'Histoire**,[1] worth the climb of eighty-eight steps up a monumental Louis XIII staircase. (The Archbishops went up on mules. The broad, low steps, up which they could ride, were the contemporary equivalent of an elevator.)

Religious sculptures in alabaster seem to have been almost the only English artistic export of the Middle Ages. I have come across them in places as far apart as Naples and Sigüenza, and there are three fourteenth-century Nottingham alabasters in this museum, a Scourging, a Crucifixion and a Burial of St Catherine. The Museum has one of the finest collections of ceramics in France, and the apartments in themselves give an idea of the state which these princes of the church kept during the Ancien Régime. The Archbishop's dining-room, with its elaborate stucco decorations of food and game, has a rich silver dinner-service laid out on the table. The French painters of the Midi, such as Mignard and Rigaud, are well represented. Provincial galleries are generally strong in portraiture and there are some good heads by David, Nattier and Greuze. For my taste the one which stands head and shoulders above the others is a 'Portrait of a Man' by Philippe de Champaigne.

If the Art Museum contains little of the very first class, the **Archaeological Museum**,[2] which one enters from the same courtyard in the Palace, is a 'must' for anyone who has not a most active

1. Open daily between May 15 and September 30; closed on Mondays during the rest of the year.
2. Open daily between May 15 and September 30; closed on Mondays for the rest of the year.

and positive allergy to flint implements. The Musée de la Préhistoire et des Antiquités narbonnaises, to give it its full title, traces the development of *homo narbonensis* from the earliest eoliths to the eve of the barbarian invasions. Cast aside all ideas of shelves filled with dusty bits of bone and flint. This museum is modern, beautifully arranged, well lit and clearly labelled. The doors are unlocked for each visitor and locked behind him, and he is tailed by a melancholy man in a cloth cap to make sure he does not smash a case and pocket an arrowhead – or at least he was when I last visited it just after the St Tropez robbery.

Beginning with animal bones and casts of footprints, the glass cases progress through objects hardly recognizable as artifacts at all to rude Paleolithic implements from Bize, La Crouzade and the other great caves of the Narbonnaise. On we travel in time through the New Stone Age, the workmanship getting finer all the while, to the earliest dawn of art, a crudely painted stone at the Azilian level. Then pottery is found, simple and plain at first and later elaborately decorated. We witness the beginning of surgery in the shape of a trepanned skull, with a neat round hole drilled in it. The first axeheads of imported jadeite mark the birth of commerce. In the Bronze and Iron Ages it is evident from their highly-developed ornaments, weapons and even vases that the local tribes carried on a vigorous trade with the Greeks. The last room of all is Roman. Do not miss the cippus with a homely scene of a donkey turning a mill, watched by a dog in front of the family altar; or the very curious carving of a man in his bath being attacked by a bear, whose intention baffled even the man in the cloth cap when I asked him.

The cream of what is left of Roman Narbonne has been skimmed off for this room. The rest is in the Lapidary Museum (same times of opening as for the Archaeological Museum), in the old Gothic church of Lamourguier. Thousands of broken stones and inscriptions are piled up in six rows, but the collection, though the largest in France, is of interest only to the specialist. Not far from the Lamourguier Church is the curious **Maison des Trois Nourrices**, where Cinq-Mars was arrested by Richelieu. It earned its name from a window supported by five (not three – the Narbonnais have miscounted) ample and corpulent Caryatids who reminded the townsfolk of wet-nurses.

A little further on the ancient Gothic **Church of St Paul** contains one of those rather mysterious ecclesiastical jokes. In a holy-water stoup near the door in the right aisle reposes a marble frog. The story is that on a high feast the frog tried to mingle its own uncouth

215

music with that of the lutes. Judged guilty of presumption rather than excess of piety, it was turned to stone and put into the basin.

The drive to Narbonne-Plage and Gruissan from Narbonne is one of the most attractive short runs on account of the calcareous ridge of the Montagne de la Clape which rises to some seven hundred feet, a rare eminence between here and the Rhône delta. It is reminiscent of a Palestinian landscape, dry, stony and rather wild in appearance. On the seaward side is another Cimetière Marin (as at Sète), dedicated to the sailors of Gruissan who have lost their lives at sea.

A drive along the lane by the side of Narbonne's nearest lagoon, the Étang de Bages, gives an intimate glimpse of the brilliant light and flat horizons that characterize the Languedoc coast. With any luck, you can see a colony of flamingoes feeding and cackling like geese close inshore.

A few miles west is the **Abbey of Fontfroide**,[1] at the entrance to a gorge. Founded in the eleventh century by Aymeri I, it became a Cistercian monastery in 1143. It has suffered the usual vicissitudes of suppression in 1791 and 1900, and for a quarter of a century has been slowly restored, so that it can now rival its sister-abbeys of Sénanque, Silvacane and Le Thoronet in Provence. Indeed, its cloister can lay claim to be the loveliest in the South of France.

Inland from Narbonne, you can look over a number of villages, such as Capestang, Ginestas or Olonzac, before entering the vine-patched slopes of the Minervois (whose wines are becoming better known in Britain). Buried deep in the Cesse canyon is **Minèrve**, a little fortress that suffered at the hands of Simon de Montfort in 1210 during the Albigensian Crusade. He destroyed the sole source of water and burned all the inhabitants. Minèrve's tiny church contains what is probably the oldest altar in Gaul; the date 456 appears on it. Recently, a little **Archaeology and Palaeontology Museum** has been opened, and it can be visited every day.

1. Guided visits daily.

Chapter 28

Carcassonne

✤

The Cité – the Château – the Walls – St Nazaire – Rennes-le-Château

The autoroute is the direct way from Narbonne to Perpignan, but the traveller should take a detour by way of Carcassonne, whence a picturesque road leads down to Perpignan through Quillan. It is an easy hour's run inland from Narbonne before the skyline is cloven by the walls and towers and turrets of Carcassonne.

To avoid being disillusioned later on, the visitor should be warned at the beginning that what he is looking at is the appearance of a great medieval fortress and not, for the most part, the actual stones of one. He has before his eyes the best restored, and not the most miraculously preserved, medieval city in Europe. A hundred years ago the Cité of Carcassonne, as it is called to distinguish it from the newer town of Carcassonne on the banks of the Aude, was a ring of crumbling walls and ruined towers like so many others. A decree for its demolition had already gone out (and the destruction actually begun of the Tour de Trésau, which had been sold for two hundred francs to the local hospital) when a local archaeologist, Cros-Mayrevieille, launched a successful movement not only to save it but to restore it.

In 1844 the task was entrusted to the famous architect Viollet-le-Duc, who restored the great Abbey of Vézelay in Burgundy and re-built the walls of Avignon. He raised the crumbling ramparts to their former height, re-erected the fallen towers and capped them with their original candle-snuffer turrets. He seems to have gone wrong on the roofing, by the way, for, on the assumption that the slate-using Northerners who built the towers would have used that material, he roofed them with slates, whereas modern experts have discovered evidence that they were really roofed with flat tiles. Be that as it may, he was an expert medievalist and on the whole did a very remarkable, if perhaps rather over-imaginative, job.

The ethics of restoration, of course, will remain an unending source of argument. The purists shudder at anything which goes be-

217

yond the very barest running repairs. Most people will probably feel that, out of the hundreds of ruined cities and castles of Europe, one of them could well be spared in order to display a perfect example of medieval military architecture belonging to a period when that art was at its apogee. Apart from those unfortunate slates, one is seeing, in all probability, exactly the sight which presented itself to the eyes of the Black Prince in 1355.

The picturesque legend, of the etymological character so popular in the Middle Ages, is that Carcassonne was being defended against Charlemagne by the Lady Carcas, widow of Balac, the last Saracen governor of the city. When, after a siege of five years, the town was on the verge of being starved out, Carcas ordered the last sack of grain to be fed to the last surviving pig. Then she had the bloated beast thrown over the battlements. It burst like a bomb, scattering all the grain among the Franks, who drew the intended deduction that there was no hope of starving out a garrison which fed grain to pigs. Charlemagne was in process of raising the siege, when a trumpet sounded for a parley, and the cry went up: 'Carcas sonne!' Charlemagne married the resourceful lady to Trencavel – 'Cleave well' – one of the bravest of his peers and bestowed on them the city as a wedding present.

That is the legend. (Very similar stories are told of ancient Rome and of sixth-century Perugia, besieged by Totila and his Goths.) In actual fact, the first place called 'Carcaso' was a fort belonging to the Arecomic Volcians, and the Trencavel dynasty only succeeded some time after Charlemagne. It was still ruling Carcassonne and Béziers when in 1209 the civilization of the troubadours was suddenly shattered for ever by the incursion of fifty thousand Northerners – Burgundians, Normans, Flemings and Germans – who, in the name of the Crusade, swept joyfully down to the loot of the South and the ruin of the Southern lords. After Béziers it was the turn of Carcassonne to be attacked. Raymond Roger was seized when on a parley under safe conduct, the leaderless city surrendered and, when the young Viscount died in captivity three months later (as prisoners were apt to do), the lordship of Carcassonne, won by treachery, was contemptuously refused in turn by the Duke of Burgundy and the Counts of Nevers and St Pol. Eventually it was accepted by the Crusader Simon de Montfort, father of that Simon de Montfort, Earl of Leicester, who led the English Barons against Henry III. As was later said of the missionaries in Hawaii, he came to do good and he did well.

After an abortive attempt by Raymond Roger Trencavel's son, a

protégé of King Pedro of Aragon, to recover the city in 1240, St
Louis razed the suburbs, which had declared for their rightful prince,
but seven years later he allowed their inhabitants to return and build
the Ville Basse on the far bank of the Aude. It was laid out chequer-
board-fashion like Aigues Mortes and all the towns built in the late
Middle Ages. (Vallauris and Valbonne are only two examples on the
Riviera of old villages destroyed in the wars at the end of the fourteenth century and rebuilt with straight streets and right-angled
corners.) Then the King set to work to strengthen the fortifications of
the city, at that time still consisting of little more than the single wall
built by the Visigoths. Most of what we see now, when it is not the
work of Viollet-le-Duc, is the work of St Louis and his son Philip the
Bold. They rendered the town impregnable by the standards of the
time and thus earned it the name of the Maid of Languedoc. The
Black Prince himself, faced with its double walls, its barbicans and
its fifty towers, did not dare to attack but turned away after burning
the Lower Town. The city lost its military importance with the invention of artillery in the fifteenth century. The era of feudal castles
was over and with the aid of his new weapon Charles VII captured
sixty of them from the English in the course of a single year. They
were to be succeeded in the next century by the low, squat, immensely thick fortresses which we have seen at Antibes, St Paul and
Marseilles.

The starting point for a visit to this unique re-creation of a medieval
city is the Ville Basse beyond the Aude. (The Musée des Beaux Arts,
at 1 Rue de Verdun, is the only municipal museum I know of with a
surrealist room – Salvador Dali, Max Ernst, André Masson and Yves
Tanguy.) If one is on foot one climbs a long ramp and enters by the
Porte d'Aude near the Château Comtal; if one is car-borne one
drives up to the great Porte Narbonnaise and leaves the car outside;
if one is intending to stay at the comfortable Hôtel de la Cité, one
waits for the red light eventually to turn to green and then drives in
through the Porte Narbonnaise, for there is only one-way traffic in
the Cité, even though the olde oake beams may be made of concrete
and stucco.

The **Porte Narbonnaise** was built to protect the most vulnerable
part of the city, the so-called 'throat' (or isthmus) where the plateau
(or peninsula) of the Cité abuts on the high ground (or mainland)
which commands it. It dates from the reign of Philip the Bold. The
style is that of his father's time except that the flat rectangular stones
of St Louis's period are now replaced by bossed stones to lessen the
ricocheting of arrows and the effects of battering-rams. Thus the

work of the two reigns can be distinguished at a glance. The external 'beaks', like the prows of ships, on the flanking towers were designed as protection against catapults and battering-rams, and particularly the kind of ram known as a 'bore'. The whole ensemble is one of the finest and best preserved things in the city and it needed no heightening from Viollet-le Duc except the addition of the slate roofs (which, as we have said, was probably a mistake).

The narrow street leads up to the nine-towered **Castle**, or Château Comtal, of the Trencavels. Built of yellow sandstone, it is the donjon of the great castle which was Carcassonne, a citadel of its own separated from the city by a barbican, a moat and portcullised gates and even cut off from the rest of the fortifications so that if they were taken it could hold out alone. It was the last defence of Carcassonne. The curious wooden projections round the tops of some of the towers are the brattices erected by Viollet-le-Duc, wooden machicolations built out to enable the defenders to drop boiling oil and molten lead on the heads of their assailants below.

In the interior is a museum with an interesting collection of local antiquities, notably the lovely Calvary of Villanière. It contains a fine English alabaster of Christ at the column, Christ on the cross, Christ in limbo and the Resurrection (with Christ stepping on and apparently blessing a soldier who does not wake from his sleep). The Salle du Donjon is decorated by a spirited fresco of a cavalry action between Franks and Saracens.

In the Castle you take a ticket and assemble for a conducted tour of the inner walls (on any day you choose except July 14), most of which are the work of Philip the Bold, although about a third, the northern and north-western section, are Visigothic. The Visigothic work can easily be distinguished by its smallish, cube-shaped grey stones, broken at regular intervals by courses of red brick in a herringbone pattern. The Visigothic towers are all rounded on the outside and flat on the inside, and the thickness of the walls is half the height. An example can be seen from the garden of the Hôtel de la Cité in the (restored) shape of the Tour Visigothe close beside it.

The great Tour St Nazaire, which is by Viollet-le-Duc after Philip the Bold, stands at the highest point of the city and from it one can obtain a good idea of the fortification scheme. St Louis's great addition was the outer circle of walls with its nineteen towers and its barbicans, and the levelling of the slope between the two ramparts to form the Lices. (We have met 'Lices' before at Arles and St Tropez. The word has come to us in the form of 'lists', for jousting and tournaments were held in these flat spaces outside the walls.) This wall, built much lower than the more imposing inner one so as to give an attacker no vantage point even if he should take it, was the feature above all which rendered Carcassonne impregnable. In the first place, it protected the main wall from sapping and mining, always one of the greatest dangers to the defenders of a castle. (The technique was very simple; the besiegers burrowed under the ramparts, made a cavern, propped its roof with beams and at the right moment set fire to them so that it caved in and brought the wall down.) Secondly, it meant that anyone who did break through it found themselves caught in the death-trap of the narrow Lices, at the mercy of the defenders on the walls above and those in the towers holding out behind them. Some of these towers were completely enclosed and had their own cisterns, kitchens and store-rooms, so that they could survive even when cut off.

Carcassonne contains a single gem of architecture in the shape of the former Cathedral, now the **Church of St Nazaire**, which rises between the Château Comtal and the Tour St Nazaire. The nave and the crypt are part of the original Romanesque cathedral which was begun in 1096 and finished in 1150. After the victory of the Crusaders the choir and transepts were rebuilt in the purest Gothic style of the Île de France, perfectly proportioned and of an exquisite lightness and grace. Everything here is clearly the work of architects, sculptors and glass-workers from the North, although none of the artists who contributed to this collective masterpiece has signed his work or is even known by name. (Gislebertus of Autun was one of the very few medieval sculptors who signed his work.) The early fourteenth-century statues on the slender columns would not be out of place in the great cathedrals of the North of France. The transepts with their large rose-windows seem to be modelled on those of Notre Dame, while the choir with its lovely Gothic windows is in the style of St Louis's Sainte Chapelle. Both these Paris churches were built only a few years before St Nazaire, which may well have been copied from them or at any rate created by the same artists.

Most of the glass in the choir and transepts is contemporary with the building, thirteenth- and early fourteenth-century work. As in Notre Dame de Paris, the rose-windows in the transepts are dedicated to Christ and to the Virgin. The central window of the choir illustrates scenes from the life of Christ, and those on either side the acts of SS Peter and Paul and of SS Nazaire and Celsus, the patrons of the church. In the chapels on either side of the choir are two particularly beautiful windows. The one on the left represents the Tree of Jesse, and the one on the right the Tree of Life, with Adam and Eve at its foot, which stands for the period between the Fall and the Redemption.

Among the excellent statues and monuments in the church is a powerful sixteenth-century Flemish *Pietà* in the north transept. Contemporary with the church are the tombs of Bishop Pierre de Rochefort and of Bishop Radulph, which centre round a moving death-bed scene. The most unusual sculpture, and the one which seems somehow to typify Carcassonne, is a fragment of a bas-relief in the Rodier chapel, representing the siege of a city with a few woefully-outnumbered defenders behind their walls in the top right-hand corner. One recalls that the Crusaders took Carcassonne from the last of the Trencavels, the valiant young Viscount Raymond Roger, with odds of fifteen to one. Even so they would not have done it without the aid of drought, for it was August and all the twenty-two wells of the city ran dry. Treachery came to the aid of drought to put an end to the freedom of Carcassonne. Its new master was the fanatical Simon de Montfort, and it is thought that this bas-relief may be a fragment of his tomb, for when he was killed by a stone launched from a mangonel at the siege of Toulouse in 1218 his body was brought here for burial.

Carcassonne's long connection with the wars was not finished for good, however, with the invention of cannon. During the First World War three hundred German officers were imprisoned in the Château Comtal, and in March, 1944, the German occupiers made the Cité into a headquarters, expelled the inhabitants and walled up all the gates except the Porte Narbonnaise. They were still busy digging tunnels under the Lices on August 20 when the Liberation put a stop to their mole-like labours.

From Carcassonne some of the emptiest roads twist steeply and narrowly through the Corbières hills in the general direction of Perpignan. The landscape has a sedate and rough beauty which is a mixing-bowl of the climates of Atlantic and Mediterranean. The longer way round by main road offers a little more in the way of history. First, by following the Aude valley upstream, come **Limoux**, to be saluted for its dry, sparkling white wine, Blanquette de Limoux. The locals say it was being made at Limoux long before sparkling Champagne was ever heard of. Then comes the little spa of **Alet-les-Bains**, whose twelfth-century cathedral was destroyed by the Huguenots in 1577. It was never repaired, but the copper-coloured ruins are impressive.

From Couiza, still in the Aude valley, travellers with a taste for bizarre conundrums and tales of hidden treasure can go up to the handsomely-set village of **Rennes-le-Château** which has been the subject of a couple of programmes on British television recently. Towards the end of the last century, Rennes's new village priest, Berenger Saunière, unaccountably acquired great wealth and spent it on himself and the village church. When challenged, he said he merely sold masses and received donations, a patently improbable story. Word spread that he had found secret treasure in the vicinity – Visigoth treasure, for Rennes had been Rhedae, capital of the Razès Visigoths, with a population of thirty thousand. Or else he had found Cathar gold, or treasure hidden by the Knights Templar as they fled to Spain on the suppression of their Order. People came to Rennes to look for the treasure; authors have concocted fantastical explanations of the bizarre church decorations which, they say, are secret messages that lead to the site of Saunière's hoard. There have been unexplained deaths and a machine-gunning incident. It has all been erected into a paranoid rebus-maniac's delight. The real truth is probably very simple and shabby.

Chapter 29

Perpignan

*

The Castillet – the Loge – the Cathedral – the Rigaud Museum – the Palace – Rivesaltes – Salses – Thuir – Céret – Elne – Collioure – Banyuls

To pass the low, vine-clad hills of the Corbières, famous for their rather bitter wine, is to cross into another country, for it is here that Spain overflows into France. The Roussillon is the French portion of Catalonia, which after various vicissitudes was finally partitioned between France and Spain by the Treaty of the Pyrenees in 1659. Catalan is the language of the countryside and is still generally spoken in Perpignan itself outside the smart shops and cafés. There are, for example, two pleasant bistros in the Place François Arago, where you can sit and listen to everybody arguing football in Catalan. (One is called the Continental and the other the American Palace, but there is another just across the stream with the even more exotic name of Drinck Hall.) Be careful about getting caught up in a 'school', for all the *pastis* are doubles in the Roussillon, and a Catalan is insulted if you demur at him buying a drink back when you have given him one. A double *pastis* is stronger than it seems.

The atmosphere of Perpignan is a happy blend of France and Spain. Although the Roussillonnais are intensely proud of being Catalan, they are equally loyal to France and have not the slightest wish to unite with their compatriots across the border. *'Nous sommes des Catalans français,'* they will tell you. On summer evenings they dance in the streets. They have all the natural gaiety of the Catalans without being embittered by politics, civil war and defeat like so many of the Spanish Catalans. Nearly half the population of Perpignan are, in fact, Spanish Catalans. Barcelona is the local metropolis and the people cross frequently into and out of Spain. There are very few nowadays who are unable to do so, for nearly all the hardshell anarchists, gunmen and war criminals who fled here in 1938 have long ago moved on to Cuba and Mexico. 'They come here because they get higher wages and better living conditions,'

The Roman triumphal arch at Orange, the most richly decorated in France

The Mediterranean

a Frenchman explained to me rather sourly.

Two of the principal hotels, the Grande and the France, are on the Quai Sadi-Carnot, where the Route Nationale 9 runs into the centre of the town, and it makes a good base from which to explore Perpignan. On either side plane trees line the quays along the Basse, a stream which runs sedately between well-kept green lawns and flower-beds, rather as in an English cathedral city. At the end, just beyond the Hôtel de France, is the **Castillet**,[1] a crenellated and machicolated building of mellow red brick, half fortress and half gate, which has survived the demolition of the city walls in 1904. On the wall is a niche with a very beautiful Madonna, who is generally crowned with fluttering pigeons. Originally built in 1368 by the King of Aragon to defend the city from the north, it was later turned into a prison. The seventeenth- and eighteenth-century Annals of Justice (as it was called), have survived and reveal many interesting details. In 1698, for example, the census of the Castillet showed, in addition to a number of convicts and women of evil life, a Basque pilgrim, an Italian pilgrim, an old pilgrim accused of espionage, another pilgrim arrested without a passport, two Turks, a deacon of Toul, and a girl called Marion, the servant of an officer who had had her put in to prevent her marrying a soldier. Truly a mixed bag. The fees of the executioner, in addition to a living allowance of 400 livres, were: 60 livres for a burning alive, a strangulation or a breaking on the wheel; 30 livres for a hanging or a 'putting to the question'; 15 livres for a flogging or a branding; 7 livres for the carcan or a mutilation. In the Castillet is the Casa Pairal, a museum of Catalan arts and popular traditions.[1]

A hundred yards up the Rue Louis Blanc the street widens into the **Place de la Loge**, with a bronze of Venus by Aristide Maillol. Here on summer evenings after dinner the people assemble to dance the *sardana*, the national dance of Catalonia. The music strikes up. Then two or three people rise from their table, join hands and dance. Others come up. There is no smiling, greeting, recognition or asking of permission. The ring expands until suddenly you notice that there are twenty people in it. Generally there are several rings going at once. They bud off like amoebae. If a ring grows too big for the space, the dancers form another in the middle of the original one. Sometimes there are two or three concentric circles. It is a grave and beautiful dance expressive of dignity and joy. At first it is slow and measured, with a complicated series of steps to left and right. Then all of a sudden the music quickens in tempo. The clasped hands rise

1. Open daily.

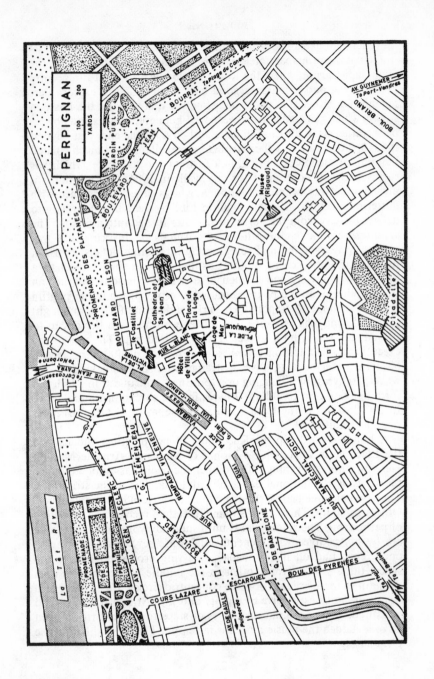

in the air over the dancers' heads, and the dance turns from a ritual to a jig. Equally suddenly the music stops and the dancers melt away, as gravely and silently as they came.

The *sardana* has its origins with the Greek trading posts which were established along this coast, according to Mr Vivian Rowe, and with the *Iliad* in which Homer tells of the dancers who form a wheel and the boys and girls hold hands aloft. The music begins with an introit played by a single shepherd's pipe, followed by a leisurely air, eight bars long, then changing to a rondo tempo, these two tempi alternating. Where there is an orchestra, it is called the *cobla*; its instruments usually consist of two *tiples*, tenor and treble valveless trumpets; a serpentine *fluviol*, the bass trumpet; a *cornamusa*, a simple brass horn (not the Breton bagpipe of similar name); a *tamborino*, a small drum, the ancient *tabor*, and not a tambourine. All seem to be descended from the *shawms* of the Bible and the trumpets which blew down the walls of Jericho.

The **Loge**, or Llotja, is the former Loge de Mer built in the fourteenth century to house the Consulat de Mer, which handled all shipping and commercial disputes. It is a handsome grey stone building, rather Venetian in style, with pointed arches and an open loggia below, which is now a café. In the Middle Ages Perpignan, now some eight miles from the sea, was a flourishing port, and a very fanciful and improbable picture in the Church of St Jacques even shows the sea washing the steps of the Loge itself. Symbolic of the maritime function of the Loge are the iron weathercock in the form of a ship and the curious framed sculpture on the wall representing the waves of the sea. (This was not simply a carving of 'the sea', for there was formerly a caravel which has vanished.) Next door, also on the Place de la Loge, is the thirteenth-century **Hôtel de Ville**. In the courtyard there is a reclining figure in bronze representing the Mediterranean by Maillol, an artist very well represented hereabouts, for he was a native son of the Roussillon. The three bronze arms protruding from the wall represent the 'three estates' of Perpignan.

Like the Hôtel de Ville and the Palace of the Kings of Majorca, the façade of the fourteenth-century **Cathedral of St Jean** is built of a material much favoured by the late medieval masons of Perpignan, rounded pebbles from the river bed, alternating with courses of red brick. Inside the Cathedral the little windows let in only just enough light for one to descry several fine altarpieces, notably the Virgin in the right apse, and to notice the typically Spanish style of religious decoration, the flamboyant gilded altarpieces, with painted saints, angels, twining vines, garlands and flowers, the kilted Christs with human hair, and the Virgins in velvet and rich brocade. Perhaps the most Spanish of all the Perpignan churches is St Jacques, whence on Good Friday the Confraternity of the Sanch, a procession of black-robed penitents with high pointed hoods, issues to perambulate the town carrying images and floats representing the Five Dolorous Mysteries, in true Sevillian style, as they have done for four hundred years.

If you go out of the Cathedral by the door in the right aisle you will find yourself in a side-street with a chapel on the left. Inside is one of the least known among Europe's breathtaking works of art, a dark wooden crucifix known as the *Dévot Christ*. The Christ is wasted and emaciated as though flayed. The ribs stand out like the hoops of a perished barrel, and the veins rise from the tense muscles like cords. The toes are clenched and contorted with agony. The thorn-crowned head droops to within a fraction of an inch of the chest, and the local people believe that when the chin finally sags to touch the breastbone the world will come to an end. Long thought to be Spanish, the crucifix is now believed to be German work of the early fourteenth century.

The year 1659 saw the definitive annexation of Perpignan to France and the birth of her most famous son, Hyacinthe Rigaud, who became court painter to Louis XIV. In the **Musée Rigaud**[1] there are nine of the master's pictures in the main hall, all of them, with sturdy local patriotism, labelled '*Jacint Rigau i Ros, dit Hyacinthe Rigaud.*' It is a good and catholic collection for a provincial gallery and ranges from Luca Giordano and Nicolas Maes to Ingres. Outstanding among the Catalan and Valencian primitives are the thirteenth-century Catalan series on the Life of St Christopher and the fifteenth-century 'Trinity' by the Master of Canapost.

While we are on the subject of primitives, the blackened frieze running along the medieval house in the Rue de la Main de Fer is, so the local people assure one, of a pornographic nature, but I could see nothing in it – and indeed precious little of it at all. A really enterprising Municipality would have it properly cleaned up and turned into a tourist attraction, one feels.

Vauban's great citadel at the top of the town encloses the old **Palace of the Kings of Majorca**. It might not seem immediately clear why the Kings of Majorca should have had their capital in Perpignan, but Jayme I of Aragon, called the Conqueror, who expelled the Moors from Majorca in the thirteenth century, united under his rule all the Catalan lands, besides one or two that were not Catalan.

1. Closed on Tuesdays.

When he died he bequeathed Aragon, Barcelona and Valencia to his elder son Pedro III and Majorca, the Roussillon and Montpellier to his second son Jayme II. In all, three Kings of Majorca ruled from Perpignan before the Roussillon was reabsorbed by Aragon. The restored Palace is built round an immense inner court surrounded by Gothic-arched arcades, and in the middle of the east side are two superimposed chapels – or a two-storeyed chapel. The great Salle de Majorque, the old throne-room, heated by three immense fireplaces, occupies the whole of the south side.

North of Perpignan is Rivesaltes, famous for its grenache and muscat wines, and as the birthplace of Marshal Joffre. Beyond is the massive **Fort of Salses**,[1] built of mellow brick and stone, and standing over the route Hercules was supposed to have taken, and Hannibal did take in 218 BC, and which became Rome's highway into Spain, the Via Domitia. A Roman camp had been on the site; later Alphonse II, King of Aragon, erected a castle in 1172, vestiges of which can still be traced. At the end of the fifteenth century the present castle was built, one of the oldest in France designed to repulse artillery.

From Perpignan three roads lead into Spain. One runs up the Conflens valley to the Cerdagne through Prades, long the home of the exiled Catalan 'cellist, Pablo Casals, and the seat of an annual music festival in his honour. Between that and the second road rises the Canigou, the last great shoulder of the Pyrenees, where I have seen snow as late as June. The second and most used road runs through Le Boulou to cross into Spain at Le Perthus. Not far away is Thuir, where Byrrh[2] is made and which boasts the largest cellars in Europe, and the largest single vat in the world.

From Le Boulou a road turns right to the peaceful little town of **Céret**. Maillol's Monument to the Dead of 1914–18 in the Place de la Liberté is effective and original, consisting of a Mourning Woman, who symbolizes Céret, weeping for her sons. In the spring visitors come to Céret to look at its famous cherry orchards, which produce the earliest cherries in France. The main artistic interest of the town is that it was one of the birthplaces of Cubism in the early years of the century and there is a Musée d'Art Moderne[3] containing examples of the work of the artists who lived here. There is a Picasso

1. Conducted tours daily except Tuesdays.
2. Open daily. Closed on Sundays and public holidays between November 16 and March 15.
3. Open daily in summer; on Wednesdays, Saturdays and Sundays for the rest of the year. Closed in December.

Room and a Manolo Room, while other painters represented are Matisse, Juan Gris, Marchand, Lhote, Braque, Marquet, Chagall, Dufy and Masson. These are the more important names in this important collection, started by the painter Pierre Brune in 1950.

The third road to Spain runs by way of Argelès through the ancient city of **Elne**, which was the Iberian Illiberis, beneath whose walls Hannibal camped, and the Roman Castrum Helenae, said to have been called after the mother of Constantine. Now a quiet country town, it was once the capital of the Roussillon and still clusters round its eleventh-century Cathedral. (In the square outside is Maillol's 'Pomona', the 1914–18 War Memorial.) While the attractive interior holds little of outstanding interest, the cloister, whose south gallery, the one next to the Cathedral, dates from the twelfth century, is one of the masterpieces of Catalan medieval art. The Romanesque sculptures show an abounding imagination. There are fanciful carvings of mermaids, dolphins and serpents swallowing frogs. The odd little men peering over a wall with a large door, three times repeated, represent St Peter in prison. Particularly fine are the Descent from the Cross, the Creation of Adam, and Herod receiving the Magi (and, not very surprisingly, brushing them off with regal scorn).

From Elne the road continues to the sea at **Collioure**, one of the most picturesque little ports on the Mediterranean and an early discovery of Derain, Friesz, Lhote and the *fauve* painters. Had it been anywhere east of Marseilles it would have shared the fate of St Tropez but, being where it is, it is relatively unspoilt, though undoubtedly congested in July and August. As the local guide-book justly remarks, it has '*beaucoup de gloire artistique, de snobisme et de véritable beauté*'. It also has three beaches, arranged like a clover leaf. The first two, where the fishing boats are drawn up on the pebbles, are separated by the great castle, and the central beach is separated in its turn from the bathing beach, the Plage St Vincent, by the Church. This is built of black volcanic rock like Agde and its round tower, with a pink dome which reminds one of Palermo, was once the lighthouse at the entrance to the harbour, perhaps originally a Greek *pharos*, for the Greeks of Marseilles traded with the Ibero-Ligurian peoples of Collioure. The interior is completely Spanish, with the high altar and all the side altars in the gilded, ornate style of Churriguerra. From the hill above, Le Balcon de Madeloc, I have counted no fewer than eight castles and forts, for this region was for many centuries the frontier zone and frequently the battle-ground between France and Spain.

Behind the glacis of the thirteenth-century pink-stoned Château des Templiers which belonged to the Kings of Majorca, is the medium-priced Hostellerie des Templiers. Rather like the more famous Colombe d'Or at St Paul-de-Vence, it contains more than three thousand paintings of modern art which are on show throughout the year.

Port Vendres, the ancient Port of Venus, used to thrive on the regular steamship service to Algiers and Oran, and is now a small commercial port. Beyond that again, through the cork-woods, lies the bay of **Banyuls**, the most southerly seaside resort on the mainland of France, which is famous for its sweet dessert wine. The wine co-operatives can be looked over every weekday. Drive round the bay to the far end of the town and leave your car at the beginning of the quay by the Laboratoire Arago. François Arago, a native of Perpignan, was actually an astronomer but the Laboratory (founded in 1887) bearing his name is mainly devoted to marine biology, and also to oceanography and terrestrial ecology. There is an aquarium, open to the public daily except between December 1 and 20, which, as far as Mediterranean fish only are concerned, is even better than the one in Monaco. All life is here contrasted. Ferocious hermit-crabs eternally fight out a terrifying struggle for existence, while in the next tank delicately tinted sea-anemones languidly wave their fronds like chrysanthemums. After looking at the aquarium, walk out to the islet at the end of the jetty. On it is Maillol's moving war memorial in grey stone, representing a dying man flanked on either side by mourning figures. Between the two islets of Grosse and Petite is the marina, opened to yachtsmen in 1967, the most southerly bit of the great Languedoc-Roussillon development scheme.

After Banyuls comes what even the *Guide Bleu*, startled for once out of its customary phlegm, describes as a 'brutal and dangerous descent' to the Spanish frontier at Cerbère.

Heureux qui comme Ulysse a fait un beau voyage.

Practical Suggestions

❧

There are so many ways of getting to the South of France that the choice of route and transport is a matter of individual preference that takes into account the time available, the season of the year and costs. As to costs, a rule of thumb for the motorist is that the less he uses public transport the cheaper his journeying becomes. In spite of today's high fuel costs, to drive to the south and spend three nights at modest hotels on the way will work out more economically than using the overnight Motorail from Boulogne to Avignon – even with couchettes and not first-class sleepers. However, the motorist with an accountant's view of things, may be able to calculate that wear and depreciation make the Motorail a paying proposition, after all.

Here is a brief *aide-mémoire* to the choice of scheduled services.

CROSS-CHANNEL CAR FERRIES
British Air Ferries: Southend–Le Touquet.
Brittany Ferries: Plymouth–Roscoff; Plymouth–St Malo; Portsmouth–St Malo.
Dan Air: Lydd–Beauvais.
Hoverlloyd: Ramsgate–Calais (hovercraft).
Irish Continental Lines: Rosslare–Le Havre.
Normandy Ferries: Dover–Boulogne; Southampton–Le Havre.
Olau Line: Sheerness–Dunkirk.
Sealink: Dover–Dunkirk; Dover–Calais; Dover–Boulogne; Folkestone–Calais; Folkestone–Boulogne; Newhaven–Dieppe; Weymouth–Cherbourg.
Seaspeed: Dover–Boulogne; Dover–Calais (hovercraft).
Townsend-Thoresen: Dover–Calais; Portsmouth–Cherbourg; Southampton–Cherbourg; Southampton–Le Havre.

MOTORAIL
Making a connection with a number of afternoon cross-Channel sailings are the overnight trains from Boulogne to various destina-

tions in the south. On these French Railways (SNCF) trains, cars are conveyed on double-deck trucks, and passengers' overnight accommodation is in either second-class couchettes or wagons-lits sleepers, or else first-class wagons-lits.

Boulogne–Avignon: once a week between April 1 and September 23; twice a week between May 22 and September 25.

Boulogne–Fréjus/St Raphaël: once a week between May 23 and September 26; twice a week between June 22 and September 7.

Boulogne–Narbonne: once a week between May 24 and September 20; twice a week between June 18 and September 10.

From Paris there are more frequent Motorail services to Avignon, Fréjus/St Raphaël, Gap, Narbonne, Nice and Toulon. Yet another service is the Car-Carrier; passengers are conveyed by one train; their cars go by overnight freight train. Car-Carriers operate between Paris, Marseilles and Toulouse every night, and in the daytime between Paris and Lyons.

FLY-DRIVE AND CAR HIRE

All scheduled air services operate the Fly–Drive, by which a car awaits you at the airport of arrival, it having been booked at the time of ticket-purchase. A similar scheme is operated by French Railways. For a short holiday of a week in the south a car is provided free by scheduled airline operators when a minimum of two people buy return tickets. There are, of course, many well-known car-hire firms in the resorts of the south; they supply the car of choice with the minimum of fuss. The only document you need to bring is a valid British driving licence.

WITHOUT A CAR

Regular flights are operated by Air France and British Airways from London to Marseilles and Nice (to the latter from Manchester, too, by Air France); by Dan Air to Perpignan and Montpellier. There are French internal flights by Air Inter from Paris to Perpignan, Nîmes, Montpellier, Marseilles, Toulon, St Raphaël and Nice. These can be booked through Air France in Britain, but work out rather expensive. Paris–Béziers is served three times a day by Air-Languedoc.

French Railways feed all the major littoral towns by overnight trains. Regular coach services to the Côte d'Azur and Languedoc–Roussillon are run by Clipper Coaches, while Europabus links the Côte d'Azur to Paris.

Now that France is felt to be no more expensive than other tourist countries in Europe, there has been an expansion of package tours to the South of France. They cater for a wide range of interests, from camping holidays to ornithological tours in the Camargue. Information about all this can be gleaned from the French Government Tourist Office's magazine, *The Traveller in France*, which is free from 178 Piccadilly, London W1V 0AL, or 610 5th Avenue, N.Y., N.Y.

ROADS TO THE SOUTH

Old hands will tell you that you can drive for a lifetime from one of the French car-ferry ports along the Channel to the South of France and work out a different route each time. This is no exaggeration, so excellent is the network of major and minor roads across the country. It demands a more leisurely approach and a recognition that the journeys out and back are a part of the holiday, and part of its variety.

Travellers making for Languedoc and Roussillon gain an early morning start by taking an overnight ferry to St Malo, Cherbourg, Le Havre or Dieppe. Travellers in a hurry can now keep to an autoroute almost all the way from Dunkirk to Menton or Perpignan. If they have a mind to, they can go flat out to be stopped only at road tolls which are steep, but they may nonetheless undercost overnight hotels. The autoroutes are adequately supplied with lay-bys, garages and gas stations, restaurants with toilet facilities and rest-rooms.

Those who have, say, three or four weeks to spare and want to cover the whole Mediterranean coast would do well to take three or four bites at the cherry. They might start with a week at Nice, a lively and attractive city from which the whole Riviera is within comfortable reach. Thence it is easy to make various excursions by car or bus into the Alpine and sub-Alpine valleys of the hinterland, as well as to San Remo and to the other resorts on the Italian side of the border. Those who come mainly for the bathing should, however, be warned that there are practically no sandy beaches east of Juan-les-Pins. Nice, Roquebrune and the other beaches are mostly made of pebbles, or else the bathing is from rocks. A few small beaches have had a face-lift with imported sand. To find extensive sand you must go to Cannes, Golfe-Juan or the coast between Ste Maxime and La Ciotat. A good compromise would be to base yourself at Cannes, where you can enjoy sandy beaches and still be within an hour or two of the eastern part of the Riviera.

West of the Rhône are the biggest sandy beaches of the whole of the French Mediterranean coast. They extend for miles and the bathing is safe almost everywhere. A few of the resorts such as Sète and Agde are old and delightful to stay in, but the beaches are at a little distance from the town. Most of the other seaside resorts on the Languedoc coast are in full development. This coast is quite different geologically and scenically from the Côte d'Azur, for it is flat and lacks the shade and variety of the eastern seaboard, but as the beaches are less crowded in summer, they have much to recommend them to devotees of the seaside holiday. The area gets at least as much hot sun as the Riviera. Inland sightseeing, both in towns and the hill ranges, is full of delight and interest.

There are hundreds of hotels and pensions of all classes and price-levels in Nice, Cannes and the other large resorts of the coast, so that there is no point in picking any of them out, and the reader is referred to the hotel lists on pages 244–255. I have gone into the question of local hotels in the chapter on Arles, which I recommend as an ideally situated centre for exploring Lower Provence and the Camargue. Allow at least a week there before moving on to Montpellier.

Here again, now that we are in the church-and-museum belt, a word of warning is necessary. Opening times of museums and picture galleries have been indicated in the text, but they should not be taken as gospel; they are modified occasionally. Even churches, for the most part, close for the sacred two hours of *déjeuner*, from noon until two o'clock, though it must be said that in other respects the long *déjeuner* is no longer quite as sacred as it used to be.

Finally, a few days may well be spent in the agreeable city of Perpignan, which is near not only Carcassonne and Narbonne but a number of sandy beaches such as Canet-Plage and Argelès. As Nice for Italy, so Perpignan is a good base for a short excursion into Spain, to the ancient city of Gerona and the lovely coast of the northern Costa Brava, Rosas and Cadaquès. Then, if you have not already covered it from Arles, I suggest a day or two in Avignon to break the journey home. If you travelled from Arles to Montpellier by way of St Gilles on the way out, you can go from Montpellier to Avignon by way of Nîmes.

The most important thing to remember is never to arrive in a town and take a chance on a room during the summer season, but always reserve in advance. In the high season hotels are apt to ignore letters and even telegrams and grasp the bird which flies into their hand. The safest thing is to get your hotel porter of the morning to telephone through to your destination and assure your reservation for that evening. He will be able to call other hotels if one is full and it is some sort of guarantee that you are on the way and will actually turn up. Otherwise you may find yourself with nowhere to lay your head.

This is not, of course, necessary during the winter months, when few people are on the road, but it is prudent to do so even in the spring and the autumn, outside the peak months of July and August, as there may be a festival, a fair or a bullfight which will have filled up the town you are making for.

Reference to the different seasons is a good excuse for finishing with a reminder about the pleasures of the South of France in winter. Our grandparents knew all about it then, for they would not have dreamed of being seen there in summer. We, overconcerned with summer delights, tend to neglect the winter virtues. Our grandparents usually stayed at least six months, and any poor weather they experienced was submerged by the fine. We, on the other hand, with our preference for short breaks may be unlucky and run into sustained winter rain and cold, but if the sun is out, the brilliant clarity of the light surpasses anything summer can offer. The best colour transparencies are taken in winter. True, the mistral may strike the exposed plain of Bas–Languedoc, but in Roussillon there are sheltered valleys with small resorts whose hotels are open in winter. They may be fairly quiet but winter, down south, can be marvellously exhilarating.

Principal Coastal Resorts

In the lists on pages 238–243, the name of the resort is followed by the address of its *Syndicat d'Initiative*, the official tourist information office where callers are supplied with (mostly free) brochures, hotel lists, sightseeing itineraries, etc. When making inquiries by post, it is advisable to write in French and essential to enclose an International Reply Coupon (obtainable from any post office).

Name of Resort	*Address of Syndicat d'Initiative*
1 Antibes-Cap d'Antibes	12 Place de Gaulle, 06600 Antibes
2 Beaulieu-sur-Mer	Place Gare, 06310 Beaulieu-sur-Mer
3 Cagnes-sur-Mer	26 Avenue Renoir, 06800 Cagnes-sur-Mer
4 Cannes	Palais des Festivals, La Croisette, and Gare SNCF, 06400 Cannes
5 Cap d'Ail	87 Avenue 3-Septembre, 06320 Cap d'Ail
6 Eze-Bord-de-Mer	Mairie, 06360 Eze-Bord-de-Mer
7 Golfe-Juan	84 Avenue de la Liberté, 06220 Vallauris
8 Juan les Pins	Boulevard C. Guillaumont, 06160 Juan-les-Pins
9 Menton	Palais de l'Europe, Avenue Boyer, 06500 Menton
10 Monaco-Monte Carlo	2a Boulevard des Moulins, Monte Carlo
11 La Napoule	Place St Fainéant, 06210 La Napoule-Mandelieu
12 Nice	32 Rue Hôtel-des-Postes, and Place Masséna, and Gare SNCF, 06000 Nice
13 Roquebrune-Cap Martin	Hôtel de Ville, 06190 Roquebrune-Cap Martin
14 St Jean-Cap Ferrat	12 Avenue Claude Vignon, 06290 St Jean-Cap Ferrat
15 Théoule-sur-Mer	5 Place Liberté, 06590 Théoule-sur-Mer
16 Villefranche-sur-Mer	Square F. Binon, 06230 Villefranche
17 Agay	Boulevard Mer, 83530 Agay
18 Aiguebelle	10 Quai Gabriel Péri, 83980 Le Lavandou
19 Anthéor	Place Gallieni, 83700 St Raphaël
20 Bandol	Allées Vivien, 83150 Bandol
21 Île de Bendor	Allées Vivien, 83150 Bandol
22 Carry-le-Rouet	6 Boulevard Moulins, 13620 Carry-le-Rouet

The main resorts (with brief indications of some amenities) are numbered so that the four coastal regions of Mediterranean France are divided in this way:

1–16	Riviera–Côte d'Azur
17–46	Provençal Riviera
47–61	Languedoc
62–69	Roussillon–Côte Vermeille

	Type of beach	Sailing facilities	Casino	Tennis	Golf	Skin-diving centre
1	fine sand	●		●	1	
2	shingle	●	1	●		
3	shingle	●		●		●
4	fine sand	●	3	●	4	●
5	shingle					
6	shingle					
7	fine sand	●				
8	fine sand	●	1	●	1	
9	sand	●	2	●		
10	sand	●	1	●	1	●
11	fine sand	●	1	●		●
12	shingle	●	1	●	2	●
13	shingle			●		
14	shingle	●		●		
15	sand and shingle	●				
16	shingle	●		●		
17	fine sand	●				
18	fine sand					
19	fine sand					
20	fine sand	●	1	●		●
21	fine sand	●				●
22	sand	●	1			

239

Name of resort	Address of Syndicat d'Initiative
23 Cassis	Place Baragnon, 13260 Cassis
24 Cavalaire-sur-Mer	Square De Lattre de Tassigny, 83240 Cavalaire-sur-Mer
25 Cavalière	—
26 La Ciotat	Vieux Port, 13600 La Ciotat
27 Fos-sur-Mer	Quai Paul Doumer, 13500 Martigues
28 Fréjus-Plage	Place Calvini, 83600 Fréjus
29 Hyères-Plage	Place Clemenceau, 83400 Hyères
30 Les Issambres	Place San-Peïre, 83380 Les Issambres
31 Le Lavandou	10 Quai Gabriel Péri, 83980 Le Lavandou
32 Les Lecques	Pavillon du Tourisme, 83270 St Cyr-sur-Mer
33 Port Cros	Place Clemenceau, 83400 Hyères
34 Port Grimaud	—
35 Porquerolles	Place Clemenceau, 83400 Hyères
36 Le Rayol-Le Canadel	—
37 St Aygulf	Place Poste, 83600 Fréjus
38 St Clair	10 Quai Gabriel Péri, 83980 Le Lavandou
39 St Raphaël	Place Gallieni, 83700 St Raphaël
40 St Tropez	Quai Jean Jaurès, 83990 St Tropez
41 Ste Maxime	Avenue Charles de Gaulle, 83120 Ste Maxime
42 Les Stes Maries-de-la-Mer	Avenue Van Gogh, 13460 Les Stes Maries-de-la-Mer
43 Sanary	Jardins de la Ville, 83110 Sanary-sur-Mer
44 Sausset-les-Pins	Boulevard Charles Roux, 13960 Sausset-les-Pins
45 Six-Fours	Place de Bonnegrâce, 83140 Six-Fours
46 Le Trayas	Place Gallieni, 83700 St Raphaël
47 Cap d'Agde	S.I. Cap d'Agde, 34300 Agde
48 Carnon-Plage	Office de Tourisme, 34280 La Grande-Motte
49 La Franqui	—
50 La Grande-Motte	Office de Tourisme, 34280 La Grande-Motte
51 Grau d'Agde	Arcades Hôtel de Ville, 34300 Agde
52 Le Grau-du-Roi	Mairie, 30240 Le Grau-du-Roi
53 Gruissan-Plage	—
54 Leucate-Plage	—

Type of beach	Sailing facilities	Casino	Tennis	Golf	Skin-diving centre
23 sand and shingle	●	1	●		●
24 fine sand	●		●	1	
25 fine sand					
26 sand and shingle	●	1	●		
27 fine sand	●		●		
28 fine sand	●		●		
29 fine sand	●	1	●	1	●
30 fine sand	●		●		
31 fine sand	●		●		●
32 fine sand	●		●		●
33 fine sand	●				
34 sand	●	1	●	1	●
35 fine sand	●				
36 fine sand			●		
37 fine sand	●				
38 fine sand					
39 fine sand	●	1	●	1	●
40 fine sand	●		●		
41 fine sand	●	1	●	1	
42 fine sand					
43 fine sand	●		●		●
44 fine sand	●	1			●
45 fine sand	●		●		●
46 rocks					
47 sand	●		●		
48 fine sand	●		●		
49 fine sand					
50 fine sand	●	1	●		
51 fine sand					
52 —	●	1	●	1	
53 sand	●				
54 fine sand					

Name of resort	*Address of Syndicat d'Initiative*
55 Narbonne-Plage	2 Rue Jean Jaurès, 11100 Narbonne
56 Palavas-les-Flots	Hôtel de Ville, 34250 Palavas-les-Flots
57 Port Camargue	S.I., 30240 Port Camargue
58 Port Leucate	Centre d'Information, 11370 Leucate
59 Sète	22 Quai d'Alger, 34200 Sète
60 Valras-Plage	24 Rue Charles Thomas, 34350 Valras-Plage
61 Vias-Farinette Plage	Arcades Hôtel de Ville, 34300 Agde
62 Argelès-Plage	Place Arènes, 66700 Argelès-sur-Mer
63 Banyuls-sur-Mer	Hôtel de Ville, 66650 Banyuls-sur-Mer
64 Canet-en-Roussillon	Place de la Méditerranée, 66140 Canet-en-Roussillon
65 Cerbère	Mairie, 66290 Cerbère
66 Collioure	Avenue Camille Pelletan, 66190 Collioure
67 Port-Barcarès	—
68 Port-Vendres	Quai Joly, 66660 Port-Vendres
69 St Cyprien	S.I., 66200 Elne

PRINCIPAL COASTAL RESORTS

Type of beach	Sailing facilities	Casino	Tennis	Golf	Skin-diving centre
55 fine sand	●				
56 fine sand	●	1	●		
57 fine sand	●		●		
58 —	●	1	●		
59 fine sand			●		
60 fine sand					
61 fine sand					
62 fine sand		1	●		
63 shingle	●		●		●
64 fine sand	●	1	●		●
65 shingle			●		
66 shingle			●		●
67 fine sand	●	1	◉		●
68 sand and shingle	●		●		●
69 fine sand	●		●	2	

Hotels

The business of recommending hotels in France has been brought to a fine art in the multiplicity of advice which is available. The *Guide Michelin* (which is the pillar of bourgeois establishment taste, with all the strengths and weaknesses this label implies) claims the greatest following; élitists may prefer *Kléber-Colombes*; more modestly cautious aspirations are amply looked after by the *Guide des Logis de France*; the socially upgraded workman's bed and board places have been popularized by the *Guide des Relais Routiers*. These are only some of the annually revised guides, and they can be bought in some of the larger American and British bookshops.

A bureaucratically impersonal approach is adopted by the French Government Tourist Office, 178 Piccadilly, London W1V 0AL or 610 5th Avenue, N.Y., N.Y., which dispenses annually revised free price-lists of tourist hotels, 'Guide des Hôtels', by regions. A tourist hotel is rated with four, three, two or one stars by the French Government — ratings not of quality, necessarily, but only of amenities (such as number of public rooms or private bathrooms). In a general way, prices correspond to star-status, with four stars at the 'luxury' or 'palace' and 'first class' end, down to the adequate and simple one star. For the area covered by this book, three 'Guides des Hotels' are to be had: Riviera-Côte d'Azur, Provence-Côte d'Azur-Alpes du Sud, and Langudoc-Roussillon.

Local Syndicats d'Initiative supply more detailed town or regional hotel lists, as they include non-tourist hotels, graded by local authorities.

A supplementary service provided by the FGTO in London is a selection of photographs and data about hotels (and camping sites) which callers can consult. The FGTO free 'Hotels in France' hotel telex-booking service is run in association with many of the major hotel chains, representing a wide range of categories. Members of the public can use this rapid booking system only through the medium of an accredited travel agent who is supplied with the official list of hotels in the 'Hotels in France' scheme.

For the motorist on the road who does not know where to lay his head as evening approaches there is the emergency service offered by 'Accueil de France', not only in a hotel in the place where the office is sited but also in the surrounding area. In the South of France their centres are at:

Avignon: Office de Tourisme, 41 Cours Jean-Jaurès (covering Gard, Vaucluse, Alpes-de-Haute-Provence and Hautes-Alpes);

Marseilles: Syndicat d'Initiative, 4 La Canebière, and Poste autoroutier Salon-Lançon-Provence (covering Bouches-du-Rhône);

Cannes: Syndicat d'Initiative, Palais des Festivals et des Congrès, and Bureau Accueil de France, Gare SNCF (covering Alpes-Maritimes west of the river Var);

Nice: Office de Tourisme, 32 Rue de l'Hôtel des Postes, and Gare SNCF, and Hall Havas, 13 Place Masséna, and Nice Parking Ferber (covering Alpes-Maritimes east of the river Var).

At present, coastal Languedoc and Roussillon are not similarly supplied (the 'Accueil de France' at Toulouse deals with inland areas), but there are hotel reservation centres and strategic points along the 'Languedocienne' and 'Catalane' autoroutes, A9 and B9 respectively. They are at Tavel, Vidourle, Montpellier-Fabrègues, Narbonne-Vinassan, and Banyuls-dels-Aspres. Similar reservation points exist on the Provençal autoroutes: on A8 between Aix and Brignoles is Aire de Brignoles; on A52 between Aubagne and Toulon is Aire du Lioquet near St Cyr-les-Lecques.

For those who feel that hotel lists or guides are somewhat impersonal, the recommendations given below are drawn from the present editor's years of journeying in the south. They consist not only of his own selections, but also those of other travellers whose judgements are valued.

This kind of recommendation is fallible, of course. The annually revised guide has the advantage of being up-to-date which this list, in the nature of things, cannot claim to be. While every effort has been made to give a fair proportion to the grand and the expensive, there is no denying the bias towards the small and modest. This is not merely on the grounds of cost, but more on the grounds of atmosphere and intimacy and the sense of Frenchness which smaller places are usually more successful in preserving. The hotels here have given value for money, in one way or another, perhaps for some quality of repose or generosity, for good food or comfort, for aesthetic finesse or a view that has built itself into memory. In short, each one has given something lasting. Not that all characteristics are ever found in one place; were such the case, its name would never be revealed in a well-thumbed list like this one. That all these criteria are built on the shifting sands of subjectivity is fully recognized. That tomorrow's new owner will emanate a totally different atmosphere is an unavoidable hazard in the unending pleasure of searching out new hotels in the South of France. It is a little like looking for heaven on earth; if one found it, one would search no more, and the construction of hotel lists would cease.

Each hotel in this list is preceded by 3, 2 or 1, a rough indicator of the price range – expensive (3), moderate (2), or inexpensive (1) – you can expect to pay outside the July/August period. Places follow in alphabetical order within their *départements* (our equivalent is a county but with a great deal less political power), and these progress from east to west, following the book's itinerary through the eight *départements* and the Principality of Monaco.

Alpes-Maritimes

ANTIBES **2** Le Caméo, Place Nationale. *Central, simple food.*

BEAULIEU **2** Frisia, Boulevard Général Leclerc. *Comfortable, view over port.*

BIOT **2** Les Arcades. *Old, simple, artists' haunt.*
1 Les Terraillers. *Handsome sixteenth-century building, Provençal cooking.*

CABRIS **1** L'Horizon. *Fine views, rural setting, comfortable plain bedrooms.*
1 Lou Vieil Casteou. *Tiny, quiet, full board only.*

CAGNES **2** Savournin, 17 Avenue Renoir. *Spacious, comfortable.*
1 Le Grimaldi, 6 Place Château, Haut-de-Cagnes. *Small and simple.*

CANNES **2** Devihôtel, 7 Rue Molière. *Small, modern, bed-and-breakfast only, near La Croisette.*
1 El Puerto, 45 Avenue Petit Juas. *Simple and quiet.*

CAP D'ANTIBES **2** La Garoupe et Réserve du Cap, Boulevard du Cap. *Secluded among pines.*

ÈZE-VILLAGE **1** Mas Provençal. *Small, simple and homely.*

ÈZE-BORD-DE-MER **2** Bananeraie. *Comfortable old house, without restaurant.*

LA GALÈRE **3** Guerguy. *Exciting position and views over sea, garden, distinguished food.*

GOLFE JUAN **1** Relais Impérial, 21 Rue L. Chabrier. *Pleasant atmosphere, garden and food.*

GRASSE **3** Régent, Route de Nice. *Modern, comfortable.*

JUAN-LES-PINS 3 Juana, Avenue G. Gallice. *Luxurious elegance of rooms and cuisine.*

2 Mimosas, Rue Pauline. *Quiet, shady garden.*

1 Cecil, Rue Jonnart. *Very simple and cheap for this resort.*

MAGAGNOSC 2 Vieux Moulin. *Quietly elegant in old olive-oil mill.*

MENTON 3 Parc, 11 Avenue Verdun. *Large and spacious, quiet garden.*

2 Orly, 27 Quai Laurenti. *Modern, functional, some balconied rooms view port and sea.*

2 L'Aiglon, 7 Avenue de la Madone. *Charming old villa in own garden; no restaurant.*

1 Auberge des Santons, l'Annonciade. *Small, garden, near monastery with view, good food.*

MONTI 1 Pierrot-Pierrette, Route de Sospel. *Small rooms, welcoming, resourceful restaurant.*

MOUGINS 3 Mas Candille. *Spacious, quiet, delightful décor.*

2 France. *Good Provençal food.*

LA NAPOULE-PLAGE 2 Le Rocamare. *Nice position and views.*

NICE 2 Résidence Petit Palais, 10 Avenue E. Bieckert. *Quiet residential area with good views, agreeable ambience.*

1 Colbert, 34 Rue Lamartine. *Centrally placed, room and breakfast only.*

1 Gourmet Lorrain, 7 Avenue Santa-Fior. *Well-equipped new hotel with solarium, garden, good food and cellar.*

1 Bali, 21 Boulevard Cambrai. *Quiet, residential west Nice, spacious and pleasant rooms; no restaurant.*

OPIO 2 Mas des Géraniums. *Peaceful rural atmosphere.*

ROQUEBRUNE-CAP MARTIN 3 Vistaëro. *Severely modern style, spectacularly 'balanced' on cliff, immense views, good service.*

2 Princessias, 15 Avenue Drin. *Lovely terraced views, garden, suited to seekers after quiet.*

1 Westminster, 14 Avenue L. Laurens. *Small, for boarders only, good menus.*

ST JEAN-CAP FERRAT 3 Résidence della Robbia, Boulevard Général de Gaulle. *Quiet villa in own grounds, distinguished meals.*

STE AGNES 1 Le St Yves. *Very simple, small, glorious views of Menton, copious meals.*

SPÉRACÈDES 1 La Soleillade. *Agreeable country inn.*

THÉOULE-SUR-MER 2 Hermitage Jules César. *Pleasantly sited; no restaurant.*

TOURRETTES-SUR-LOUP 1 Belles Terrasses. *Simple, fine views.*

1 Grive Dorée. *At edge of village, good fare.*

LA TURBIE **2** France. *Garden, Provençal décor.*

VALBONNE **1** Auberge Provençale. *Simple accommodation, lively generous restaurant.*

VALLAURIS **1** Sports, Rue de la Gendarmerie. *Interesting menus, shady terrace, simple but lively.*

VENCE **3** Auberge des Seigneurs, Place Frêne. *Splendid medieval Provençal house interestingly furnished, high quality meals.*

VILLEFRANCHE **2** St Estève, Rue Duhamel. *Modern, charming, room and breakfast only.*

Principality of Monaco

MONTE CARLO **2** Europe, 6 Avenue Citronniers. *Modernized, simple furnishings, quiet.*

1 Olympia, 17 bis Boulevard Général Leclerc. *Modernized, well-run bed-and-breakfast hotel.*

Var

AGAY **3** Sol et Mar, Le Dramont. *Handsome, comfortable, well-equipped with modern amenities.*

ANTHÉOR **1** Les Flots Bleus. *Pleasant atmosphere, near beach.*

BANDOL **2** Goéland, Avenue Albert Ier. *Peaceful and elegant, with charming terraced gardens down to beach, high standard of food and service.*

1 Coin d'Azur, Rue Raimu. *Quiet, simple, garden, steps to beach.*

BEAUVALLON **3** Marie-Louise, Guerrevieille. *Small, secluded.*

BORMES-LES-MIMOSAS **1** Bellevue, Place Gambetta. *Renovated and comfortable.*

BOULOURIS **3** La Potinière. *Secluded in own grounds, handsomely modern, attractive bedrooms, restaurant for residents only.*

CABASSON **1** Les Palmiers. *Ordinary pension de famille in idyllic surroundings of woodlands, hills, vineyards, within sound of sea and curved, sandy beach.*

CANADEL-SUR-MER **3** Roitelet, Route de la Môle. *Fine cuisine.*

1 Plage. *On main road near sea, small, plain.*

CARQUEIRANNE **1** La Réserve, Les Salettes. *Unpretentious, fine views from terrace, interesting menus and wines.*

CAVALAIRE-SUR-MER **2** Chez Raymond. *Plain, modern amenities.*

CAVALIÈRE **3** Le Club. *Highly efficiently run modern hotel, outstanding food, service, amenities, own beach.*

LA CROIX-VALMER **3** Parc. *Peacefully enfolded in own grounds, stylish, no restaurant.*

FRÉJUS-PLAGE **2** Palmiers. *Sizeable hotel, pleasant bedrooms with sea views or round garden.*

1 Il était une fois. *Plain, agreeable rooms, few amenities other than shady garden.*

GIENS **3** Relais du Bon Accueil. *Surrounded by rich vegetation of isthmus, comfortable and quiet.*

GIGARO **3** St Michel. *Hilltop views of coast, garden, tennis.*

HYÈRES **1** Soleil, 4 Rue Remparts. *Simple bed-and-breakfast base near old town.*

1 Chez Marius, 1 Place Marché. *Clean, plain, good restaurant, in old town.*

HYÈRES-PLAGE **2** La Potinière. *Some good dishes prepared in restaurant, near sands.*

LES ISSAMBRES **2** La Quiétude. *Garden, pool, views out to sea, lives up to its name.*

LE LAVANDOU **3** Auberge de la Calanque, Avenue Général de Gaulle. *Fairly smart, well equipped, gardens looking over port.*

2 Rabelais, Rue Rabelais. *Pleasant, simple, room-and-breakfast only, near port away from congested area.*

1 Plage, La Favière-Plage. *Straightforward, comfortable, reasonable charges in relation to amenities and position.*

LES LECQUES **2** Les Pins, La Madrague. *Quiet, close to extensive sands.*

1 Petit Nice. *Near beach, comfortable and relaxing, well-cooked dishes.*

ÎLE DE PORQUEROLLES **3** Mas du Langoustier. *Old, solitary Provençal farmhouse, suitably furnished, private grounds and beach, island wines and seafood specialities.*

ÎLE DE PORT CROS **3** Le Manoir. *Beautiful, elegant, secluded house in own grounds surrounding bay.*

PORT GRIMAUD **3** Giraglia. *Handsome, modern, luxurious, tasteful style, private beach.*

PRAMOUSQUIER **2** Beau Site. *Pleasantly sited above road near beach, small bedrooms, dining terrace.*

ST AYGULF **3** Catalogne. *Old style décor in modern building, garden, pool, no restaurant.*

ST CLAIR **2** Flots Bleus et Mar é Souléou. *Cheerful, bustling family hotel on fine sandy beach.*

ST RAPHAËL **2** Beau Séjour, Promenade Président Coty. *Balconied*

rooms face beach, good and varied menus.
1 Nouvel Hôtel, Rue H. Vadon. *Simple little bed-and-breakfast inn.*
ST TROPEZ 3 Treizan, Quartier Treizan. *Outside St Tropez among trees, bed, breakfast and midday snacks, delightful atmosphere and furnishings.*
3 La Ferme d'Augustin, Plage de Tahiti. *Handsome farm buildings in own grounds, quiet and spacious.*
3 Yaca, Boulevard d'Aumale. *Modernized, elegant, courtyard garden, great charm and comfort.*
2 Colombier, Impasse des Conquettes. *Bed-and-breakfast hotel at lower end of St Tropez price scale.*
STE MAXIME 2 Maxima 2000, Route du Plan de la Tour. *Woodland bungalows, club house, swimming pool, successful large-scale exploitation of modern semi-collective holiday formula.*
1 Revest, 48 Avenue Jean Jaurès. *Modernized, simple, pleasant.*
SANARY 2 Roc-Amour, Quartier Beaucours. *Comfortable, isolated, modern, gardens, private beach.*
1 Primavera, Avenue Port Issol. *Small villa and garden, cosy, informal.*
TOULON 3 Frantel Tour Blanche, Super-Toulon. *Superb site and views, excellent amenities including pool.*
1 Maritima, 9 Rue Gimelli. *Sizeable, convenient bed-and-breakfast.*
LE TRAYAS 2 Relais des Calanques. *Bedrooms and restaurant hang over Esterel rocks, tiny beach, extended shady terrace.*

Bouches-du-Rhône

AIX-EN-PROVENCE 3 Paul Cézanne, 40 Avenue Victor Hugo. *Furnished down to smallest details with taste and elegance, no restaurant.*
1 Croix de Malte, 2 Rue Van Loo. *Pleasant, rambling old house, centrally situated, no restaurant.*
1 Les Terrasses, 21 Chemin du Belvédère, Val St André. *One of a small number of modestly priced tourist hotels to offer full- and half-board.*
ARLES 2 Nord-Pinus, Place Forum. *A 'quaint character' with reminders of famous clients of past, rather antique and eccentric, in delightful square.*
2 Calendal, 22 Place Pomme. *Charming, friendly, quiet, central, no restaurant.*
1 Le Cloître, 18 Rue Cloître. *Old, comfortable, summer restaurant*

in courtyard adjoining cloister of St Trôphime.

1 Mireille, 2 Place St Pierre, Trinquetaille. *Large rooms, friendly reception, lively, swimming pool, in suburb away from congested centre.*

LES BAUX-DE-PROVENCE 3 La Benvengudo. *Garden, pool, stylish and modern, Provençal furniture, agreeable atmosphere.*

2 Hostellerie de la Reine Jeanne. *Simply furnished, pleasant rooms some with terrace, theatrical views, good food.*

CARRY-LE-ROUET 1 Beau Séjour, Route Sausset. *Functional, modern, fine views, garden, pool.*

CASSIS 3 Roches Blanches, Route Port-Miou. *Quiet, outside village by sea, comfort and elegance, interesting menus.*

MARSEILLES 3 Beauvau, 4 Rue Beauvau. *Famous hotel with historical associations, totally and discreetly renovated, very comfortable, near port, no restaurant.*

2 Européen, 115 Rue Paradis. *New, central, agreeable rooms, no restaurant.*

1 St Dominique, 11 Rue St Dominique. *One of numerous low-priced bed-and-breakfast hotels, some rooms with showers, garage.*

MARTIGUES 3 Hostellerie Ste Anne-Riva, Route Marseille. *Elegant restaurant and interesting dishes, view over lagoon.*

1 Provence, 48 Boulevard C. Pelletan. *Very simple, inexpensive.*

ST RÉMY-DE-PROVENCE 3 Calabrun et Auberge de la Graio, 12 Boulevard Mirabeau. *Small, beautifully furnished, good service and restaurant.*

2 Arts, 30 Boulevard Victor Hugo. *Lively, modern, comfortable, good food, central.*

LES SAINTES MARIES-DE-LA-MER 2 Mirage. *Reasonably priced bed-and-breakfast hotel in village.*

2 Les Arnelles, Pont de Bannes. *One of many riding hotels, less costly than most, simple, quiet, pleasant.*

SALON-DE-PROVENCE 1 Poste, 1 Rue Président Kennedy. *Centrally placed, pension not obligatory.*

SAUSSET-LES-PINS 2 Plage. *Small, simple, agreeable views, garden.*

TARASCON 1 Provençal, 12 Cours A. Briand. *Spacious rooms in hotel, more expensive fine rooms in annexe; Provençal specialities on menu.*

Vaucluse

AVIGNON 2 Auberge de France, 28 Place Horloge. *Next to Palace of Popes; noted table, Comtadin specialities.*

1 Le Jaquemart, 3 Rue F. David. *In heart of old town; simple, inexpensive bed-and-breakfast base.*

ORANGE **2** Arène, Place Langes. *Pleasant rooms, large restaurant and Provençal dishes.*

1 Commerce, 4 Rue Caristié. *Modernized, quiet, no restaurant.*

VAISON-LA-ROMAINE **3** L'Oustaü, Route Villedieu. *Outside town; quiet, agreeable menus.*

1 Théâtre Romain, Place Chanoine Sautel. *Suitable for short stay to see excavations.*

Gard

AIGUES-MORTES **2** St Louis, Rue Amiral Courbet. *Some spacious bedrooms, respected restaurant.*

BEAUCAIRE **3** Vignes Blanches, Route Nîmes. *Well run and equipped hotel, copious meals, own wines.*

1 Glacier, 36 Quai Général de Gaulle. *Plain to stark, large and busy restaurant, very moderate prices.*

LE GRAU DU ROI **3** Splendid, Boulevard Front-de-Mer. *Comfortable, pleasant views, good restaurant.*

NÎMES **2** Louvre, 2 Square Couronne. *Well equipped rooms, reliable restaurant and brasserie, garage, near arena.*

1 Provence, 5 Square Couronne. *Modest, sizeable and convenient bed-and-breakfast establishment.*

PONT DU GARD **1** Auberge Blanche. *A pleasant base just north of Roman bridge, above Gardon river.*

PORT CAMARGUE **3** Le Chabian. *Garden, tennis, pool, recently opened.*

ST GILLES **2** Cours, 10 Avenue F. Grifeuille. *Suitable for short visit to abbey church.*

UZÈS **1** Hostellerie Provençale, 3 Rue Grande Bourgade. *Seventeenth-century inn, small, rather faded but with atmosphere and memorable dishes in restaurant.*

VILLENEUVE-LÈS-AVIGNON **3** La Magnaneraie, 37 Rue Camp de Bataille. *Beautiful fifteenth-century silkworm rearer's house converted with distinction for comfort and cuisine.*

2 Atelier, 5 Rue Foire. *Sixteenth-century house, expertly furnished with antiques, patio, no restaurant.*

Hérault

AGDE **1** Araur, Avenue Vias. *Small, on right bank of Hérault,* *garage, no restaurant.*

BÉZIERS **2** Compagnie du Midi, 20 bis Boulevard Verdun. *Near station, run with distinction in all departments.*

CAP D'AGDE **3** Sablotel. *Very new and large, garden, pool, lifts, by beach.*

2 La Grande Conque. *Long established, comfortable, fine views over bay.*

CARNON **1** Gédéon. *Simple, near sandy beach.*

FLORENSAC **1** Léonce. *Pleasant, modernized, in centre of village, varied menus.*

LA GRANDE-MOTTE **3** Méditerranée, Allée de Vaccarès. *Perhaps the least expensive of the new hotels, set back from sea.*

MARSEILLAN **1** Château du Port. *Overlooking Bassin de Thau, yachtsmen's haunt, informal, recently enlarged, interesting food, nice local wine.*

MONTPELLIER **3** Demeure des Brousses, Route Vauguieres. *Eighteenth-century farmhouse in fine grounds 3 km. outside Montpellier, peaceful, very comfortable, cuisine to match.*

2 Nice, 14 Rue Boussairolles. *Plain little hotel, good menus.*

NISSAN-LEZ-ENSÉRUNE **2** La Résidence. *Quiet, furnished with dignity, small enclosed garden, no restaurant.*

1 Acropole. *Unvarnished and serviceable, wine included with meals.*

PALAVAS-LES-FLOTS **2** Alexandre, Route Carnon. *2 km. outside Palavas, quiet, high standards, outstanding cuisine, by seafront.*

2 Languedoc, 4 Rue Carrière. *All rooms with private facilities, no restaurant.*

PÉZENAS **1** Génieys, 19 Avenue A. Briand. *Simple rooms, but extremely good value for money, thriving restaurant, good and varied menus.*

SÉRIGNAN **1** Les Acacias. *Pool, gardens, near sea, some rooms with kitchenette.*

SÈTE **2** Les Abysses, 24 Quai Général Durand. *Overlooking canal, comfortable, splendid choice of seafoods.*

1 Le Floride. *2 km. west on Corniche, shady garden, near beach, excellent menus.*

LA TAMARISSIÈRE **2** La Tamarissière. *Long established, on right bank of Hérault, close to sandy beach and shady pines, garden, some choice dishes, wine included in pension price.*

VALRAS-PLAGE **2** Mira-Mar, Front-de-Mer. *Fairly large, most rooms with private facilities, lifts, views over sea and port.*

VIAS **1** Vieux Logis. *Very simple rooms, good standard of restaurant.*

Aude

CARCASSONNE 3 Domaine d'Auriac, Route Ste Hilaire. *4 km. southeast of city, elegantly converted old mansion, luxurious atmosphere, restful.*

3 Donjon, 2 Rue Comte Roger, La Cité. *Fine position, stylish, garden, all rooms with private facilities, no restaurant.*

2 Montségur, 27 Allée d'Iéna, Ville Basse. *Beautifully furnished, rustic décor in restaurant, noteworthy meals.*

1 Auriol, 52 Rue 4-Septembre, Ville Basse. *Satisfactory and inexpensive.*

LA FRANQUI 1 Plage. *Facing wide sands, functional, modern, resourceful kitchen, seaside family hotel.*

LIMOUX 2 Moderne et Pigeon, 1 Place Général Leclerc. *Somewhat hemmed in but comfortable, wine included in table d'hôte.*

NARBONNE 1 Le Floride, 66 Boulevard F. Mistral. *On main road, small, all rooms with bath or shower, good menus.*

1 Midi, 4 Avenue Toulouse. *Near Place des Pyrénées, modest prices in relation to comfort and quality of restaurant.*

NARBONNE-PLAGE 2 La Caravelle, Boulevard Front-de-Mer. *On beach, all rooms with bath or shower, varied dishes.*

PORT LEUCATE 2 Étoile du Sud. *Large, amenities to match, pool, garden, some rooms with kitchenettes, half-pension terms.*

SIGEAN 2 Château de Villefalse, Villefalse. *5 km. from Sigean above lagoon, not far from sea, country club atmosphere, pool, quiet surroundings.*

Pyrénées-Orientales

ARGELÈS-PLAGE 2 Le Lido, 50 Boulevard Mer. *By sea, shady garden, pool, most rooms with own facilities.*

1 Solarium, 9 Avenue de Vallespir. *Simple but adequate in relation to modest charges.*

BANYULS 3 Le Catalan, Route Cerbère. *Lovely views of coast, very attractive position, tennis, swimming pool, high standard of service and catering.*

CANET-PLAGE 2 Font le Patio, Front-de-Mer. *Sizeable, modern, well and considerately run.*

2 Aquarius, 40 Boulevard du Roussillon. *Pool, garden, lifts, all rooms with baths.*

CÉRET 3 La Chàtaigneraie, Route de Fontfrède. *2 km. west of Céret, lovely views, peaceful, pool, garden, no restaurant.*

2 Arcades, 1 Place Picasso. *Small, modern, all rooms with bath or shower and wc, some with kitchenette, no restaurant.*

COLLIOURE **2** Le Bon Port, Route de Port-Vendres. *Garden terraced with views over bay, all rooms with own facilities, pleasant and comfortable.*

1 Hostellerie des Templiers, Rue C. Pelletan. *Large and comfortable, original atmosphere, valuable collection of paintings.*

ELNE **1** Le Carrefour, 1 Avenue P. Reig. *Simple and better accommodation available, good Catalan dishes.*

PERPIGNAN **2** Delseny, 14 Cours Lazare-Escarguel. *Very large, well equipped, no restaurant.*

1 Le Helder, 4 Avenue Général de Gaulle. *Near station, inexpensive rooms, some with bath or shower, agreeable restaurant.*

PORT BARCARÈS **2** La Presqu'île. *Modern, lively, suited to young people.*

PORT VENDRES **3** Compagnie du Midi. *Overlooking port, elegant, comfortable, interesting Catalan dishes.*

PRADES **1** Glycines, Route Nationale. *Modest hotel with prices to match, all rooms with own facilities, garden.*

RIVESALTES **1** Debèze, 11 Rue A. Barbès. *Quiet, plain, small, some well-prepared dishes.*

ST CYPRIEN-PLAGE **1** Glycines, 1 Rue E. Delacroix. *Close to beach, agreeable atmosphere, succulent seafood dishes.*

SORÈDE **2** St Jacques. *A little inland from Argelès, quiet, pleasant views, no restaurant.*

Index